EYEWITNESS TO
INFAMY

EYEWITNESS TO
INFAMY

AN ORAL HISTORY
OF PEARL HARBOR

December 7, 1941

PAUL JOSEPH TRAVERS

Guilford, Connecticut

An imprint of Rowman & Littlefield

Distributed by NATIONAL BOOK NETWORK

Copyright © 1991 by Paul Joseph Travers
First Lyons Press paperback edition, 2016

British Library Cataloguing in Publication Information Available

Library of Congress Cataloging-in-Publication Data Available

ISBN 978-1-4930-2343-1 (pbk.)
ISBN 978-1-4930-2344-8 (e-book)

∞™ The paper used in this publication meets the minimum requirements of American National Standard for Information Sciences—Permanence of Paper for Printed Library Materials, ANSI/NISO Z39.48-1992.

To Frances and Herman,
Loving parents whose legacy
of love and life is the greatest
gift of any survivor.

The Island of Oahu, due to its fortifications, its garrison and its physical characteristics, is believed to be the strongest fortress in the world.

—GENERAL GEORGE CATLETT MARSHALL, 1940

It was lovely. . . . We were about to change an island of dreams into a living hell.

JAPANESE PILOT TATSUYA OHTAWA,
ON THE MORNING OF 7 DECEMBER 1941

Contents

7 DECEMBER 1941: THE DAY OF INFAMY

ON THE ISLAND

Contents

CONTENTS

8 DECEMBER 1941: THE DAY AFTER

ACKNOWLEDGMENTS

This oral history of Pearl Harbor was inspired decades ago with a handful of Pearl Harbor survivors who wanted to document their contributions to the Day of Infamy. From proposal to publication, the project was a journey encompassing thousands of hours and thousands of miles. Along the way, I made new friends and renewed old acquaintances who helped me reach journey's end. When questioned about the book's publication date, I often responded with the cliché that good things come to those who wait. To my friends, I can now say that the waiting has ended. I hope you enjoy reliving one of the most significant and dramatic days in American history.

I am indebted to the Pearl Harbor Survivors Association for their initial support, which allowed me to develop a network of vital contacts. Without their assistance, the book would never have been completed. I am equally indebted to the hundreds of Pearl Harbor survivors who contributed their narratives, contacts, and moral support. Their voices will live on as echoes in the wind that whisper a warning to keep America at-the-ready. A special thanks goes to Jane Warth for her skill in the art of editing; she waved her magic pencil and transformed a diamond in the rough into a sparkling gem.

I would also like to express my sincere gratitude to the following organizations who eagerly provided their assistance: the American Legion, *Baltimore Magazine* (for the interview with Joseph Taussig), the US Naval Academy, the US Naval Academy Alumni Association, the US Naval Historical Center, the Veterans of Foreign Wars, and Mr. Paul Cora, curator for Historic Ships in Baltimore.

PREFACE

"We interrupt this program . . ." For many Americans tuned to their radios on 7 December 1941, the announcement stirred only casual interest. Interruptions of this type were usually an update on the events of World War II. Those who turned an attentive ear were most likely to be first- or second-generation Americans with strong familial and patriotic ties to their country of origin. Despite the concern of the American public with military aggression across both oceans, thoughts of America entering the war were as distant as a small chain of islands in the Pacific Ocean, some three thousand miles off the coast of California. No one suspected this interruption would be the prologue to a four-year nightmare of death and destruction. Radio bulletins and newspaper headlines, which announced "War with Japan" and "Jap Planes Bomb Oahu," stunned a suspicious, but unguarded, nation. While the announcement of war was a surprise, the way it happened was a shock.

Across the Atlantic Ocean, war was already a way of life. European powers were dueling in a life-and-death struggle, which threatened political stability around the world. To many political observers, war came as no surprise. Renewed hostilities were an inevitable continuation of World War I. The armistice on 11 November 1918 ended the first global conflict. But by 1941, Adolf Hitler had conquered the enemies of Germany and steered his war machine to the western and northern shores of the Continent.

The situation across the Pacific Ocean was even more volatile and threatening. In an effort to stop Japanese expansion into China and protect American, British, and French interests in the Far

East, President Franklin D. Roosevelt in July 1941 demanded that Japan withdraw all forces from Indochina. To enforce his demands, Roosevelt ordered Japanese assets in America frozen and placed an embargo on oil supplies to Japan. When Great Britain took similar action, Japanese leaders faced a major crisis in foreign and economic policy. To agree to Roosevelt's demands would be a humiliating political and military defeat. War production in Japan was already hindered by the July 1940 embargo placed on the exportation of American scrap iron and steel to Japan. Oil supplies were vital to keep the Japanese war machine rolling across Asia. If the supply of oil was cut off, Japan would be forced to abandon military activity in China. A more feasible alternative for Japan was to find a new supplier. A defensive pact with Hitler and Benito Mussolini would offer the opportunity to concentrate military resources and provided a new supplier of oil and raw materials. When Roosevelt anchored the US Pacific Fleet at Pearl Harbor, Japanese leaders saw this as the first step to armed intervention into the foreign affairs of Japan. Japan was being slowly backed into a corner by a show of force. There would be no compromise in its position. War was no longer an option; it was the only course of action.

Although Americans spoke of neutrality and prayed for peace, in their hearts they knew it was only a matter of when and where before America was drawn into the conflict. The when and where became 7 December 1941, Pearl Harbor, Oahu Island, Territory of Hawaii. The two-hour attack on Pearl Harbor had such far-reaching and lasting effects that it became an event imprinted in the minds of most Americans living at the time. For a split second, their lives stopped, and this memory was preserved in a time capsule buried in their consciousness. For decades afterward, Americans would be able to respond in detail to the question "Where were you on Pearl Harbor day?" However, as the date slowly receded into the past, the memory of the event slowly receded from the American memory. Although time faded the memory of that day for the majority of Americans alive during World War II, it would always be a day of memory to the servicemen, servicewomen, and civilians who were on Oahu. For most members of postwar generations, that day would mean only a few lines in a history textbook. Pearl Harbor day was associated with black-and-white newsreel footage of Roosevelt, who immortalized "a day which will live in infamy" in his address to a joint session of Congress on 8 December 1941.

When I first mentioned the idea of this book to people, many asked: "Why write a book on Pearl Harbor? What could possibly be said that has not already been said in books and films?" People often mentioned that previous historians had covered every aspect of the attack, from factual accounts to theories of conspiracy and military misconduct. Despite their efforts to complete the unabridged story of Pearl Harbor, historians overlooked one of the most obvious and important segments. The role of the participants who were directly involved in the event was somehow forgotten. Historians focused attention primarily on political and military leaders and strategy. Chronicling and documenting the participants' history of the event was left incomplete.

This book is more than a factual recount of the attack on Pearl Harbor. It is the personal history of Pearl Harbor survivors and a personal odyssey of a group of unsung heroes who survived 1,347 days of war between 7 December 1941 and V-J Day, 15 August 1945. The narratives enable the reader to relive the attack through the senses of those who were there. Even knowing the battle's outcome, the reader is easily swept into the drama.

The survivors' narratives make history human. The narratives cover the full range of military activity, while portraying the human side of a historical event. Most important, they span the emotional spectrum—the heroic, the tragic, and, at times, the comic. The narratives are intriguing because they offer a rare look at the action behind the scenes. The survivors are the children of the Great Depression, who journeyed to Pearl Harbor from the cities, towns, and farms across America.

The seeds for this book were planted during the late 1950s when I was a young boy listening to my father's war stories. The stories were not tall tales about heroic feats in mortal combat, but brief accounts of battles in faraway places. They were short history lessons that stirred my curiosity and imagination. The stories spanned a period from 1939 to 1944 and covered an area from Fort Slocum, New York, to Pearl Harbor, Guadalcanal, and the Palau Islands. My father's Pacific campaign ended with a battle wound and a medal for bravery, but his stories continued. Although my interest in great battles diminished during adolescence, I remained fascinated by one battle.

This book began in fall 1979, when I placed a short advertisement in the classified section of several local and regional newspapers in the Middle Atlantic region. The advertisement, which asked Pearl Harbor survivors to document their experience and preserve a chapter in American history, was buried among hundreds of other advertisements. It was impossible to predict a response. Chances of the advertisement being found by a Pearl Harbor survivor were slim. My expectations were greatly exceeded when I received more than thirty responses. I then notified veterans' groups and slowly established a network of contacts. My patience and perseverance paid off in fall 1980, when the Pearl Harbor Survivors Association agreed to run an announcement in its national newsletter, the *GRAM*. The announcement proved the turning point for the project. The response was immediate and overwhelming. I received over one hundred narratives within a month. As the months passed, my network of contacts slowly expanded. Distance proved no obstacle in spreading the word. Leads were as close as my neighborhood in Baltimore and as distant as a Catholic mission in the mountains of Malawi, Africa. By summer 1981, I had collected approximately 250 narratives through the mail and personal interviews.

Reducing the massive collection of narratives to a workable number was my most difficult task in preparing this book. Deciding whether a personal chapter of American history was suitable for the book proved emotionally trying. Although some narratives overlapped, each had a unique style and character.

In the course of collecting the narratives, I became friends with numerous survivors. Their narratives helped to bridge a generation gap of over thirty years. The survivors' eagerness to communicate and my sincere interest quickly helped to overcome the awkwardness of an outsider intruding into their past. Survivors supplied not only narratives but also photographs, drawings, and other personal memorabilia.

The survivors provided vibrant chapters in American history. They talked with pride about their wartime experiences. For many of them, Pearl Harbor was the central point in their lives, and they could remember the attack as if it were yesterday. The details were vivid and exact. Time had the paradoxical effect of sharpening their focus. The survivors played back events and analyzed them as they would a slow-motion film.

This book has several interesting footnotes. A number of wartime friends regained contact with one another, resulting in happy reunions. Many of these people were last together more than forty years ago. A sad footnote was the quiet and dignified death of several survivors.

In the light of surveys conducted on the role of Pearl Harbor in American history, the role of preserving the experience of it assumed added importance. In November 1981, during an Associated Press-NBC News poll, 1,602 adults were telephoned in a nationwide scientific random sampling and asked: "Do you know why Pearl Harbor is important in American history?"

Eighty-four percent gave accurate responses, and 16 percent said no, were not sure, or incorrectly identified Pearl Harbor. A correlation between education and an accurate response surfaced in this limited poll. The more educated respondents responded accurately, whereas almost two-thirds who had not graduated from high school were unable to answer the question. Most surprising were the statistics about the younger respondents. Only seven out of ten of those between eighteen and twenty-four years of age knew the significance of Pearl Harbor, as compared to nine out of ten who were between fifty and sixty-four years of age.

A 1981 poll conducted in Japan by *Yomiuri Shimbun*, a major Japanese daily newspaper, indicated that 80 percent of Japanese men and women in their twenties were unable to connect Pearl Harbor and their country's role in World War II. They most often associated Pearl Harbor with honeymoons. Hawaii had become popular with Japanese newlyweds.

Media polls, current world situations, and attitudes of world leaders sharply underscore the words of twentieth-century philosopher and man of letters George Santayana, who prophesied that "those who cannot remember the past are condemned to repeat it."

Since the American Revolution, patriots have rallied the fighting spirit of their fellow citizens with inspiring slogans. To past generations of Americans, "Remember the Alamo" and "Remember the *Maine*" were two popular battle cries that were rooted in gallant stands by American fighting forces. Today such slogans, preserved in folklore and legend, bring to mind eras, events, and lessons learned through ordeals of fire. Although many Americans have forgotten the Pearl Harbor attack, the significance of 7 December 1941 guarantees that "Remember Pearl Harbor" will always be more than a slogan.

The history of Pearl Harbor may fade with the passing of time, but the north winds will blow forever over Oahu and echo a haunting refrain to the memory of those who served and sacrificed.

APPROACHING THE 75TH ANNIVERSARY

Black smoke billowing towards the bright blue sky from exploding ammunition magazines and fires from ruptured oil bunkers, mighty warships capsized and sunken with twisted and crumpled steel breaking the surface of the water, airplane hangars and airplanes smoldering on tarmacs in heaps of molten metal junk, broken and burned bodies bleeding into the earth and bobbing lifelessly in the harbor, and tattered and torn American flags flapping proudly and defiantly in the tropical breeze—These are the images of Pearl Harbor that have been seared into the historical DNA of our country.

These are the pictures that will tell the story of 7 December 1941 at the hundredth anniversary and beyond. In some medium when paper photographs are extinct, they will undoubtedly survive the ravages of time. Inevitably, what will not survive are the survivors themselves. Their ranks have been irrevocably vanquished over the years, proving that Father Time is one foe that can never be defeated, not even by the noblest of warriors.

For the fiftieth anniversary in 1991, there were numerous voices to remember the Day in Infamy. Gatherings around the country were celebrations of life for Pearl Harbor survivors and the remainder of the Greatest Generation who were popularized by journalist Tom Brokaw in his best-selling book of the same title. Now in 2016, only a few of those voices remain. Although many are barely above a whisper, they still resound with a steadfast determination that recalls their younger years when they witnessed that apocalyptic day in American history that forever changed the course of a country. So, once again, we spiritually and emotionally gather on the diamond jubilee to celebrate those faltering voices. We pause to remember their stories for the simple reason that it is our patriotic duty to honor those who served and sacrificed for our freedom.

With the first edition of this book in 1991, I enjoyed my so-called fifteen minutes of fame as a Pearl Harbor author and historian, one of many. As I traveled to various functions to promote the book, I always deflected any accolades to the actual Pearl Harbor survivors, the real heroes in the book. In turn, they deferred to me, even though I was only a messenger. This was not an exception but their calling card. Their humility and sincerity characterized their generation at every level of life. During my research interviews, I quickly discovered they were simply ordinary people cast into extraordinary circumstances, who in their own unique way became unsung heroes during and after the war. On 7 December 1941, they began America's epic march to victory. Now in the long shadows of the fading light as they take their final steps, I am honored to walk alongside their ranks and carry the message, possibly for one last time, before we say good-bye.

The past twenty-five years have been marked by reunions, remembrances, and even a revision or redemption, depending on your point of view. The revision, called a rewriting of history by its harshest critics, remains a flashpoint for historians, survivors, and military personnel. The resulting flames of fact and fiction, which may never be extinguished, continue to illuminate the ghosts of two survivors who lurk in the shadows of the fire. Even though the subjects, the highest-ranking officers on Oahu at the time of the Japanese attack, are deceased, the controversy over their culpability at Pearl Harbor has simmered for seventy-five years.

Ten days after the attack, four-star Admiral Husband Kimmel, Commander in Chief of the US Pacific Fleet, and Lieutenant General Walter Short, commander of US military installations in Hawaii, were relieved of their commands. It was reported that during the attack, Kimmel, who watched the devastation of his fleet from his office window at the submarine base, was struck in the chest by a spent fifty caliber bullet. As the casing tore his white jacket and raised a welt on his chest, Kimmel was reported to have said: "It would have been merciful had it killed me." Another witness recalled that during the attack Kimmel tore off his four-star shoulder boards in despair, acknowledging the end of his command and career.

The Roberts Commission, the fact-finding panel hastily convened by President Roosevelt in the days following the attack, conveniently found Kimmel and Short guilty of "dereliction of duty" and "solely responsible" in a report before Congress on 28 January 1942. Both men, who were reduced two stars in rank, retired in disgrace shortly after the report. Subsequently, the "dereliction of duty" charge was changed to "errors in judgment." This technicality did little to mitigate their guilt in the eyes of the public when all military officers were allowed to retain their highest rank after the war except Kimmel and Short. In 1949, Short passed away from chronic heart ailment, which many supporters claimed was a broken heart. His charge to clear his name quickly faded from the public eye and the media.

His counterpart on the other hand mounted a one-man crusade that lasted for twenty-six years. Until his death in 1968, Kimmel fought relentlessly to clear his name. During subsequent hearings after the war, Kimmel vigorously defended his actions, testifying that he was not given access to vital intelligence information. After his death, his sons and grandson championed the cause to restore Kimmel and Short to their four-star rank.

Through the years, the heated rhetoric has always focused on whether Kimmel and Short were sufficiently forewarned about a possible Japanese attack and, if so, did they take appropriate countermeasures. For the supporters of Kimmel and Short, the issue revolves around "Operation Magic," the cryptanalysis project that had broken Japanese military and diplomatic codes. Their key pieces of evidence are the decoded diplomatic cables indicating that Pearl Harbor would be attacked, which were never disseminated to the commanders at Pearl Harbor.

Opponents, dismissing unsubstantiated claims that Kimmel and Short were scapegoats for the Roosevelt administration, counter with the fact that both commanders had been issued a "war warning" on 27 November 1941, by Washington. Despite orders to initiate a defensive employment, they argue that neither commander took adequate measures. Kimmel failed to disperse his fleet, did not put them on alert, and did not order long-range air or naval patrols after the navy lost track of the Japanese carrier fleet. Meanwhile, Short failed to protect his airplanes by gathering squadrons together in tight groups and deployed only one of six air defense radar stations. Proponents for Kimmel and Short claim the "war warning" concluded that Japan would attack US bases in the western Pacific and not Hawaii.

Since 1941, there have been ten official reviews of Kimmel and Short and their conduct on 7 December 1941. The last in 1995 by the Pentagon stated that both men were accountable for the island's state of unpreparedness but also concluded "responsibility should be broadly blamed." On 25 May 1999, the US Senate passed a non-binding resolution by a vote of fifty-two to forty-seven to exonerate Kimmel and Short and requested the president posthumously restore both men to their previous full rank, which requires a presidential nomination. To date, no president has taken action.

HAIL AND FAREWELL

As for the living survivors, there are no controversies to rival the Kimmel and Short saga. For them, all that remains are the here-and-now and the hereafter. There is no controversy, only conversation when they gather to remember. Their reunions are a celebration of life, a time to reflect on their lives and remember deceased comrades, especially those who paid the ultimate sacrifice on 7 December 1941. For the rest of Americans like myself, their reunions are an opportunity to connect with Pearl Harbor through the actual participants—living history personified and glorified. But whether it is honoring the living or the dead, we must stop and listen to their voices before they fade to a whisper and disappear from our memory. In all likelihood, the seventy-fifth anniversary will be our last chance to document the final footnotes to the Pearl Harbor story. For me as an author, it is another chance to share some human-interest stories that are heart breaking, heart felt, and heroic.

On Friday, 3 July 2015, Ray Chavez, age 103, and Jim Downing, age 102, the two oldest known survivors at the time, met for the first time in San Diego to share their Pearl Harbor memories.

In the early hours of the morning on 7 December 1941, Chavez was at the helm of the USS *Condor*, a wooden-hulled purse seiner converted to a minesweeper, patrolling the restricted waters of the channel entrance to Pearl Harbor. Between 0350 and 0357, the *Condor* reported a periscope sighting by visual signals to the destroyer USS *Ward* also in the area. At 0637, the *Ward* sighted a periscope tailing the unarmed cargo ship USS *Antares* near the entrance to Pearl Harbor and opened fire with several rounds from its main guns and several depth charges.

The two-man midget submarine had been apparently attempting to enter the harbor by following the *Antares* through the anti-submarine nets. In August 2002, the kill was finally confirmed when a team of scientists from the University of Hawaii discovered the seventy-eight-foot submarine about three miles outside Pearl Harbor in 1,200 feet of water. It was theorized that major flooding caused by shell holes sank the vessel.

After completing his tour of duty at 0600, Chavez returned home to his navy housing in Ewa Beach and hit the rack. At around 0800, his panic-stricken wife hurriedly awakened him with news of the attack. Staggering to the front door, the still-groggy Chavez rubbed his eyes as the fleet disappeared in clouds of smoke and fire. After catching a ride back to his ship, the crew was ordered to sweep the channel. As preparations to sail were underway, a destroyer steaming out of the harbor cut the cable to their minesweeping gear. The crew could only stand by and helplessly watch the aftermath of the attack unfold. Chavez remembered crying as the bodies of charred and oil-soaked sailors began floating on the surface.

Ironically, Jim Downing, gunner's mate and postmaster aboard the USS *West Virginia*, was also at home on that fateful morning. While hosting breakfast with his bride of five months for eight of his shipmates, he heard muffled explosions from nearby Pearl Harbor. When an antiaircraft round cratered a twenty-five-foot hole in his backyard, the gravity of the situation just a few miles away was apparent.

Racing back to his ship with his shipmates in a commandeered truck, he arrived about twenty minutes after the first wave of Japanese dive-bombers. By then, his ship was slowly settling in the harbor mud from nine torpedo hits. Fires from ruptured fuel tanks were sweeping across the decks. Downing spent the day aiding the wounded and fighting fires with a borrowed water hose from the inboard USS *Tennessee*. He watched in horror as sailors, who were blown overboard into the fiery oil-covered waters, became human torches once they surfaced.

Covered in oil and dodging bullets from the second wave of Japanese planes, Downing raced along the decks in the midst of the chaos and carnage, memorizing the names of his fallen comrades from their dog tags. Later, he visited stricken shipmates at the naval hospital to collect names and messages for families back home. Many were burn victims near death. With access to addresses as the postmaster, he penned personal letters to as many families as possible about the last days of their loved ones. He felt that gold-star families deserved more than a standardized Western Union telegram from the Secretary of

War announcing with "deep regret" that their son had been killed in the performance of his duty and in the service of his country.

Of the thousands of heroes on the island of Oahu on 7 December 1941, there were fifteen recipients of the Medal of Honor, the nation's highest military award for personal valor above and beyond the call of duty. Only five survived their Day in Infamy and four survived the war. On 27 May 2010, a final chapter in the Pearl Harbor story was completed with the death of John Finn. Finn, who passed away at the age of one hundred, was the last Medal of Honor recipient from Pearl Harbor.

On the morning of 7 December 1941, Chief Petty Officer Finn, an aviation ordnanceman assigned to the Naval Air Station Kaneohe Bay, was at home when he heard gunfire coming from the direction of Pearl Harbor. Alerted to the attack by a neighbor, he drove to the hangars and found the airbase under siege. Commandeering a thirty-caliber machine gun from one his men, Finn attached it to a moving tripod and pushed it to an open area for a clear line of fire that left him exposed to the enemy. He blazed away at strafing Japanese planes until the attack was over two hours later.

Wounded numerous times, the affable and self-effacing Finn best described his injuries during an interview with Larry Smith for his book *Beyond Glory*, an oral history of Medal of Honor recipients. "I got shot in the left arm and shot in the left foot, broke the bone. I had shrapnel blows in my chest and belly and right elbow and right thumb. Some were just scratches. My scalp got cut, and everybody thought I was dying: Oh, Christ, the old chief had the top of his head knocked off! I had twenty-eight, twenty-nine holes in me that were bleeding. I was walking around on one heel. I was barefooted on that coral dust. My left arm didn't work. It was just a big ball hanging down."

On 7 December 2014, four of the nine survivors from the USS *Arizona*, John Anderson, Lauren Bruner, Louis Conter, and Donald Stratton, gathered at the USS *Arizona* Memorial for what they believed would be the final "official" reunion of the USS *Arizona* Reunion Association. In the future, they still planned to informally gather at some location on Pearl Harbor Day to remember, but today they would mark the end of a tradition with a grand flourish.

While at the memorial, the group poured a "final toast" to their shipmates. Drinking from champagne glasses that had once been aboard their ill-fated ship, they shared a bottle of wine that had been a gift from President Gerald Ford to the association in 1975. After the toast, one of the glasses was handed to a team of navy and National Park Service divers and placed at the base of the *Arizona's* gun turret four. Gun turret four serves as the final resting place for *Arizona* survivors who wish to have their ashes placed aboard the ship. Since 1980, thirty-eight *Arizona* survivors have been reunited with their fellow shipmates on the ship.

After the reunion, the remaining survivors overruled the association and declared the final "official" reunion would be in Hawaii for the seventy-fifth anniversary with the hope that there would be someone still alive. In 2015, only Lauren Bruner and Clarendon Hetrick attended the anniversary ceremony on the University of *Arizona* campus in Tucson. Once again, both men came to peruse the library's special collection of USS *Arizona* memorabilia and bring back to life the bittersweet memories

On the morning of 7 December 1941, Bruner and Stratton with about one hundred other sailors miraculously cheated death. They escaped the inferno aboard the decks of the *Arizona* by scaling a rope that had been thrown from the repair ship *Vestal*, which was moored inboard. The intense heat from the burning battleship melted their skin as they slowly made their way hand over hand with charred hands, dangling sixty feet above the fiery harbor. Each man suffered severe burns over 60 to 70 percent of their bodies that required a painful, long-term convalescence.

Bruner was the "Second to the Last to Leave" before Alvin Dvorak, who succumbed to his injuries seventeen days later. Seven months later, Bruner was back on duty with the destroyer USS *Coghlan*. Stratton's injuries were so severe that he was medically discharged in 1942. After going through boot camp for a second time, he later rejoined the navy in the Pacific and served in a number of campaigns until being discharged in December 1945.

For two survivors of the *Arizona*, 2014 would be their last reunion. On 4 February 2015, Joe Langdell passed away at the age of one hundred, at the time the oldest Pearl Harbor survivor and the oldest surviving officer from the *Arizona*. On the morning of 7 December 1941, Ensign Langdell was not aboard his ship. Taking advantage of his math skills, the navy had temporary assigned him to a project with navy photographers to accurately measure firing range on a ship's guns. At the time of the attack, he was asleep in his barracks on Ford Island about one hundred yards from the *Arizona*.

Awakened to the sounds of the battle, Langdell could only watch in horror as his ship exploded in a fireball and heaved out of the water before breaking in half and settling in the harbor mud. Minutes later, he was pulling wounded sailors out of the water and carrying them to first-aid stations.

Three days later while sitting down to breakfast in the wardroom of a nearby ship, he was approached by a navy officer and ordered to report to the pier. Waiting at the pier was a motor whaleboat and a party of twenty enlisted men with large bundles of bed sheets and pillowcases. For the next two days, Langdell and his work party scoured the decks of the *Arizona* for any remains of his shipmates. Bodies were carefully wrapped in sheets, and body parts and bones were placed in pillowcases. While viewing the charred hulk of his ship, Langdell saw that the last bomb to hit the ship had shattered the gun turret directly above his assigned battle station.

On 14 November 2015, John Anderson, one of the four survivors who attended the 2014 reunion in Hawaii, passed away at the age of ninety-eight due to complications from hip surgery. In 1940, Anderson was transferred to Hawaii and later reunited with his twin brother Jake aboard the *Arizona*. Both men had joined the navy in March 1937 and now served on the same ship as turret gunners on different turrets.

On the morning of 7 December 1941, Anderson was heading below deck for breakfast after setting up chairs for Sunday-morning worship services. After hearing a "kaplunk," he looked out a port-hole and saw Japanese planes bombing Ford Island. He immediately raced to his gun turret while all the time looking for Jake. Before he could load the gun, a bomb bounced off the turret's top and penetrated the deck, killing many of his shipmates in a thunderous explosion. Minutes later, the ship's deathblow was struck when the forward ammunition magazine with 1.5 million pounds of gunpowder exploded. Ordered to abandon ship, he climbed aboard a barge taking wounded men to the beach. Later, he returned to the ship and searched for his brother, who was never found.

There are ships, such as the USS *Oklahoma*, that embrace only a final footnote to Pearl Harbor. Ed Vezey, who passed away on 2 January 2016, had the distinction of being the last man standing, the last survivor from that battleship. Since 2007, he had traveled to Pearl Harbor to attend the *Oklahoma* memorial ceremony and honor all of those who served and sacrificed on that day, especially his former shipmate and best friend Francis "Frank" Flaherty.

On the morning of 7 December 1941, Ensign Vezey and Ensign Flaherty were in their quarters when they heard the call to man battle stations. Vezey raced to his antiaircraft turret while Flaherty raced to the ship's turret. It was the last time they would ever see each other. Eleven minutes after taking nine torpedo hits broadside, the *Oklahoma* rolled over with its mast and superstructure jammed into the mud. When the order came to abandon ship, Flaherty remained in the turret, holding a flashlight so the turret crew could escape. When the ship rolled onto its side, Flaherty was entombed with over four hundred of his shipmates. For his bravery and courage, he posthumously received the Medal of Honor. On his living room wall, Vezey proudly displayed a painting of the USS *Oklahoma* Memorial and a portrait of Frank Flaherty, which he talked to every day while working out on a treadmill.

In 1943, the *Oklahoma* was righted and refloated for salvage purposes. The skeletal remains of the 429 men entombed in the ship, presumably to include Flaherty, were interred in mass graves at the National Memorial Cemetery of the Pacific in Honolulu, commonly known as the Punchbowl. The austere grave markers were simply inscribed with the words: "Unknowns, USS *Oklahoma*, Pearl Harbor, December 7, 1941." With no dedicated monument, the legacy of the crew languished in obscurity for sixty-six years along with the location of some burial sites.

Beginning in 2000, Vezey rallied support around his fellow shipmate Paul Goodyear, who single-handedly spearheaded the effort to erect a monument to their fallen shipmates. In addition to making personal appearances in support of the memorial, Vezey also worked on the committee that oversaw the building of the memorial.

Finally, on 7 December 2007, near the spot where the *Oklahoma* was moored, the USS *Oklahoma* Memorial was solemnly dedicated with Vezey and Goodyear as keynotes speakers. With black granite walls representing the formidable hull of the ship and white marble standards (columns inscribed with each casualty) symbolizing the naval tradition of "manning the rail" in full dress whites, the memorial had returned the lost crew to her ship.

With crew and ship symbolically reunited, many families with names of loved ones on the monument felt it was now time to symbolically and physically bring their boys back home by identifying their remains. After a protracted battle with the navy, which desired to leave the gravesites undisturbed, their request was granted. In November 2015, the military announced that seven servicemen from the *Oklahoma* had been identified using dental records. Only thirty-five had been identified immediately after the war. In June, the Defense POW/MIA Accounting Agency began exhuming the sixty-one caskets containing the remains of nearly four hundred "unknowns." Using advanced forensic science, the agency hoped to have 80 percent of the crew identified within five years.

CLOSER TO HOME AND HEART

Closer to home, the relentless march of time exacted its toll on a number of cherished friends whom I met while researching the book. On 28 October 2000, Admiral Kemp Tolley passed away at the age of ninety-two. Tolley, who bore an uncanny resemblance to the movie swashbuckler Errol Flynn, graduated from the US Naval Academy in 1929 and served in the navy for thirty years before retiring in 1959. Unlike Flynn's daring fictional exploits on the silver screen, Tolley's real-life adventures on the high seas created a swashbuckling naval legend.

When the book was first published in 1991, most readers glossed over the introduction, unaware of Tolley's connection to Pearl Harbor because there was no link in the way of an explanation, footnote, or story. That was not an oversight; it was a direct order from the admiral. Only the most astute historian or history sleuth would have known that his Pearl Harbor experience in the Philippines was a tale of mystery and intrigue that baffled conspiracy theorists throughout the decades. In his book *The Cruise of the Lanakai*, the admiral regaled readers with stories about his incredible escape from the Japanese. In the spring of 1991, he regaled me with those same tales on the front porch of his Victorian mansion overlooking the rolling countryside just down the road from where I lived.

While wrapping up research at the US Naval Academy and still searching for someone with a Pearl Harbor connection to write an introduction for the book, I struck up a casual conversation with one of the librarians at the front desk. When I mentioned that I lived in northern Baltimore County, a sly smile creased his face before he offered the name of the admiral as an option. In the same breath, I was warned that my odds of meeting my ideal candidate, much less convincing him to write an introduction, were next to impossible. I was advised to draw up a long list of possible candidates.

Although long since retired, the admiral was still a regimented sailor who prized his privacy and shunned even the occasional visitor from outside his inner circle. A swabbie like myself stood no chance. Much to my surprise, I received a phone call from the admiral a few days after mailing him my request letter. After a brief telephone interview, I was more than welcome to meet with him and make my sales pitch with a copy of the manuscript. A few meetings later, while enjoying the early evening with a pitcher of gin and tonic (our meeting ritual) overlooking the bucolic rolling countryside, a deal was struck. In return for writing the introduction, he was to receive three signed copies of the book with one stipulation. His Pearl Harbor story would not be included or even mentioned in the book. He believed the focus of the book should be on the men and women who witnessed the attack firsthand. And make no mistake, my cause in convincing the admiral was also aided by my father's connection to Pearl Harbor and my connection to the military. So with the admiral's passing, it is only fair to share his story with my readers.

In late November 1941, President Roosevelt and his military staff knew that a large flotilla of Japanese naval forces was steaming south from the Formosa Straits. What they didn't know and desperately wanted to discover was location and direction, which might possibly indicate destination. On 2 December, Roosevelt ordered Admiral Harold R. Stark, Chief of Naval Operations, to charter three small vessels to form a defensive information patrol and observe and report by radio Japanese movements in the west China Sea and Gulf of Siam.

On 5 December 1941, Lt. Tolley was given command of the lightly armed USS *Lanakai* and ordered to "patrol off the entrance of Cam Ranh Bay and report the direction by the Japanese fleet when it emerges." The *Lanakai*, an eighty-nine-foot schooner-rigged, diesel-powered yacht, last saw action in 1937 as a movie prop for *The Hurricane*, starring Dorothy Lamour and Jon Hall. Built in 1914 for a German trading company, the vessel was seized in Honolulu by the US Navy three years later during WWI and renamed the USS *Hermes*. In 1926, she was bought by the Lanakai Fish Company and renamed the *Lanakai*, which means heavenly sea in Hawaiian. Before sinking during a typhoon in 1947, she served as a patrol boat, tender for leper colonies, and company yacht.

While at anchor near the entrance to Manila Bay in the early morning hours of 8 December (7 December east of the International Date Line), Tolley and his crew received word of the Japanese attack at Pearl Harbor and orders to return to Manila.

On 10 December, the *Lanakai* survived the devastating Japanese air raid, which destroyed the Cavite Navy Yard. On Christmas Day, she assisted in the evacuation of Manila, carrying army officers and equipment to Corregidor.

On the evening of 26 December, carrying Dutch and American officers and manned by a Filipino crew, the *Lanakai* set sail for "destination unknown." Traveling primarily at night and hiding in dense jungle coves during day, the schooner sailed from island to island, battling Japanese bombers and fierce storms while trying to outrun the Japanese navy. Three months and four thousand miles later, the *Lanakai* arrived at Fremantle, Western Australia. Tolley's journey in the South Pacific became one of the greatest sea adventures of the twentieth century.

Years later, Tolley wrote that the mission provided evidence that the Roosevelt Administration not only suspected a Japanese attack but was doing its best to provide the enemy with an easy target. In an interview with *The Sun* in 1981, Tolley stated: "Roosevelt's fear was that the Japanese would knock the British and Dutch fleet out there and leave us holding the bag alone. But meanwhile he was hoping he could get an incident cheaply by sinking me . . . I thought the whole thing was damn peculiar."

On 11 February 2012, Myrtle Watson passed away at the age of ninety-eight. After Pearl Harbor, the army nurse spent the rest of the war in Hawaii before being discharged in 1945. She resided there for several years before returning to her home in Baltimore, where she continued her career as a nurse. Following her retirement in 1975 as the head of a neonatal intensive care unit, she became active in the Maryland Chapter of the Pearl Harbor Survivors Association (PHSA).

On trips to Hawaii to see her daughter, she would always visit the closed Schofield Hospital to remember her Day in Infamy. Staring up at the lanai (overhanging balcony) and wiping away the tears, she was always overcome with what she described as an eerie and spooky feeling. Her story was so emotionally compelling that it was later used in an American history textbook for middle and high school students. I will always remember her as a sweet, kind, and energetic lady who finally convinced my father to join the PHSA.

Just as fate would place her on Oahu, where my father was also stationed, many years later it would bring her to the front counter of the Hamilton Post Office, where my father worked as a window clerk. For most of her life, Watson had lived in the Hamilton area of the city and frequented the post office to buy stamps and mail parcels. However, it wasn't until that one day when she was mailing a package to her daughter in Hawaii that the two Pearl Harbor survivors finally realized their common bond. Years later, when the book was taking shape, my father introduced me to Myrtle, one of the true unsung heroes from 7 December 1941.

The losses for the Maryland Chapter of the PHSA were staggering in 2009 when eight members passed on. One of those survivors was Ed Robertson, former chapter president who served with the 64th Coastal Artillery at Fort Shafter on 7 December 1941. Ed became another Pearl Harbor mentor and a motivating force in seeing the book to its completion. Whenever I became discouraged over the lack of progress in collecting narratives or disappointed with the lack of interest from publishers, Ed was always there with an encouraging word or sound suggestion. To my disappointment and not Ed's, his story, like many others, fell victim to the editor's pen and opinion.

Closer to my heart, that year also saw the passing of my father, Herman J. Travers, who ironically died on the same day as Ed Robertson. If there was ever a poster boy for the Greatest Generation, it was my dad. Born and raised in the Canton area, one of Baltimore's many waterfront industrial areas, he left high school in the ninth grade at the height of the Great Depression to support his family.

Despite the hard economic times reflected in the long lines at soup kitchens and employment offices, there were manual labor jobs, literally for the picking, at the packinghouses and canneries that lined the waterfront. Hours were long, wages were short, and working conditions deplorable as seasonal fruit and vegetables were cleaned, steamed, canned, and shipped. These were not the ingredients for childhood dreams come true. A few years later when the next eldest sibling found work, my father was finally free to follow his dream. His journey of a lifetime began with a long walk downtown to the recruiter's office with a handful of neighborhood friends.

In prewar America, my father quickly discovered it was as difficult to join the military as it was to find a good paying job. Rejected by the navy for bad teeth and the marines for bad feet, he joined the army, ironically as an infantryman. He always admitted with a quick laugh that he was an easy mark for the recruiter. Just one look at sharply dressed soldiers in khaki uniforms with spit-shined boots and polished brass, parading against a background of palm trees and sandy beaches, was enough to seal the deal. Racing home, he packed a small duffle bag and headed out the door for an adventure of a lifetime in the tropical paradise of Hawaii.

In January 1941, the outstanding recruit in basic training found himself proudly posing for pictures against the backdrop of Schofield Barracks. My father had finally found his calling with the 27th Infantry Regiment. The Wolfhounds, renowned for their bravery in battle and gentleness in peace, would come to characterize my father's life. Not only did he find a budding career in the army, he also found a home.

One of my father's favorite movies was *From Here to Eternity*, the 1953 Academy Award–winning blockbuster that featured most of Hollywood's biggest stars, including my father's favorite singer, Frank Sinatra. Set against the background of army life at Schofield Barracks, the romance-drama portrayed the emotionally entangled lives of three soldiers in the months before the Japanese attack. One of the major plot themes, a true test of manhood in the army, was boxing on the regimental boxing team. And unlike the main character "Prew," who refused to box, my father was looking forward to the boxing smokers to be held around Christmas as a member of the team. Prior to joining the army, he was an aspiring welterweight under the tutelage of Lee Halfpenny, former amateur lightweight champion of the world and local boxing legend, who taught boxing at the Central YMCA.

The Japanese attack ended my father's idyllic peacetime deployment as an enlisted man, but certainly not his dream of a military career. In late 1942, my father was commissioned a second lieutenant after attending Officer Candidate School (OCS) at Fort Benning, Georgia. "Just more cannon fodder," he would always jokingly comment while downplaying his ability as a soldier. But all joking aside, my father was a "soldiers' soldier." One of his favorite OCS stories was his friendship with a Jewish lawyer from New York City whose military skills in the field were as dismal as my father's skills in the classroom. After "lights out," they would sneak off to a safe haven in the barracks for study sessions. Much to the delight and bewilderment of my father, this unlikely pairing of solider and scholar graduated with honors.

After OCS and leave at home where he meet my mother at a neighborhood social club, my father eventually returned to the Pacific campaign with the 323rd Regimental Combat Team of the 81st Infantry Division, just in time for the Battle of Peleliu. There on a remote coral island, often referred to as the Antietam of the Pacific for its bloody skirmishes, his service and sacrifice were put to the ultimate test.

On 17 October 1944, he successfully led a team of four volunteers to rescue wounded men from the battlefield while enduring deadly enemy mortar fire that killed one of his men and wounded another. Two weeks later on 30 October, while on patrol near Bloody Nose Ridge, he was seriously wounded while directing a counterattack after being ambushed by enemy machine-gun fire. But Peleliu was not the first time that my father had lost men under his command. While training on the California coast in 1943, two of his men drowned in a rubber raft accident during a mock amphibious assault. After the incident, my father wrote letters of condolences to the families, the hardest task he ever had to do in his life.

Like most infantryman, my father rarely talked about his combat experiences. What he did on the battlefield was expected not extraordinary. He always said that he was just doing his duty and deflected any glory to his fellow soldiers, especially those who made the ultimate sacrifice. For the book, I had to strike a deal similar to that with the admiral and agree not elaborate on any battlefield encounters. My father's selflessness and humility personified his generation, but in fairness to the readers and in order to set the historical record straight, Lt. Travers received two medals for heroism in combat during his time on Peleliu.

Sent back to the States, my father spent the next three years in and out of military hospitals while doctors attempted to reconstruct his foot, which had nearly been severed by a bullet. Discharged from Valley Forge Army Hospital in 1947, he returned home to begin a new life with his wartime sweetheart, whom he married in 1945. A lover of the outdoors, his dream of a career as a state trooper, park policemen, or even a mailman was scuttled by his war injury. Seeking job security for his family, he worked for thirty-two years as a window clerk for the US Post Office.

After retiring, my father, like so many other veterans, lived a life of quiet and stoic virtue that focused on faith and family, especially the grandchildren. While sailing blissfully into the sunset of retirement, my father was called to duty for one last battle. This time Alzheimer's was the foe, another heartless and ruthless enemy from which there was no escape or victory. Despite the many dark days in the confinement of a nursing home, there was always that melancholic memory from the shores of Hawaii that always brightened a few minutes of those days for the family. As the illness progressed and his memory faded, my father could still recall with clarity his Day of Infamy at a time when he couldn't remember his name.

On 17 November 2009, after a four-year battle with the disease, my father, bowed but not broken, fell exhausted on that battlefield. The "Old Soldier" didn't die; he just faded away. A humble and compassionate man, my father endured his illness with a spiritual grace that reflected an inner peace beyond comprehension. In dying, he taught those around him how to live. At the nursing home, he was remembered as a small island of tranquility in a vast ocean of heartbreaking sadness. That was his legacy to the staff, residents, and visitors. However, there were times at sundown when the enemy would advance without warning and shatter that stillness in an explosion of distant memories. During those dark nights of the soul, the ghosts of the battlefield would silently drift across his mind. The nursing staff often heard my father barking out orders and shouting out the names of forgotten soldiers that had risen from the dead.

The brutal combat and the death of his men were burdens that my father carried to the grave. On a windy and rainy November morning, we laid my father to rest as the sound of "Taps" echoed across the barren hillside. His headstone is a flat bronze marker atop a granite base. Affixed to the marker directly below his name are two bronze medallions, the replica medal for the Military Order of the Purple Heart and a folded flag indicating service as a US Army veteran. It is an unpretentious memorial, a tailor-made and well-suited cloak of tribute to an unsung hero.

Three weeks later on 7 December my wife and I attended the Pearl Harbor Memorial Service at the Maryland WWII Memorial overlooking the scenic Severn River and the historic US Naval Academy. Sponsored by the Maryland Department of Veterans Affairs, the Maryland Chapter of PHSA, and the Maryland Chapter of the Sons and Daughters of Pearl Harbor Survivors, the program highlights included the placing of a wreath on the Pearl Harbor monument at exactly 12:55 p.m. (the time the first wave of Japanese planes descended on Pearl Harbor), the playing of "Taps," and a remembrance ceremony. On a bitter cold day with tears in our eyes, we stood at attention as the final roll call was taken for those survivors who had recently fallen. My father's name echoed across the river as the ship's bell was rung in his honor. After the benediction, I walked away believing that the final page in his Pearl Harbor story had been written and his book of life closed, or so I thought.

THE LAST SURVIVORS FORGED IN STEEL
In addition to the Pearl Harbor remembrance at the WWII memorial outside Annapolis, there is also a memorial service held aboard the fantail of the USCGC *Taney* in Baltimore's inner harbor. It is the place where the last survivors meet another last survivor. Commissioned in 1936, the 327-foot cutter served for more than fifty years before being decommissioned by the Coast Guard on 7 Decem-

ber 1986 and donated to the city of Baltimore as a memorial and museum. Part of the fleet operated by Historic Ships in Baltimore, the *Taney* is a virtual time capsule for American maritime history, having participated in WWII, the Korean War, and the Vietnam War. During WWII, she fought in both the Atlantic and Pacific theaters, performing antisubmarine patrols and convey escort duty. Her many special assignments included sailing as an admiral's flagship and evacuating Allied prisoners from Japan at the end of the war.

Following the war, she was reconfigured for Coast Guard peacetime duties. Home ported in California for over twenty-five years, she earned the title "Queen of the Pacific." From 1973 to 1977, she carried out weather patrols and hunted hurricanes off the East Coast. From 1977 to 1986, she returned to frontline operations that included search and rescue, fisheries patrol, drug interdiction, and summer training cruises for the Coast Guard Academy.

In July 1941, the *Taney* was transferred to the navy and assigned to the fourteenth Naval District for local defense. On the morning of 7 December 1941, the she was moored alongside Pier 6 in Honolulu Harbor. Upon receiving the message: "Air Raid, Pearl Harbor. This is no drill," her crew swiftly manned her antiaircraft guns to engage Japanese planes as they flew over the city. Immediately following the attack, she commenced antisubmarine patrols near Pearl Harbor.

In the late 1960s, the *Taney* became the last US ship in commission that had seen action during the Japanese attack on Hawaii. Beginning then, she was often referred to as "The Last Survivor of Pearl Harbor." In reality, the last surviving warship (or ship by definition) of Pearl Harbor, which was actually anchored in Pearl Harbor on 7 December 1941, was the light cruiser USS *Phoenix*. In 1951, the ship was sold to Argentina and commissioned in the Argentine Navy as the *General Belgrano*. During the Falklands War in 1982, she was sunk by the British attack submarine HMS *Conqueror* with the loss of 323 lives.

However, despite the storied histories of the last warships, the distinction of being the last boat or vessel at Pearl Harbor on 7 December 1941 belongs to the 100-foot-yard tug, the USS *Hoga*.

On the morning of 7 December 1941, the *Hoga* was moored with other yard service craft near the Ten/Ten Dock when the attack commenced. Within ten minutes of the first strike, the tug and her ten-man crew (the cook was ashore) were underway with orders to assist wherever she could. Steaming toward Battleship Row, while plucking sailors out of the water, she headed toward the shattered hulk of the *Arizona*, where she pulled the crippled *Vestal* away from the burning battleship. While moving the minelayer *Oglala* away from the torpedoed *Helena*, she was ordered to assist the *Nevada*, which was making a run to open sea.

Recognizing the opportunity to sink a battleship and bottle up the fleet by blocking the harbor entrance, Japanese dive-bombers directed a fierce attack on the crippled vessel. Underway at 8:45, by 9:07 the *Nevada* was slowly steaming forward and quickly sinking from a torpedo hit during the first wave of the attack. With the help of the *Hoga* and the minesweeper *Avocet*, she was run aground and nosed in the soft sand to Hospital Point, where she was clear of the harbor entrance. The *Hoga* remained alongside the battleship to fight the raging fires above and below deck. Later returning to Battleship Row, she fought fires for seventy-two continuous hours. Following the attack, she patrolled the harbor and assisted in cleanup, salvage, and recovery operations.

In 1948, the *Hoga* was transferred on loan to the Port of Oakland for primary use as a fireboat. In 1994, she was returned to the navy and mothballed with the ghost fleet at Suisan Bay. In July 2005, she was donated to the city of North Little Rock, Arkansas, as a floating museum. After a series of financial setbacks that delayed restoration, she was finally moved to Mare Island in July 2012 for repairs to her hull and deck. Declared watertight and seaworthy by the navy and returned to her original appearance, she arrived at the Arkansas Inland Maritime Museum on 23 November 2015, after an arduous three-month journey that was spotlighted by the media. On 7 December 2015, the *Hoga* served as the backdrop for the Pearl Harbor ceremony, which honored Arkansas' last three Pearl Harbor survivors. Following a ribbon-cutting ceremony, the historic tugboat was officially opened to the public.

For nearly twenty years, the main deck of the *Taney* has been my destination on 7 December. The memorial ceremony follows the same format as the one at the WWII memorial overlooking Annapolis. However, since it is aboard the last surviving warship, there are some added flourishes. The Fourth Engineer Battalion, US Marine Corps, presents the colors and the US Coast Guard Honor Guard sounds the rifle salute. The flag that flutters on the stern of the ship was flown over the USS *Arizona* at the *Arizona* Memorial and the forty-eight-star American flag carried by the St. Andrew's Society of Baltimore was at Pearl Harbor on 7 December 1941. Highlighting the program is the Pearl Harbor Memorial conducted by the Escort to the Colors, the St. Andrew's color guard outfitted in the traditional highland dress of kilts, kilt hose, and glengarry caps. Following the keynote address, a member of the color guard steps front and center with an Enfield rifle to execute a British rifle drill in honor of the fallen. The ship's bell is then rung in memory of those ships and units at Pearl Harbor that suffered casualties. At exactly 12:55 p.m., "Taps" is played and a wreath is dropped into the water. Following benediction, a bagpiper plays "Amazing Grace" before the colors are retired.

One of those honored guests to participate in the wreath ceremony has been Pearl Harbor survivor Thomas Talbott. For the last few years, he has the distinction of being the only survivor to attend, another one of the last men standing. On 7 December 1941, Talbott was a nineteen-year-old marine corporal on roving guard duty at the dry docks. In the stillness of a Sunday morning, he could hear the ticking of his Bulova watch that he had purchased a few days earlier and still has today in good working order.

Counting the minutes until his relief arrived, he watched in disbelief as torpedoes fell from the sky in the direction of Battleship Row before the harbor erupted into fireball. Instead of spending the rest of the day at the beach swimming with his friends, he spent hours trying to rescue tarred and charred sailors who had jumped ship into the burning oil-soaked water. "You could hardly breathe. That smell and that stench stayed in my body and my mind. I still smell it once in a while today," Talbott said at the 2012 ceremony. "I still have dreams about that day."

Before 2011, most of the Pearl Harbor ceremonies around the country were held in conjunction with local chapters of the PHSA. At Pearl Harbor on 7 December 2011, about 120 survivors gathered to mark the seventieth anniversary. At the end of the ceremony, President William Muehleib, citing age and poor health of the remaining members, announced the Pearl Harbor Survivors Association would officially disband on 31 December. Started in 1958, the association listed 2,700 members from an estimated 7,000 to 8,000 living survivors. Approximately 84,000 uniformed men and women were on Oahu on 7 December 1941. Local chapters would continue to function as long as possible, but there would be no national group to head the members or organize the annual trip to Hawaii. The mantle of their legacy was passed to the Sons and Daughters of Pearl Harbor Survivors. With about twenty local chapters, the Sons and Daughters would continue with the scholarship program and newsletter.

The seventieth anniversary in Pearl Harbor also witnessed ash scattering and interment ceremonies for five survivors. On Tuesday, 6 December, the ashes of Lee Soucy were placed inside the battleship USS *Utah*. On 7 December 1941, Soucy, a pharmacist's mate, swam to shore after his ship capsized and administered to the wounded from a makeshift first-aid station. Over the ensuing years, he frequently gave talks and met with Japanese pilots who attacked Pearl Harbor and survived the war. Unlike many survivors, he was one who was able to forgive. On his Pearl Harbor Survivors garrison cap was a button that read in Japanese: "Love not war."

On Wednesday, 7 December, the ashes of Vernon Olsen, a three-time survivor of the Pacific in WWII, were placed in gun turret #4 on the *Arizona*. On the morning of 7 December 1941, while on mess duty, Olsen raced to his battle station, which was 150 feet above the deck on the aft mast behind a fifty caliber machine gun. With all of the ammunition locked away, all he could do was watch as Japanese planes buzzed the ship at close range. When the order came to abandon ship, Olsen climbed down from the mast into a cauldron of smoke and fire on deck, burning his arms and hands on the steel rungs. Taken ashore by boat, he watched the rest of the attack from Ford Island.

Five months later in May 1942, Olsen was aboard the carrier USS *Lexington* during the Battle of the Coral Sea. When the order to abandon ship was given, Olsen once again found himself in the water, swimming safely away from the ship before being rescued. Severely damaged by Japanese torpedo bombers, the burning carrier, drifting dead in the water, was scuttled by the destroyer USS *Phelps*.

With the surrender of the Japanese in August 1945, Olson found himself left with one year of a six-year enlistment. Seven months later in March 1946, he found himself in the armada of ships, sailors, and scientists that were assembled for nuclear tests at Bikini Atoll in the Pacific. Operation Crossroads, the US military's first postwar nuclear testing, included ninety-five target ships that would be subjected to the effects of an atom bomb near ground zero.

Like thousands of other sailors, Olsen, dressed only in every-day work clothes with no protection from radiation, was involved in clean up operations aboard the highly contaminated ships that had been blasted with winds nearing 1,000 mph and thermonuclear heat exceeding temperatures on the sun. Medical tests were also conducted on the thousands of rats, goats, and pigs that had been placed aboard the target ships. Olsen, like many other veterans who witnessed the tests and became the first generation of "atomic vets," believed the navy was also secretly conducting medical tests on military personnel who were also exposed to high levels of radiation. Olsen and his fellow shipmates had never been warned about the dangers of radiation exposure.

On two occasions, I have been asked to be a keynote speaker at the *Taney* ceremony. I always considered the invite an honor, even more after the death of my father. My theme for the 2015 service was the legacy of the sons and daughters of Pearl Harbor survivors. It was a timely topic because I had never paused in life to consider my place in the hierarchy of Pearl Harbor. Like my father before me, I had been busy raising a family and working a career during my middle years. After some pondering, I quickly realized it was a topic that needed to be urgently addressed. With the death of many Pearl Harbor survivors in recent years, their children, my generation, were the next generation of Americans facing their own mortality. Before we passed on, what would be our Pearl Harbor legacy? That was the question to be pondered.

On the fantail of the *Taney* on 7 December 2015, I humbly and sincerely answered the question. My father's death was not the end of his Pearl Harbor story, but the birth of his Pearl Harbor legacy. As the son of a Pearl Harbor survivor, that legacy provided a source of pride as a child, bragging rights, if you will, among the neighborhood kids. As a young man, that legacy served as a role model, leading the way to military service in the Marine Corps. Later in life, that legacy served as a rallying cry to keep the memories alive, resulting in a book about Pearl Harbor survivors. On that sunny afternoon, the torch of that legacy was passed to every American with the words: "Today, I stand before you as the son of a Pearl Harbor survivor. Today, we stand together, each and every one of us, as sons and daughters of Pearl Harbor survivors. Together we raise our voices in unison—Remember Pearl Harbor! Keep America Alert! Lest we forget!"

INTRODUCTION

History professors produce a majority of the "definitive" histories of war that are based on statistics, dates, battle scenarios, and reports and casualty figures. Sometimes the author will have actually witnessed an action but understood little of what he saw. His glasses may be roseate, or distorted, darkly tinted, or even clear. But alas! Rather than allowing the reader to judge the facts for himself, the facts are often bent by opinion.

In the story about to follow, living men—not statistics, not the opinions of historians—speak living history in the first person. Just as a dozen Boy Scouts given ten seconds to view the contents of a store window will arrive at a dozen different inventories, our forty-eight witnesses to the destruction of Pearl Harbor manifest differing reactions, observations, feelings, and conclusions. The result is a conglomerate total that in no manner could be amassed by a single individual.

You will find no mock heroics here. People act like people, clearly displaying the discipline and comradeship engendered in the military service, along with the normal gripes, sometime boredom, naïveté of youth, and wholesome diversity of our countrymen.

A history such as this, a type rarely encountered, can never be duplicated in the case of Pearl Harbor. Those who wrote it are transitory; in another ten years, the last of them will be serving their final assignment, without replacement, ever.

Kemp Tolley
Rear Admiral USN (Retired)

Pearl Harbor: Geographical and Historical Background

Pearl Harbor is a natural inlet on the southern coast of the island of Oahu, Hawaii. Located approximately six miles west of the city of Honolulu, the harbor has a surface area of eight and one-half square miles, and there are some twelve miles of docking facilities around its perimeters. The harbor has no distinctive shape, but is marked by distorted dimensions and uneven boundaries, which give it the appearance of a watery maze. The main body of water is joined by smaller bays, called *lochs*. The four main lochs—West Loch, Middle Loch, East Loch, and Southeast Loch—take their directional names from positions around the edge of the harbor complex. Ford Island is located in the center of the main body of water. The landlocked harbor, which has only one access channel, has an average depth of fifty to sixty feet. The harbor's natural attributes made it a sanctuary for ships seeking refuge.

The harbor takes its name from the Hawaiian *Wai Momi* (Water of the Pearl). The first English name for the harbor was Pearl River, which eventually became Pearl Harbor when fleets of sailing ships used it for anchorage. The first English visitors to the islands arrived in 1786, in the HMS *King George* and the HMS *Queen Charlotte*, both of which were under the command of Captain Nathanial Portlock. He recorded an account of that brief visit in his captain's log, and it became the first public description of Wai Momi, when it appeared in British journals in 1789. In 1792, the HMS *Discovery*, under the command of Captain George Vancouver, visited the harbor. The first military action ever recorded at Pearl Harbor occurred in 1794, when Captain John Kendrick, aboard the HMS *Lady Washington*, landed a small detachment of men, who assisted the king of Oahu in a battle to retain control of the island after the death of King Kahekili in the same year.

In the early 1800s, pearl oysters still remained the harbor's main attraction. After visiting the harbor in 1818, Englishman Peter Corney returned to England and published a descriptive account of oysters and their harvesting in the *London Literary Gazette* in 1821. The article stated that there were "many divers employed here diving for pearl oysters which are found in great plenty." However, in 1825, with the arrival of the HMS *Blonde*, a new and different interest was taken in the harbor. The ship's naturalist, Andrew Bloxam, viewed the harbor for its military rather than its pearl potential. In his scientific ledgers, Bloxam had written that "it would form a most excellent harbor as inside there is plenty or' water to float the largest ship and room enough for the whole Navy of England." Despite these words praising the military potential of the harbor, it was overlooked as a military base until later in the century. In 1840, America staked an unintential claim to the harbor, which would lead to control and possession. In that year, King Kamehameha II asked Charles Wilkes, a navy commodore who had arrived with the US Exploring Expedition after an extended cruise to the Antarctic, to survey the harbor. The resulting chart, "South Side of the Island of Oahu, Hawaiian Islands, Showing the Harbours of Honolulu and Ewa or Pearl River," was the navy's first engineering survey of the harbor.

Until the late 1880s, this work would be the only project undertaken in developing the harbor for commercial and military use. In October 1887, the Hawaiian Senate ratified a treaty giving America exclusive right to establish a coaling station and repair yard in Pearl Harbor. Surveys were made in 1887 and 1897, but little was done to remove the obstructing sandbar at the harbor's entrance. The sandbar, which extended across the mouth of the harbor, decreased the water's depth to ten feet and limited access by larger and deeper-drafted vessels. When the ownership of the islands was assured by annexation in 1898, America proceeded to make Pearl Harbor a first-class naval base. The base was designed to provide ample pier accommodations for the discharging and loading of naval supplies, and it was never intended to enter into commercial competition with Honolulu. In 1900, with an appropriation of $100,000, the first dredging began. A channel four and one-half miles in length was dredged from the sea and across the sandbar and coral reef to the yard site. More dredging ensued, and in 1908 the channel was cleared to a width of six hundred feet and a minimum depth of thirty-five feet. The harbor was now available to the largest ships afloat. The dredging was finally completed in late 1911. On 14 December 1911, Rear Admiral Chauncey Thomas made the official entry into the harbor, in the flagship USS *California*. The celebration involved Hawaii's biggest ribbon-cutting ceremony. As the cruiser steamed through the channel, she broke a red, white, and blue ribbon stretched across the entrance from shore to shore. After the outbreak of World War II in 1939, the navy began to expand Pearl Harbor Navy Yard's dry-dock and repair facilities, using large appropriations from Congress. When the US Pacific Fleet began using the harbor as an operating base in 1940, military observers noted deficiencies, which led to their questioning of the harbor's reputation as the "Gibraltar of the Pacific." These deficiencies remained speculation until the morning of 7 December 1941.

At the time of the dredging, the navy began to construct a number of forts at the harbor's entrance. In 1909, the largest of these fortifications, named Fort Kamehameha after the great Hawaiian king and warrior, was completed at the southeastern corner of the harbor entrance, below Hickam Field. Fort Weaver and Fort Barrette were later constructed on opposite sides of the channel entrance in order to solidify the defensive position. These two fortifications were armed with twelve-inch mortars and sixteen-inch naval guns converted to use for coast artillery.

The Hawaiians had named the natural centerpiece of Pearl Harbor *Mokuumeume* (Island of Strife). The first recorded owner was

Don F. Francisco de Paula y Marin, a Spanish interpreter for King Kamehameha. A British survey in 1825 listed the island as Rabbit Island. In 1865, James L. Dowsett bought the island for $1,040, and he later sold it to Miss Caroline Jackson for $1. It acquired the name Ford Island when Miss Jackson married Seth Porter Ford, a Boston physician. The island was transferred to the US government during World War I. It became home to the army's Sixth Aero Company. After World War I, the navy began to use the island and eventually took control of all of its aviation facilities. At one time, both the army and the navy had air stations on the island. The army had Luke Field on the Pearl City side, and the navy had the Naval Air Station on the opposite side. In 1939, the army moved its air units to Hickam Field and left Luke Field to the navy. The Naval Air Station continued to operate until March 1962, when it was decommissioned.

The Battle of Pearl Harbor:
The Official Account of the US Navy

On Oahu, 7 December 1941 began as another typical Sunday. It was the day of the week when military activities centered around relaxation and recreation. For military personnel, it was the time when the paradox of living in the Pacific became most evident. In this tropical paradise in the middle of the Pacific Ocean, they were preparing for a war that raged thousands of miles over the eastern and western horizons. In this island setting, it would have seemed more appropriate if the personnel were training to become tourists ready to embark on an extended vacation instead of a military campaign.

On military maps, the tiny island chain of Pearl Harbor appeared as an isolated, impenetrable fortress. The expanse of ocean surrounding the islands would certainly make it impossible for an enemy fleet to advance to them without being detected hundreds of miles at sea. Most Americans believed that their country's entrance into the global conflict would be by a formal declaration resulting from continued military aggression on the continents. Although Admiral Husband E. Kimmel, Commander in Chief, US Fleet (CINCUS) and Commander in Chief, Pacific (CinCPac), warned of the possibility of a surprise air-raid attack, few people thought the Japanese had the capability to "pull it off." Most people believed that the Japanese would not attack any American forces without a formal declaration of war. The fact that Japan had attacked China in 1895 and Russia in 1904 without a formal declaration of war was dismissed as neither pertinent nor practicable. After all, this was the mid-twentieth century, and Japan was now a world power operating under the unwritten code of modern warfare. Surprisingly, no prominent US military leaders excused the surprise attack on the grounds that Japan had violated its solemn agreement in the Hague Convention.

A factual narrative of the attack compiled from official navy files, military archives, congressional records, and other government sources provides insight into the immensity of death and destruction resulting from the air raid. The narrative is a list of cold, hard facts; it is a bookkeeper's ledger listing credits and debits, with a bottom line showing the losses sustained to personnel and equipment. As with any major battle, conflict, or disaster, in the Pearl Harbor attack the statistical data become the reference point to measure the total spectrum of human experiences, which gives the event its emotion, intensity, and meaning.

THE US PACIFIC FLEET

Contrary to initial reports coming from Pearl Harbor after the attack, the major part of the US Pacific Fleet was not present there on 7 December 1941. A ship count showed that only about half of the fleet was anchored in the harbor. All three of the fleet aircraft carriers were elsewhere, but eight of the nine fleet battle ships were present at the time of the attack. Several ships were absent due to overhauls on the West Coast, while others were assigned to task forces on special missions.

A special task force under the command of Vice Admiral William F. Halsey on the USS *Enterprise* was about two hundred miles west of Hawaii en route to Pearl Harbor, after having delivered Marine Corps fighter planes to strengthen the defensive capability of Wake Island. The task force consisted of one aircraft carrier, three heavy cruisers, and nine destroyers. A second task force under the command of Rear Admiral J. H. Newton on the USS *Lexington* was about four hundred miles southeast of Midway, en route to deliver Marine Corps scout bombers. This task force was composed of one aircraft carrier, three heavy cruisers, and five destroyers. A third task force under the command of Vice Admiral Wilson Brown on the USS *Indianapolis* was deployed off Johnston Island to test a new type of landing craft. The task force consisted of one heavy cruiser, five destroyers, and a number of minesweepers.

In addition to these three task forces, two heavy cruisers were on convoy duty in Samoa and the Solomon Islands to protect commercial shipping to Australia, and one heavy cruiser and four destroyer minesweepers were conducting tactical exercises about twenty-five miles off the coast of Oahu. Two submarines were in the Midway Island area, and two others were near Wake Island. Other noncombat support ships, such as oil tankers, transports, and cargo vessels, were in transit between Hawaii and the West Coast. All ships at sea were on wartime alert and fully armed. The absence of this portion of the US Pacific Fleet left the following ships in Pearl Harbor on 7 December:

eight battleships

two heavy cruisers

four ten-thousand-ton cruisers

two seven-thousand-ton cruisers

thirty destroyers

four submarines

one gunboat

nine minelayers

fourteen minesweepers

twenty-seven auxiliary vessels, such as repair ships, tenders, store ships, tugboats, and yard craft

All vessels at Pearl Harbor, except for those undergoing overhaul at the Navy Yard, were in readiness condition three, as prescribed by fleet orders. This required one-quarter of the antiaircraft batteries and their control stations to be in a ready status, with gun crews and ammunition at hand. All major combat ships were in condition "X," with two machine guns and two five-inch antiaircraft guns in a ready status, with gun crews and ammunition at hand. In addition, all vessels were required to be on twelve-hour notice for getting underway for sea duty. The degree of closure for watertight doors and hatches was determined by the alphabet code for battle-ready status. Condition "X" was the minimum-readiness condition, whereas condition "Z" was the maximum-readiness condition, with full watertight integrity. Most of the ships in the harbor had been in port for at least a few days and were almost filled to capacity with fuel oil.

RECONNAISSANCE

Although the high command at Pearl Harbor knew the need for aerial reconnaissance, the shortage of planes and personnel prevented commanders from establishing an effective reconnaissance system. It was estimated that a 360-degree patrol of the islands at a distance of eight hundred miles would require eighty-four planes on sixteen-hour flights. To perform such a patrol on a round-the-clock basis would require about 180 planes with accompanying crews. In December 1941, the planes and personnel were not available. Most of the aerial reconnaissance was conducted during combined training exercises and operations conducted by the army and navy. Other reconnaissance efforts were made by aircraft and destroyers deployed on antisubmarine searches, as well as by aircraft-carrier reconnaissance planes that escorted task forces leaving and entering Pearl Harbor. On the morning of 7 December, a small number of reconnaissance planes were in the air, and an equal number were on stand-by-ready status. Three patrol planes were scanning the fleet's operating areas, while three others remained grounded on thirty-minute notice. A submarine task force and four planes from Ford Island that were in the air took part in a joint exercise. Three Marine Corps/scout bombers at Ewa Field were on standby with two-hour notice, and fifteen bombers and fifteen utility planes were on standby with four-hour notice. Task forces at sea were conducting air and sea searches, as mandated by fleet orders.

High command decided that, with such a limited range for reconnaissance, the existing aerial reconnaissance was sufficient for the fleet and Oahu in a peacetime status. The belief prevailed that Japan's initial act of war would not be a surprise attack on Pearl Harbor. However, the Japanese high command was able to turn American deficiencies, misconceptions, and speculative theories to its advantage, with devasting results.

Another form of aerial reconnaissance, which received considerable publicity and attention after the attack, was radar. Radar installations on the islands were considered in the experimental stage at the time of the attack. Although the navy was installing radar units as fast as they could be obtained, by the end of 1941 only a handful of ships were equipped with these long-range reconnaissance devices. At the same time, the army was in the process of installing three large field radar units, as well as six mobile units on trucks. The effectiveness of radar to detect moving objects depended on the height of both the installation and the target. Large ships in open water could be detected by shipboard radar units at a distance of twenty miles. Aircraft equipped with radar had a range of up to two hundred miles, depending on elevation.

The First Shot of the Battle

Although a number of US ships claim to have fired the first shot of the Pearl Harbor attack, the distinction of having fired the first shot of the Battle of Hawaii and World War II belongs to the destroyer USS *Ward*.

At 3:45 a.m. on 7 December 1941, the minesweeper *Condor*, while making a routine sweep for magnetic mines off the channel entrance to Pearl Harbor, spotted a mysterious object riding in the water. A closer look through binoculars revealed the object to be a midget submarine. The submarine was trailing a large steel barge being towed by the minesweeper *Antares*, which was waiting for the antisubmarine net across the channel entrance to be opened. The *Condor*, equipped only for minesweeping, with no armament, notified the *Ward* by yardam blinker: "Sighted submarine on westerly course speed five knots." The *Ward*, which was also on patrol duty in the area, proceeded to head on a course to cut off the submarine before she was able to make her way into the harbor. At 4:58, the submarine net gate opened to allow the *Condor* to enter the channel entrance. The net gate remained open until 6:30, when the *Antares* approached it. At this time, the unidentified submarine was spotted by the USS *Ward* and a PBY 14-P-1, which was conducting aerial reconnaissance. At 6:45, after sounding general quarters, the *Ward* opened fire on the submarine, which was operating in restricted waters. The first shot, fired by the number-one gun at a range of one hundred yards, missed its mark. The second shot, fired from the number-three gun, hit the coming tower, causing the submarine to submerge. Depth charges were then dropped over the site where the submarine was last seen. The submarine failed to surface and was believed to have been sunk. At 6:53, the *Ward* radioed the Fourteenth Naval District: "We have attacked, fired upon, and dropped depth charges upon a submarine operating in defensive sea area."

At 7:15, the USS *Ward*'s message, which had been delayed in decoding, was delivered to the duty officer of the Fourteenth Naval District. Minutes later, the same message was delivered to the duty officer, CinCPac. At 7:25, the destroyer *Monaghan* was ordered to get underway and investigate the submarine sighting reported by the USS *Ward*. At 7:41, CinCPac headquarters received the PBY 14-P-1 report about submarine activity off the channel entrance. Like the message delivered to the Fourteenth Naval District, this one was also delayed in decoding. The message had been logged with headquarters at 7:00. At 7:51, the *Monaghan* received her orders from the Fourteenth Naval District, which had been prepared at 7:25. At 7:55, the first wave of Japanese bombers made its appearance over Pearl Harbor. Another opportunity to alert the fleet was lost.

The Attack

The attack, which lasted an hour and fifty minutes, was carried out in four phases: 1) 7:45–8:25: concentrated attack by an estimated total of sixty-five torpedo planes, dive-bombers, and horizontal bombers; 2) 8:25–8:40: lull in the attack and sporadic bombing and strafing runs by an estimated fifteen dive-bombers; 3) 8:40–9:15: concentrated attack by an estimated total of thirty horizontal bombers and eighteen dive-bombers; 4) 9:15–9:45: bombing and strafing runs by an estimated twenty-seven dive-bombers; after this last attack, all planes in the area around Hawaii returned to their carriers.

Phase 1

As the preparatory signal for morning colors was being hoisted, Japanese bombers made a sudden appearance over Pearl Harbor, flying low and fast over Merry Point Landing toward Ford Island. Within seconds, nine dive-bombers hit the Naval Air Station on Ford Island. Although damage to the station was not total, thirty-three of seventy navy planes parked on runways and near hangars were destroyed or severely damaged. No further attacks were directed at Ford Island, except for a direct hit on a hangar by a bomb that had been intended for the USS *California*, but fell short of its target. At almost the same time that bombs fell on Ford Island, air bases at Eva, Hickam, Wheeler, Bellows, and Kaneohe were subject to dive-bomber attacks and strafing runs. Within the first minutes of the attack, seven formidable air bases were neutralized. During and after the attack, only a token air force was able to resist the Japanese bombers or follow them out to sea on their return trip to their carriers. Although the initial attack came as a total surprise, defensive actions and maneuvers were immediate. Battleship machine guns opened fire immediately, and within five minutes nearly all antiaircraft batteries were in action. Cruiser antiaircraft batteries were in action within four minutes and were fired within seven minutes.

Although Pearl Harbor was hit first by dive-bombers, torpedo planes inflicted the major damage during the attack's first phase. The planes launched their payloads from as low as fifty feet. The harbor's shallow water presented no obstacle because the torpedoes had been specially fitted with wooden fins to compensate for water depth. The torpedo planes made four separate attacks during this first phase. Their flight path brought them in over the southeast corner of the tank farm near Merry Point Landing and down on the decks of the ships at Battleship Row. During this phase, all outboard ships on Battleship Row received torpedo hits. The battleships USS *Arizona*, *Oklahoma*, *Nevada*, and *West Virginia* were hit first and either sunk or severely damaged.

The *Arizona* was immediately knocked out of the action. After she took several torpedoes and bombs, a higher-level bomber fired a bomb that hit near her number-two turret, which blew up her forward magazines. The ship went down so fast she did not have time to roll over on her side. Within a minute of that explosion, over one thousand men lost their lives. In the second torpedo plane attack, the *Oklahoma* took three hits and tilted to a list of 20 to 25 degrees. As the ship began to slowly roll over, men started to scramble over her starboard side. The ship continued to roll over until her masts hit bottom and stopped her roll at about 150 degrees. Many of the survivors from the *Oklahoma* made it safely to the decks of the *Maryland*, which was inboard of her. The *Maryland* escaped with relatively little damage, in comparison with the rest of the battleships. She took one bomb on the forecastle and an armor-piercing one on a hold. Her position on the inside saved her from torpedo bombers.

During the third attack in phase one, the *West Virginia* took heavy bomb and torpedo hits. The ship took so many torpedo hits that a couple passed through holes made by the first hits. One hit knocked off her rudder, which was later picked up from the harbor bottom. When a large fire broke out amidship, word was given to abandon ship. Also in the third attack, one plane flew in from the west to hit the cruiser *Helena* and the minelayer *Oglala*, both of which were at the Ten-Ten Dock. One torpedo passed beneath the outboard *Oglala* and detonated against the side of the *Helena*, buckling the side plates of the *Oglala*. Submersible pumps from the *Helena* were useless because her engineering plant had been damaged from the torpedo hit. Another bomb dropped between the two ships at around 8:00 resulted in the *Oglala's* loss of power. With the aid of a tug and a motor launch, the *Oglala* was moved away from the *Helena* and secured behind her at the Ten-Ten Dock. By 10:00, the *Oglala* had taken on so much water that she rolled over.

The fourth attack came from a wave of enemy bombers that came in over Pearl City and the Middle Lock and hit the ships moored on the opposite side of Ford Island, directly across from Battleship Row. This side of the island was the berthing place for aircraft carriers when they were in port. On this Sunday, the seaplane tender *Tangier*, the target ship *Utah*, and the light cruisers *Raleigh* and *Detroit* were in their spaces. The *Detroit* and *Tangier* escaped torpedo damage, but the *Raleigh* suffered one hit and the *Utah* suffered two hits. When the *Raleigh* began to roll over, her crew put out extra lines to the quays and held her upright until the attack was over. To keep the ship upright in the water, the crew threw overboard aircraft, lockers, and any others items fastened to the ship. The *Utah*, which from the air resembled an aircraft carrier because of her concrete decks for target practice, drew the attention of Japanese pilots. After two torpedo hits, the ship began to list rapidly to port; she capsized at 8:13.

By 8:25, most of the torpedo damage to the fleet had been inflicted. All the outboard battleships along Battleship Row had received at least one direct hit from the bombing runs. The *Arizona* was a raging inferno threatening her sister ships; the stern of the *California* was on the harbor floor; the *West Virginia* was gradually sinking to the bottom; and the *Oklahoma* was in the process of rolling over. Only the *Nevada*, which had received one torpedo hit, was able to begin preparations to get underway.

Phase Two

The second phase has been termed a lull because it marked a distinctive break in between major attacks by the Japanese. During this phase, attacking aircraft made a series of sporadic bombing runs over the harbor. An estimated fifteen dive-bombers participated in five attacks on ships in the Navy Yard, the *Maryland*, *Oklahoma*, and *Nevada*, and cruisers and destroyers anchored in various parts of the harbor. At 8:32, the *Oklahoma* capsized. Although the yard craft and other small vessels assisted the damaged ships, the larger ships in the harbor moved very little. The major action during this phase took place in the channel between Ford Island and Pearl City, where a midget submarine was sunk. The destroyer *Monaghan* was moving out of the East Loch when she passed between the *Tangier* and the seaplane tender *Curtiss* as the Japanese were firing on a midget sub that had surfaced in the harbor. The *Monaghan* put on flank speed, rammed the sub, and dropped two depth charges. Then the *Monaghan* headed out to sea, followed by the destroyer *Henley*.

Phase Three

The third phase began with the appearance of eight groups of high-altitude bombers that crossed and recrossed the harbor. Their altitude of about ten thousand feet prevented them from causing any major damage. Bombs converted from fifteen- and sixteen--inch artillery shells were dropped along Battleship Row and the Navy Yard. The *California* was hit by a fifteen-inch shell equipped with tail vanes, which penetrated to the second deck and exploded, causing a major fire. The main deck of the *Curtiss* was hit with a bomb, which killed twenty men and injured fifty-eight others. While bombers converged on their primary targets, numerous ships began to make their way out of the harbor. The tanker *Neosho*, which had just delivered part of her load of aviation fuel to Ford Island, pulled out between the *California* on one side and the *Maryland* and the *Oklahoma* on the other and made her way to Merry Point Landing. At the same time, the repair ship *Vestal*, which had been bombed, and then set on fire from the *Arizona*'s burning oil fires, started to get underway, but was beached near Aiea Point when she started to sink. A few destroyers from the East Loch and a couple of cruisers from the Navy Yard also began to make their way out of the harbor. The *Nevada*, which was anchored at the northern end of Battleship Row, behind the *Arizona*, cleared her berth at 8:40 and steamed toward the harbor entrance while under attack from a determined group of dive-bombers. With her bridge and superstructure in flames, she continued to make her way down the harbor channel. When Admiral William R. Furlong, aboard the *Oglaga*, feared that her sinking would block the harbor entrance, he ordered that she be deliberately grounded at Waipio Point, with the assistance of two tug boats. On the Navy Yard side of the channel, the destroyer *Shaw*, which was berthed in Floating Dry Dock Number Two, received a bomb hit possibly intended for the *Nevada*. The resulting fire eventually destroyed her forward magazines and produced one of the most spectacular explosions seen during the attack. In Floating Dry Dock Number One at the Navy Yard, the US Pacific Fleet flagship, the USS *Pennsylvania*, as well as the destroyers *Cassin* and *Downes*, sat high and dry on keel blocks. Soon after the USS *Shaw* blew up, a bomb hit between the *Cassin* and the *Downes*, rupturing their oil tanks and causing a raging fire, which forced the crews to abandon them. At this time, the *Pennsylvania* was hit amidships by a heavy bomb, and her captain ordered the dry dock flooded in order to extinguish the fires around the *Cassin* and *Downes*. As the water level in the dry dock rose, the burning oil on the surface engulfed the ships. The heat became so intense that it set off the magazines in both destroyers, causing an explosion, which tumbled over the *Cassin* and onto the *Downes*.

Phase Four

During the fourth and final phase of the attack, an estimated twenty-seven dive-bombers conducted nine strafing attacks throughout the harbor. The attacks were aimed at the nearby airfields with their remaining aircraft, and rescue workers who were assisting the disabled fleet were caught in the open. By 9:45, the last attack planes left the harbor area and returned to their carriers. The burning wreckage in the harbor and on the airfields reflected the losses in personnel and equipment. When finally tabulated on paper, the losses were worse than originally estimated immediately following the attack. In Pearl Harbor, eighteen warships had been sunk or severely damaged. The navy lost ninety-two aircraft, including five from the carrier *Enterprise*, and had thirty-one damaged. The army lost ninety-six aircraft. The army and navy dead numbered 2,251, and almost half had been on the sunken *Arizona*. The navy listed 2,036 killed in action or fatally wounded and 759 wounded in action; the army listed 215 killed in action or fatally wounded, 360 wounded in action, and 22 missing in action. These were the figures given before the Joint Congressional Investigating Committee on 15 November 1945.

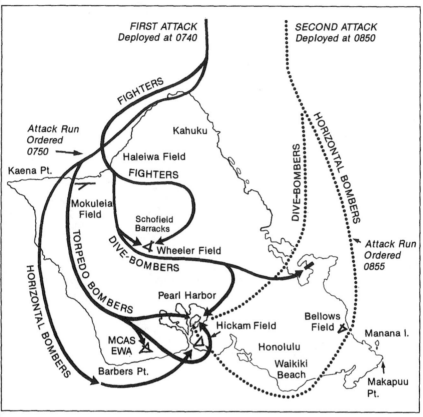

JAPANESE ATTACK ROUTES. At 0600, the first wave of 189 planes took off from carriers 230 miles north of Oahu. An hour later, a second wave of 171 planes departed. At 0753, Commander Mitsuo Fuchida transmitted the signal for a complete surprise attack, "Tora, Tora, Tora" ("Tiger, Tiger, Tiger").

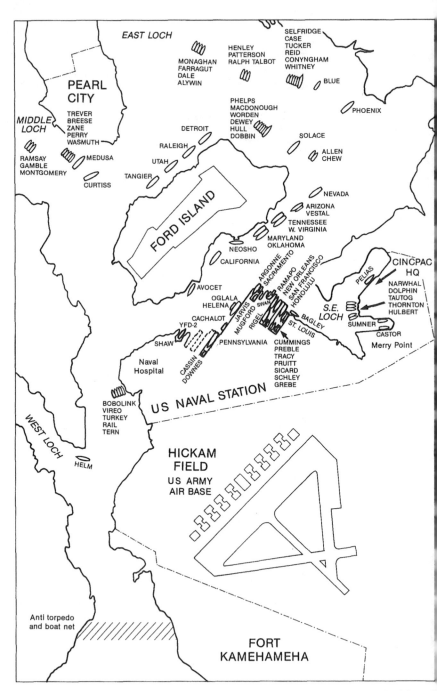

SHIP LOCATIONS. Pearl Harbor, 7 December 1941, 0755. Of the ninety-six ships positioned inside the harbor, eighteen were sunk or heavily damaged. Contrary to popular belief, only about half of the fleet was present.

7 DECEMBER 1941:
THE DAY OF INFAMY

ON THE ISLAND

Mapping a Tropical Forest

In 1932, when President Herbert R. Hoover decided that the major part of the US Pacific Fleet would be based at Pearl Harbor, Oahu was already a haven for an established network of Japanese spies. Despite keeping lists of suspect Japanese residents, American authorities were helpless to stop legal and illegal espionage activity. In 1941, a small but extremely efficient ring of secret agents was operating in and around Pearl Harbor. Due to the freedom allowed island residents in prewar Hawaii, there were few secrets unavailable to, and unknown by, Japanese-trained agents and intelligence officers. Airplane rides from nearby John Rodgers Airport and sightseeing boat tours by the navy provided easy access to virtually any sections of the harbor for the purpose of monitoring military activity. Anyone was free to roam the hills of Oahu with camera and binoculars in hand. Even in the early 1940s, such activity was not uncommon. Vacationers and servicemen were the mainstay of the Hawaiian tourist industry.

Because of such a large number of sightseers and day trippers, it would have been impossible for US government officials to stop and search anyone who appeared suspect. Although the hills of Oahu provided a safe observation post under an impenetrable tropical canopy, they were not an exclusive refuge under control of Japanese spies and sympathizers. Not all the activity in the upper and more remote reaches of the island was devoted to cloak-and-dagger adventures. The story of William Showen shows the other side of military activity taking place on the island. For him, Oahu became a personal paradise. It was a land of endless beauty, where he escaped the drudgery of everyday life by disappearing into the expanse of tropical forest covering the low mountains. After spending the winter of 1938–1939 in the Civilian Conservation Corps in Green River, Wyoming, Showen enlisted in the army in November 1939, with a first duty assignment in Hawaii. Winter in Hawaii was certainly a lot more appealing than another winter in Green River.

It was 1 October 1941, when the 21st Infantry Brigade was deactivated and reformed as the 24th Infantry Division. I was promoted to fourth-class specialist, which raised my pay to $54 a month. I was assigned to the new division headquarters G-3 Section as a draftsman. We were quartered in the Third Engineer Batallion quadrangle, at the lower end of the post next to Wheeler Field.

My work at the time included preparation of overlays to accompany requests sent through the Hawaiian Civil Defense Department to Washington, D.C., for money to build emplacements for long-range coastal defense weapons we didn't have. These would be 240-millimeter rifles and would be placed on the plateaus near the Koolau Mountains. Part of my spare time was spent "living it up" at the Kemoo Farm tavern, right outside the gate.

Although assigned a different job, I didn't lose my interest in the mountains and obtained permission to make a "reconnaisance" for three or four days of the Kawainui and Kawaiiki Streams, which drain a good part of the Koolau Mountains and empty into the Kawailoa Gulch and finally the Anahulu River at Haleiwa. Three other fellows volunteered to go with me. They were Celestino Coto from Tarrytown, New York, and two boys named Barden and Wicky.

On an afternoon in mid-November 1941, we were dropped off above the Opaeula Reservoir at the beginning of a contour trail, which we followed down into the Kawaiiki Stream. We established camp on the stream and, after a meal, told stories around the campfire and bedded down for the night. The next morning we had breakfast, policed the area, and after packing up began our trek upstream to a point I estimated was the point to begin our ascent of the north ridge.

This was a long and difficult climb and it was midday or later by the time we reached the top. Crossing over after a break, we began our descent into the Kawainui Stream and valleys. We learned to use the staghorn, which grew abundantly in areas, as a cushion and steps for our descent in very steep areas. Reaching a stream bed, we began following this downstream. I had set a main junction on the main Kawainui Stream as our destination for that night. It was tiring and as we rounded each bend in the stream I kept expecting our junction at the next bend. At least this is what I kept telling the comrades. They, of course, were as tired as I was and anxious to reach our campsite.

We finally reached our destination and our campsite was ideal. The valley was wide and open and the main stream was much larger than I had anticipated. There also were a number of large pools in which to swim near our camp. Water was within easy reach for cooking, and the place we set up our tents was comfortable. There was plenty of dry wood for the fire, which we kept going all night. We remained at this spot for two nights, making short exploratory hikes upstream and into adjacent areas. We did much swimming and relaxed as much as we pleased.

On the morning of the fourth day, we struck camp and began our move downstream. There was no jungle to cut through, although in areas we had to use the banks to bypass deep water and small waterfalls. By noon we ran into the narrows, which were a series of canyon-like sections filled with deep water and steep walls. We couldn't hike through, so we had to climb up over ridges and around these ponds. Coto, who was a large man, was not able to make the steep climbs so we carried his equipment and he swam through these areas. We repeated this operation three or four times until we finally reached a large open area and pool and decided to camp for the night.

We had our usual fire and hot chocolate and pancakes for breakfast at this our last campsite, which happened to be on large flat rocks. The chocolate was at night and the coffee was in the morning. We also brought along syrup for the pancakes, and there were usually canned vegetables and bread, which we had purchased at the commissary. After completing breakfast on the final morning of our "vacation-reconnaissance," we continued downstream to an old dam and the beginning of a tunnel and another contour trail, which we followed to the Eucalyptus Forests above Kawailea. Our transportation arrived here.

There may have been a few other camping ventures either when I was with the 21st Infantry Brigade or with the 24th Infantry Division. I recall once camping on the beach at Makua on the leeward (west) side of the island. At that time I was looking forward to returning home and seemed that I had a dream of visiting my home. In those days an overseas tour was two years and I would have been on Oahu two years on 29 December 1941. But I also admired this land and felt akin to it because of its delightful climate and beautiful sunsets. From Makua it must have been a beautiful sunset in those days. The beach was isolated and there was but one house in the area and no road north of the valley. Only the railroad continued around Kaena Point to the northwest.

It was sometime in November that all units on the island were alerted. For what we didn't know. Rumor that the Japanese fleet had disappeared had us wondering. Troops were issued live ammunition for guard duty for the first time. The only time we had ever used live ammunition was on the firing range for scores. But this died down and everything seemed to return to normal. We in headquarters were not issued weapons or ammo. One company, however, did remain in the field in the North Sector, on installation guard duty at bridges and cable huts, etc.

As always seems to happen, there are some people who complain if they think others are not doing the same duties as they are. It matters not that the others have other duties to perform. In our case those of us who worked in the headquarters were excused from normal housekeeping and guard duties. But personnel assigned to these duties were complaining to the first sergeant. Since we worked five days a week, we were not available for such extra duties during those five days. But on weekends the first sergeant began scheduling us for such details as housekeeping, kitchen patrol, supply, guard, etc. I had been listed in the roster for window-washing duty on 7 December 1941.

It was a beautiful Sunday morning and I was in the mess hall having breakfast, which was served from 7:00 to 8:00 a.m. on Sundays, an hour later than usual. I wasn't happy about the window-washing duty facing me and weighed the risks of punishment if I should fail to appear for that detail and spend the day in Honolulu at Waikiki Beach. I visualized myself at Waikiki Tavern having a few beers, or sunning myself on the beach.

Just before 8:00 a.m., as I was leaving the mess hall I heard an explosion to the south of us and saw men running toward the southwest edge of the quadrangle. There were one or two more explosions as I ran to join the others. It was Wheeler Field; there were six airplanes diving on the field and we could see the bombs released from under the fuselage and fall toward the hangars. Now there was fire and heavy black smoke rising. The planes circled over our barracks. We could see the heads of the pilots in the cockpits and the fire from machine guns in front of the cockpits. Then the red sun on the side of the planes. They were Japanese planes.

We scattered as the bullets ricocheted off the concrete walls of our barracks. I ran to the supply room. Other men were already there arming themselves. I grabbed a rifle belt and two bandoliers full of ammunition and an older rifle that I was familiar with. But as soon as I opened the bolt, I realized this was being prepared for shipment back to the States. It was loaded with cosmoline. I reached for a newer M-1 rifle and discovered that all the ammunition I had was in clips for the older rifle. Transferring the rounds from the older clips to the new clips, I listened as the radio announcer stated that Pearl Harbor was being attacked, as well as Schofield Barracks and Wheeler Field, that it was not a drill but an actual attack by Japan.

The radio was signing off and played the national anthem. "The Star-Spangled Banner" never sounded more beautiful and raised our spirits just hearing it.

Outside, noncoms (noncommissioned officers) had their squads sandbagging and setting up machine guns on the roofs. By now the smoke columns were rising high into the sky with a westward drift and we could see the larger accumulation of smoke from the Pearl Harbor area.

Rumors were circulating, and one man is alleged to have panicked so badly that he ran round wildly crying, "We're going to die, where's the priest?" The small daughter of Major Miller, our G-1, was supposedly hit by a Japanese bullet while walking home from church. Headquarters personnel reported to our division headquarters and I set up the first operational situation map for the G-3 Section of World War II. The first entry or entries were messages allegedly from an airline pilot who saw a Japanese troopship south about twenty miles headed north toward Pearl Harbor; another reported a truckload of Japanese headed up Wilhelmina Rise.

We moved the headquarters from the wooden building we had occupied into one of the artillery concrete quadrangle buildings on the north part of the post. Windows and doors were sandbagged. Guards were everywhere, and as darkness came on many were trigger-happy. A standing joke at the time was of the guard who called, "Halt, bang, bang, who's there?" Civilian dependents were evacuated preparatory for movement back to the mainland.

Other messages reported paratroops landing at Barber's Point and elements of the Nineteenth Infantry Regiment making ground contact with enemy troops of Kaena Plateau. A marine major radioed a request for permission to conduct a practice landing at Waialua Bay. I heard General Wilson state that a message might be sent back stating that any landing would be immediately fired on. We thought that night that the Japanese had returned as the shells exploding over the Pearl Harbor area lit up the sky with loud explosions and flashes of flame. Again, it must have been a result of trigger-happy gunners. The Japanese were nowhere around.

Early that morning at an isolated and newly established radar station on the north side of the island, Privates Joe Lockard and Elliot had tracked two planes that were scouting ahead of the attack group and later detected the larger flight. This station was not yet in full operation, and they were merely practicing with the equipment. The information was called into the Information Center, Fort Shafter, which was headquarters. The men were told to forget it. A flight of B-17s was expected from the States.

By custom over the years, Sunday had always been a day of relaxation and recuperation for military personnel in Hawaii. No officers visited their companies, and men were accustomed to spending Saturday nights in town or elsewhere. Families attended church on Sunday mornings. Aircraft were in their hangers, and ships clustered in Pearl Harbor. Lockard and Elliot were actually waiting for the chow truck to arrive from Schofield. Elliot had been in the old brigade headquarters unit, and I knew him there. He had hinted about some new equipment that was being installed and had something to do with what was called television. This provided a person with a receiver to actually see the people conducting a program at the broadcasting station. It was hard to visualize such progress then.

We were all issued gas masks, as well as weapons and ammunition, and were required to carry them with us at all times. Even after men were permitted leave to visit town again, they had to carry weapons and gas masks with them. There was an immediate and continuing blackout at night. No lights were permitted, and violations were noted and perpetrators punished. For a few days we were uneasy, still expecting the Japanese to come back and attack. They could have landed on the north side of the island while bombing Pearl Harbor. There wasn't a single piece of artillery in the field to oppose such a landing. Only the one company on installation guard.

Some men had suggested joining me in the mountains to conduct guerrilla warfare against the Japanese, should there be a surrender of the island to overwhelming enemy forces. We knew we had no aircraft left and few naval craft able to fight. However, on the afternoon of the third day after the attack, we received word that an aircraft carrier had arrived with a full complement of aircraft and pilots. We felt considerably relieved by this news. After that there was a constant buildup of emplacements, replacement of ships and aircraft, and repair of ships at Pearl Harbor. We finally received the authorization to build the emplacements for the 240-millimeter rifles and installed them. They never had to be used against an enemy, but we were happy they were there and knew that the sound of the "ashcan" traveling overhead after one of them fired carried a lot of explosive power against any target aimed at.

I did not remain in the headquarters long, as we seemed restricted and I wanted to be out in the field. A situation developed which permitted me to be transferred to the S-2 Section, 21st Infantry Regiment. This was located at Brigade Woods, where we used to set up Brigade Headquarters. Thus the name. But now everything had been placed underground, as in the fashion of dugouts. The command post was a rambling structure built in the ground, and earth was piled over it. Quarters were holes in the ground with logs, plywood sheets, and earth piled on top. Beds were wooden bunks built on the sides of the earthen walls. Probably similar to those used by American, French, and British forces in World War I during their trench warfare in France.

I spent a week on the plateau and later went down into the Makua Valley and spent more time down there. Abandoned buildings were used for quarters at Makua. The weather was excellent and there was no rain. I spent much of my time climbing and exploring with members of the unit. Sometimes a pig was killed and there was a little feast. The food was good, anyway, and I was outdoors, which is what I wanted. I continued sending overlays and reports back to the regimental S-2. After about a month of this pleasurable duty, I was called back to Brigade Woods and assigned to the Observation Post at Puena Point. This was just east of Soldiers' Beach.

During all my time in Hawaii, I did not become acquainted with anyone from the civilian community. Of course, I never spent much time there. A few visits to Honolulu and a few taverns, but no lasting friendship developed. My time was occupied with military-related activities or hiking and camping in the mountains. By 1943 the ratio of men to women on Oahu was about three hundred to one. This included defense workers and military, in addition to the normal male civilian population. Since the war began, martial law had been in effect and these islands were governed by the military. It was deemed advisable, considering the large male population, to provide an outlet through legal means for the normal male biological urges. So there were legally established houses of prostitution. They were licensed by the government, and the girls were regularly inspected by military doctors. This did not eliminate venereal disease, but there would likely have been many more cases if prostitution had been suppressed, as those needing treatment would not be receiving it.

It was a common sight in downtown Honolulu to see a line of men along a street and up a stairway to the second floor of a building. Everyone knew what they were there for, and those in line knew everyone knew what they were there for.

———

William Showen remained with the 24th Infantry Division, but transferred to Australia when the division was relieved by the 41st Infantry Division in June 1943. His last action of the war came in April 1944, when he landed at Tanaharmarah Bay in Dutch New Guinea, in a combined operation with the 40th Infantry Division. He arrived home on 18 July 1944 and was discharged in June 1945.

Military Intelligence

GERALD M. VANDYKE

The Pearl Harbor attack created a controversy that continues today. Although the attack was a surprise to the military commands at Pearl Harbor, many historians, political observers, and military commanders believed that Roosevelt and his military staff members had knowledge of the Japanese attack as early as 2 December 1941, some five days before the actual attack. Proponents of theories linking Roosevelt to a cover-up speculate that he feared the Japanese would abandon their attack plans if the military forces at Pearl Harbor were provided with prior warning.

Theories about conspiracies and cover-ups have been discussed in a number of books claiming to have found the evidence necessary to implicate the Roosevelt administration. The books have not been able to prove their charges and have added more confusion to the controversy. Literature supporting claims of a conspiracy had led many Americans to believe that US cryptographers had broken the Japanese military code prior to the attack. However, the only code broken was the Japanese diplomatic one.

On 6 December 1941, a number of Japanese diplomatic messages were interrupted and decoded. These priority messages, known as the "Purple" code, were aggressive and full of fighting words, and they revealed Japanese dissatisfaction with American and British peace efforts. A later message instructed Japanese ambassador Kichl-saburo Normura and Saburo Kurusu, his special envoy, to present a note already in their hands to the State Department at 1:00 p.m. on

7 December. These messages completed the intelligence picture and supplied an up-to-the-minute report on Japanese diplomatic activity. From these messages, the military command and White House staff in Washington, D.C., knew that the Japanese, some twenty-one hours before sunrise over Pearl Harbor on 7 December, had opted for war. Whether the messages were ignored, lost, misinterpreted, or conveniently destroyed by the president and his staff remains at the center of the controversy. Until proven otherwise, it is safe to say that Roosevelt remains innocent of conspiracy charges. He appears to have taken the answer and absolute truth about the issue to his grave.

The story of Gerald M. VanDyke provides an inside view of the controversy. At the time of the attack, VanDyke was a special agent with the US Army Counter Intelligence Service. His observations and reports made prior to the attack surfaced later when the question of a conspiracy was raised.

Was the Japanese treacherous attack on Pearl Harbor a complete surprise? No! Were Lieutenant General Walter G. Short and Admiral Husband E. Kimmel scapegoats for that naval disaster? Largely, yes! Was there ample warning given of an impending attack, and the military forces warned to go on the alert and "stay there"? Definitely, yes! Was the warning given by someone specifically designated to keep the high command informed on the international situation—particularly the critical relations between the United States and Japan? Positively, yes! Then, why was our fleet caught in Pearl Harbor, and why didn't the commanders of other military services take necessary—at least normal—precaution?

First, I want to state that having taken an oath of secrecy, when joining the Counter Intelligence Service, I kept quiet for twenty-five years. But now, I do not feel that I am being disloyal in any way by revealing the actual facts concerning military actions bearing on the Battle of Pearl Harbor. I consider it my duty to pinpoint, as near as possible, the blame for the way things did happen. For the sake of all concerned, directly and indirectly, and for the purpose of having a correct historical record, there should be no further delay in revealing these important basic facts.

At this point, I would like to briefly mention some of the things leading up to the Pearl Harbor attack. As far back as 1934, we had received reliable reports that Japan was planning to dominate all of Southeastern Asia, including most islands in the West Pacific. The US government was fully aware that Japan's course of action would lead to an intolerable clash of interests, and that war might become inevitable.

In a report to the intelligence officer, Hawaiian Division, on 10 April 1937, I pointed out Japan's basic plan for expansion. First, to make Japan the sole champion of the interests and welfare of the Oriental races, and the guardian of the peace of the Far East. Second, to settle once and for all with the White Race, the question of Japanese supremacy in the Far East. Third, to protect Japanese commercial interests by removing or eliminating, if necessary, all competitors from her special sphere of influence. Japan, at that time, was deeply involved in a war with China in an effort to complete the first phase of its Basic Plan for Expansion. Japanese leaders were openly advocating war with the United States and Russia, if necessary to achieve their final goal. Even before this, the United States had undertaken peacetime military measures to counter a probable Japanese expansionist move to the south and east. For example, a number of aeronautical survey expeditions were made in the South Seas with a view to locating suitable aviation facilities, to be used for protecting lines of communication between the United States and Australia in case of war. I was secretary for one such expedition.

As an indication of the clear and positive opinions of our office, I would like to refer to an essay that I wrote and showed to my chief on or about 1 November 1941, and finally published in the *Duncan Eagle* on 11 December. In part, it read: "With the first of our opponents, Hitler, we are already committed to mortal combat. By the second, the Mikado, it is felt, we are being lured by an olive branch in one hand while the other hand, constrained with a dagger, seeks our most vital organs for a fatal stab at the most propitious moment! Can that hand be stayed? Or is it decreed by fate that THAT HAND shall fall and thus plunge the peoples of the Pacific into the most gruesome holocaust of all times? The answer is not far off! The coming struggle is one in which every man, woman, and child has a part! They must know their part! They must do their part!"

Shortly thereafter, at a meeting of the FBI, Naval Intelligence, and Counter Intelligence agents, my chief declared to all: "War between the United States and Japan had become inevitable!"

I had spent eight years in the Philippines, about five years in China, and nine years in the Hawaiian Islands; and I had devoted a great deal of time and effort toward keeping up with Japanese public opinion and studied, intensively, the international situation in the Pacific area. I took two daily Japanese newspapers, read their important magazines, and many of their military books; I made frequent reports to the local intelligence officer, Hawaiian Division, on special situations as they arose.

Early in 1941, I was transferred to the Counterintelligence Service, with headquarters in Honolulu. On or about 12 May, I was informed by my chief that, in accordance with a decision of the joint chiefs of staff in the Hawaiian Islands, I had been given the assignment of writing up a Summary of Contemporary Opinion in the Japanese press, to be distributed biweekly to the FBI, to Naval Intelligence, to major echelons of the army and air corps in the Hawaiian Islands, and to the War Department, Washington, D.C.

The summary was to be considered a Combined Report for the above services. It contained my personal analysis and interpretations of information coming from the Japanese press and also a summary of opinion based on other information at hand.

On Saturday afternoon, 29 November, my birthday, I remained on duty after normal working hours in order to get out the last issue, because of the urgency of the international situation and especially because of the critical relations between the United States and Japan. The report was signed by an assistant, for the chief who was absent.

On the first page of this document, I made a summary and an assessment of the international situation and, therein, warned: "Our forces should be placed on the alert and stay there, due to the imminent possibility of an attack." Words were underlined for emphasis. Said crucial warning was never heeded!

Just whom was to blame for what happened? First, I would say, that I do not believe it was directly the fault of either Rear Admiral Kimmel or Lieutenant General Short, although they could not deny responsibility, due to their positions. I am inclined to blame the various intelligence officers for not properly weighing the information that we furnished; for not giving our opinions more careful consideration; and for not impressing the importance, or likely importance, thereof on the heads of the various military services.

The high command had confidence in my ability to interpret the situation correctly, when giving me the assignment, but failed to act on the information, it is believed, due to carelessness, or neglect, on the part of their respective intelligence officers at the most critical time. Those failures could have been due, perhaps, to the fact that the intelligence officers had never been made fully aware of the actual intent and purpose of the Summary, and the tremendous amount of background and study used in its preparation.

One more thing that could be considered of vital importance: during the development of the Hawaiian Department Defense Plans, my office in the Hawaiian Division was given much of the "spadework" to do. After considerable study of Japanese tactics in previous wars—Japan being our logical enemy—it was the opinion of our office that the first phase of the plan should be based on the possibility of an attempted surprise attack. However, when the matter was taken up with a consultant from higher headquarters, Hawaiian Department, the idea was arbitrarily ruled out!

I have always felt that said decision was crucial and proved to be a fatal mistake, 7 December! (The officer who made that decision attained considerable fame during the invasion of Europe. His death was untimely; his name will not be mentioned.)

Special Agent VanDyke's Pearl Harbor experience was related in a letter to his sister within a week after the attack. On the evening of 6 December, VanDyke spent the evening aboard the Oklahoma. Deciding to spend a leisurely Sunday at his nearby house, he left the battleship early on the morning of 7 December to return home. The letter provides a view of the attack from the streets outside the military bases.

Dear Sister,

My family and I were living in a house alongside the fence around Hickam Field, near Pearl Harbor, at a point about halfway between the large hangars, which bore the brunt of the attack at this field, and the battleships, in Pearl Harbor, which were the main objective of the bombing attack against the navy.

We were centrally located and therefore had an excellent view of the great, treacherous aerial assault. Many, and some of the first, planes flew in for the kill directly over our house at an altitude of less than one hundred feet.

There was no protection, and no place to go—it was just a case of stand by, look on, and trust that you were not going to be struck down or be blown to bits.

In the face of it all, I never saw such a fine display of calmness among men, women, and children. Hysteria was totally absent. Strange as it may seem, some people were hard to convince that the attack was real. They declared it was a mock battle by the American forces.

But we soon saw an American bomber shot down nearby, and also a Japanese plane burst into a red ball of flame, streaking down toward the dry docks. This soon dispelled all about as to what was going on!

I had just placed a pot of coffee on the stove and stepped outside when the first planes came over. I called to the family that the war was on! The coffeepot remained on the stove for four days, when I returned and found the bottom burned out!

After watching the attack for a short time, I decided to make the trip to Honolulu and report for duty at my headquarters. I also decided to go alone, without my family, as there was only a single highway, and I felt that, inasmuch as no direct attack was being made on our residential district, it would perhaps be safer to leave the family in the zone of stray bullets and falling shell fragments than to risk taking them over a main highway that was certain to be congested with traffic, making it a prime target for strafing by enemy planes.

Sure enough, as had been assumed, the road was strafed, soon after I had passed over it, killing a number of people and causing a serious traffic jam.

A friend of mine, Ray Berry, and I departed for our respective posts at the same time. A few days later I was shocked to learn that Ray had been killed on the road a few minutes after our parting and that his body had not been identified for two or three days.

I arrived in Honolulu safely and reported for duty, and four days later I got my first "cat nap." Most of that time had been spent with local police and FBI agents, picking up enemy agents, 248 in all. Their intelligence force was wiped out, and we doubted that it would ever be given a chance to reorganize (and it didn't).

My family had been safely evacuated to Honolulu, where I met them on the fourth day. Each had volunteered to donate blood for the wounded and otherwise be of assistance.

The morale here is at a high pitch, and the men in the armed services are itching for the Japs to come back and vowing that, if they do, few, if any, of the little yellow devils will ever live to tell the tale.

Chin up—that's where ours will always be.

Your brother, Mason

Gerald M. VanDyke retired as a master sergeant in 1944 with over thirty years of service in various army intelligence operations and units.

Radar Reconnaissance

RICHARD SCHIMMEL

On Sundays the army radar service operated from 4:00 to 7:00 a.m. During other days the service operated from 4:00 a.m. to 4 p.m. At 6:45 a.m. on 7 December, the army mobile radar station at Opana picked up signal of a lone aircraft flying toward Oahu. The operators were expected to plot about twenty-five patrol aircraft during their duty hours, and the aircraft was dismissed as one of their own. At approximately 7:00 a.m., when a large number of aircraft 130 miles to the north appeared on the screen, Privates Joseph Lockard and George Elliott called the air-warning Information Center at Fort Shafter to report the incident. Their call was received by a young and inexperienced second lieutenant, who was training at the center and serving as the duty officer. The officer told the pair to "forget it" and discounted the information as being a patrol from Hickam Field or the group of B-17 Flying Fortresses that was due in from California sometime that morning. The operators remained at the station and continued to plot the advance of the aircraft. At 7:45 a.m., the aircraft, now more numerous, appeared closer to the island. Within forty-five minutes, the first wave of bombers made its run over the airfields and the harbor. The last chance to alert ground, air, and sea forces at Pearl Harbor was lost when the advancing Japanese airplanes were incorrectly identified and assumed to be American aircraft. Private Richard Schimmel was at the Fort Shafter Information Center when the message was received from the mobile radar station in Opana. His story provides insight into the problems, in both personnel and equipment, experienced during the early days of radar in the military service.

My story began in the early days of August 1940, as I waited for my high school homeroom assignment. My days at school were definitely numbered. I wasn't one of the favorite subjects of my teachers. Time and time again, we would be warring in the battle of good conduct.

My father had been a wanderlust, and I must have inherited that part of me from him. I would read all the travel news in the local or Philadelphia newspapers and dream about visiting all the distant and exotic places described in the articles. By far, Hawaii had the most appeal to me. Sunning myself on a pearl-white beach with blue sky and water, surrounded by native girls, didn't seem a bad way to spend part of my youth. The only problem was figuring out how to get there.

I had a friend who was one of twelve children. I was one of eight, so money was not flowing in either one of our families. My friend got me to join the army with him. The only problem came when it was time for his father to sign the papers. He wouldn't sign because he was afraid of losing some relief money. Even without my friend, I didn't have any problem enlisting. I had already signed my father's name to the enlistment papers.

I signed up on 28 August 1940, and was put in the Signal Aircraft Company. Little did I know that as of 14 August 1940, the Signal Aircraft Warning, using radar, had been added to the army. I had pictured myself sitting with a big pair of ears listening for airplanes. I was assigned to the Hawaiian Islands, for which I was very happy. It seemed my daydreaming about Hawaii would come true after all. We sailed out of New York early in November 1940 and spent Thanksgiving doing kitchen patrol between Panama and California. We spent a week in California on Angel Island, which was farther from San Francisco than Alcatraz. We landed in Hawaii on 10 December 1940, to the sounds of "Aloha Oe" from the Army Band and the moans of the soldiers already there shouting, "You'll be sorry."

We took the Oahu train for Schofield Barracks, where we were greeted by our drill sergeant, who had been the number-one model soldier out of some thirty-five-thousand men in 1940. Within a few minutes, we found out why he was selected for that honor. He had all the charm and personality of a junkyard dog, and I firmly believed that he would come back as one when he died. I quickly learned my right from my left. If you had to carry a large rock in your left hand for a day, you wouldn't easily forget.

We didn't live in a little grass shack, but close to one. Our home was the old chemical warfare barracks. The ceiling got higher and the floor got lower from us scrubbing the floors so often. Our captain had been a West Pointer, and we lived the plebe life. The food was good, but the table manners were strictly West Point. I was beginning to wonder about those days on the beach that I had imagined. Schofield Barracks seemed as far away from Waikiki Beach as Allentown, Pennsylvania.

We started our training, which at times was like teaching us Greek, considering that none of us had ever seen a radar unit until now. By the time we put up the first radar unit outside the United States, we knew that the red paint on the antenna had to match the red paint on the tower. The whole training course was salvaged by two good electronics men. They made things click and got the equipment and men operating in the right order. After the radar had been set up at various locations around the island, we worked with the civilians in building the Information Center at Fort Shafter. We rode back and forth from Schofield Barracks to Fort Shafter each day with our peanut butter and jelly sandwich plus one meat sandwich and two cookies in a brown bag. When the Information Center was completed, we worked inside the building setting up plotting tables. I was quickly becoming a jack-of-all-trades, master-of-none in radar operations. When they needed telephone operators, my friend Joe McDonald and I got the job. It was easy duty with few calls and fewer officers and noncoms. We split shifts inside the center, and while one was on duty the other usually rode in one of the trucks past the guard gates into Honolulu, dodging the military police (we had no passes) until it was time to come back on duty. We were already in a radar unit, so we thought there weren't too many places they could send us for punishment.

It seemed that if you got in trouble in the army, a radar unit was most likely in your future. One of our friends was sent to the mobile station at Opana and later became a hero of sorts. He supposedly picked up the Japanese planes on his radar unit as the attack force was making its way toward the island. When he called the Information Center on that Sunday, Joe McDonald took the message and told the lieutenant, who was the duty officer, about what they were sighting on the radar up on the point. After the message came in to the center, Joe woke me up and said, "Shimoto (my nickname), the Japs are coming." We weren't exactly sure what the lieutenant did with the message, but Joe and I were convinced that the planes they sighted on the radar were Japanese. At the Information Center, it was thought that the aircraft were patrol planes from the island or offshore carriers, or flights due in from California. We waited inside the center to see what was happening about the sighting, but the situation was being downplayed as a false alarm. Except for Joe and me, nobody seemed to be worrying too much. About a half-hour later, we heard the bombs. I ran out of the tent I was in and made my way to a cliff looking over Pearl Harbor. We could see planes diving and puffs of smoke, but little else. Someone said that the navy was having a sham battle. At the time, that made the most sense out of anything that happened during the morning. At least that would explain why the lieutenant wasn't worried about the sighting reported by the radar unit at Opana. Just then, we heard on the radio that Japanese planes were attacking Pearl Harbor and that this was no drill. As soon as the radio announcer said "Japanese planes," we took off from the cliff and ran back to the center. We grabbed our rifles and what gear we could and took up positions inside the fort. My friend and I climbed on the top of the mess hall, but retreated down when anti-aircraft guns behind us started shooting over our heads. For us, the attack lasted only a few seconds. Jap planes passed over our heads on their way to Pearl Harbor without firing a shot.

After the attack, I went back to the Information Center and copied the message Joe McDonald had received from Joe Lockhart word for word. Joe Lockhart was the one who picked up the Jap planes and reported them to the Information Center. Joe McDonald's copy of the message was taken from him and sent to Washington, D.C. Admiral Kimmel and Lieutenant General Short were interrogated about the message by Supreme Court Justice Owen Roberts as part of the investigation into the attack. Everyone assigned to the Information Center had to make a written statement as to what they saw and heard on that Sunday morning. For a number of days after the attack, the Information Center saw a lot of military brass conducting formal and informal investigations. Most of the attention was given to the duty officer, Opana radar unit, and Joe McDonald. Rumors were in the air that there was a conspiracy somewhere in the Information Center that prevented the message from being passed on to the proper authorities in a timely manner. Within a couple of weeks, things returned to normal. I never did find out what happened to the lieutenant who was the duty officer, but I do know that all radar sightings and messages were thoroughly checked out and reported to higher command. I learned a lesson the hard way, along with everybody else in the radar units. It was a lesson which would serve me well for the rest of the war.

Richard Schimmel later became crew chief on a small radar unit on Oahu. After spending time on Canton Island, north of American Samoa, he was shipped back to Hawaii and became crew chief at the Fort Shafter Information Center. After over five years, fifty-six months of which was overseas, he was discharged as a staff sergeant in the air force.

Schofield Barracks and Wheeler Field

HUGH LAW AND ALBERT GLENN

By December 1941, Schofield Barracks was more than its name implied. The sprawling military reservation in central Oahu was the headquarters and training area for the army's 24th and 25th Infantry Divisions. The base—named after Major General John M. Schofield, US Army Pacific military division commander who in the 1870s spent considerable time on Oahu investigating its potential as a military base, was the army's counterpart to the navy base at Pearl Harbor. Prewar army life at Schofield was anything but boring. Training exercises and readiness drills were conducted on a continuous basis, much to the consternation of many of the enlisted men. On 5 December 1941, men from units of the 24th and 25th Infantry Divisions were enjoying a well-earned weekend of rest after spending a week in the field during a training exercise. At 7:55 a.m., when a major wave of Japanese bombers swept down from the north through Kole Kole Pass in the Waianae Mountain Range, the men at Schofield Barracks graduated from training exercises to the real thing. The war was delivered to the steps of their barracks.

The damage at Schofield Barracks was minor compared to that of the other bases on Oahu. If Japanese military commanders had launched an amphibious or aerial invasion of Oahu, there is no doubt that the army base would have been subjected to an intensive attack, with results similar to those at Pearl Harbor. Heavy strafing and numerous errant bombs aimed at nearby Wheeler Field pro-duced a small number of casualties and limited damage to buildings and equipment. Many military observers questioned whether Schofield Barracks would have been attacked if it were not for its proximity to Wheeler Field.

Unlike Schofield Barracks, Wheeler Field was a primary Japanese target and was devastated by the attack. The army airfield, just across the road from the army compound, posed the greatest threat to the waves of attack planes. If American fighter planes were somehow able to get airborne and mount a counterattack, the Battle of Pearl Harbor could have taken place over isolated stretches of central and southern Oahu. Within minutes, half the combat planes at Wheeler, forty-two of eighty-three, were either damaged or totally destroyed. Airplanes disappeared in the fireballs of exploding bombs. Hangars and utility buildings were blown apart. Men were cut down by flying debris and strafing as they tried to make their way across the runways to man the planes or pull them to safety. As with other airfields around the island, at Wheeler the fighter planes were lined up in neat rows in front of the hangars in order to guard them against sabotage attempts. After the attack, Japanese pilots remarked that the attacks on the airfields had been easier than the practice runs they had made weeks earlier.

The destruction at Wheeler Field was repeated at every major military airfield on Oahu. At Schofield Barracks, the few minutes under enemy fire turned into days and weeks of guarding, reinforcing, repositioning, and reconstructing defensive positions around Oahu. One Hawaiian legend is that a goddess stood guard over Kole Kole Pass in order to protect Oahu from intruders. After the main wave of the Japanese attack force passed through the mountain gap on its way to Pearl Harbor, soldiers digging in around the island remarked, tongue-in-cheek, that the goddess "was probably shacked up with some squid [sailor] in downtown Honolulu for most of the night and the better part of the morning."

Hugh Law entered the army air corps in November 1939 after spending two years at the University of Oregon. He was discharged from the army air corps in December 1939 and enlisted in the army in February 1940, and received his orders for Hawaii. On the morning of 7 December, Japanese bombers were among many of the difficulties Private First Class Law encountered.

The first time in five months that Finance visited the mess hall of the military police company, which it had been assigned to for breakfast on Sundays, proved to be a quite memorable meal. After the usual Sunday feast of bacon, eggs, toast, and milk, Sergeant Howard Ledgerwood·and I stepped out into the northeast corner of the Schofield Headquarters, Third Engineering Battalion Quadrangle, for a bit of fresh air. It was approximately 7:55.

Within seconds after we went outdoors, a flight of silver planes buzzed the quadrangle from the direction of Kole Kole Pass. As they flew past, we heard the rat-a-tat of machine guns coming from groups of planes that followed them over the base. At the time, each plane was maybe from two hundred to three hundred feet above the quadrangle. Sergeant Lawford from Headquarters and Headquarters Company was standing beside us when he somewhat nonchalantly uttered some words that should have been made part of American history. At about 7:56, while looking skyward at the swarm of planes buzzing the area, he calmly remarked, "Well, this is the end of the Japanese empire." Sergeant Ledgerwood and I assumed it was part of a naval air maneuver. The prophetic words of Sergeant Lawford were lost somewhere in the excitement and panic of the situation; however, they did galvanize us into action.

A minute or two later, we broke off the lock to the military police supply room next to the mess hall and then broke off the locks to the ammunition chests and rifle racks. By this time, it was now after 8:00, the quadrangle was filling up with G.I.'s, mostly military police. As we were tossing out 0-3 rifles, we were strafed by planes heading over to bomb and strafe Wheeler Field. After tossing out all the bandoleers of thirty-caliber ammo and all the 0-3 rifles, we went out on the lawn of the quadrangle to fire at the planes. I fired my first shot at around 8:55. By now, the Third Engineer Battalion was dragging a heavy thirty-caliber water-cooled machine gun onto the quadrangle of the west barracks. As I fired another shot, the assistant provost marshal, a major, drove into the quadrangle. Sergeant Ledgerwood and I were getting ready to fire again, when the major stepped out of his sedan and hollered to a group of military police, "Arrest those men," meaning us. The major must have been post officer of the day on duty to have been in uniform so early Sunday morning. As the group of about ten military police started to grab us, a group of bombers strafed where we were standing. From the sky, the Japanese pilots must have been wondering why we were huddling up to form such an easy target. Maybe they thought we all wanted to die together. As the bullets started to hit closer, the group split and dove and sprinted in different directions. In the meantime, the engineers had the machine gun finally in action, but without water in the jacket. The gunner fired one long continuous burst and immediately froze the weapon. Those were their first and last rounds fired at the enemy. In all the commotion, the major's sedan had been driven off, leaving him on the quadrangle and vulnerable as the rest of us. The major took the manhole cover off the parade deck and dropped into the sewer line. That was the last time we saw the major.

When everyone had scattered, Ledgerwood and I grabbed our rifles and ran up to the deck by our finance office. We fired from that position until the last of the planes buzzed overhead. We didn't down any planes. All we could do was shoot and hope that the bullets hit a fuel line or detonated one of the bombs before they could drop them on Wheeler Field. We stood on the deck and watched the planes fly over Wheeler, then listened for the explosions amid the clouds of smoke already coming from the airfield. If some of the military police would have used the rifles and ammunition we had tossed out to them or if the major had ordered them to do so, there would have been a chance that we would have downed some attackers. Since that day, I have had very little use for military police or military police officers.

Hugh Law resumed his air force career in 1942, when he was recalled as a flying cadet. He finished the war as a first lieutenant, after having flown thirty-two combat missions against Japan. He was discharged from the air force in 1970.

*　　*　　*

Albert Glenn joined the army in March 1940 out of the Boston Army Base after having been disqualified, due to poor eyesight for a job as a Massachusetts conservation officer. The results of the eye test administered by the army recruiter showed his vision to be considerably better than what the state test had indicated. Arriving in Hawaii in May 1940, he was thirty years old and had the distinction of being the oldest rookie in 35th Infantry Regiment. He was, perhaps, the oldest private in Hawaii.

I arrived at Schofield Barracks on 7 May 1940 at around 7:45 a.m., nineteen months to the exact day and almost the exact hour of the Japanese attack. I took recruit training in June 1940 at the time Norway was invaded by Germany. The army at Schofield was on alert call during most of that month.

Later in the summer, I was chosen to go to S-2-3 school for map and drafting duty. In those times very few enlisted men joined the army with anything more than a high school education, so I felt that my couple years of college certainly helped in selection. As it turned out, I had one of the highest marks in the school and was promoted to corporal on 1 July 1941 when I graduated. I was assigned to Headquarters and Headquarters Company, Third Battalion, 35th Infantry Regiment. The military occupation specialty was called chief scout and observer for my position. The title sounded as if it belonged to someone in the army cavalry on the western plains in the 1870s fighting Indians.

On the day before Thanksgiving 1941, Schofield Barracks went on alert call. Some of the troops went on island patrol to vital installations with machine guns mounted on weapons carriers. The latest alert threatened the chances of some teams in the army football championship, which was always decided on the first Saturday in December. At the time there was an eight-team league. Word had it that personnel vital to those teams in the championship would not find themselves on duty at one of the vital installations on the first Saturday in December. I always felt that the reason the first Sunday in December was chosen for the attack was the Japanese believed most of the army personnel would celebrate on 6 December after the game and would not be in too good of a condition on the following day.

On Sunday, 7 December 1941, I went to chow at around 7:00 a.m. There were about fifteen men in the chow line, so it was hard to tell if the postgame celebration and the weekend of liberty took their toll on the troops. There was usually a light turnout for Sunday breakfast. A lot of men preferred to catch up on their sleep, especially after being in the field for a week on maneuvers. Although an alert was in force, no one was forced to stand reveille on Sunday mornings. After a breakfast of cereal and fried eggs, I took an orange and went up to the second floor of M Company and put it in my footlocker. At around 7:45, I was still up on the second floor when I heard considerable commotion at Wheeler Field, which was about a half-mile away. From the window, I could see puffs of smoke and thought there must be a "jawbone" alert to get the army air corps on the ball. About a minute later, all of Schofield shook from a series of violent explosions. I wasn't quite sure what was happening. I could hear planes, but could see nothing passing overhead. It didn't take long for the planes to appear through the window. A second or two later, the planes put a few rounds through our lockers. A few minutes later, I heard the bugler on the quadrangle of the 35th Regiment blow alert call. This meant to fall out with full field packs and combat gear. I put on my gear as quickly as possible and ran over to the battalion headquarters to get my S-2-3 equipment, which was standard operating procedure when on alert. Being in such a hurry, it seemed like none of the combat gear fit right and something was always missing. At least the S-2-3 equipment was where it should have been.

While making my way across the quadrangle, planes with the rising sun on their wings could be seen. Whenever a plane passed overhead, we dove for cover regardless of whether they were strafing or not. Now that we were in full combat gear, we were ready to fight the Japs. The only problem was that we didn't have any ammunition. The captain of M Company had forgotten his key to the supply room and had to shoot the lock off the door before we could begin to fight back. A platoon from M Company put a fifty-caliber machine gun on the roof of the barracks and fired at about twelve planes going overhead. One of the artillery units elevated a 105-millimeter howitzer and was thought to have knocked down a plane. Most likely, the unit fired at the same time somebody else did and saw a plane go down and took it to its credit. It seemed hard to believe that a howitzer aimed at an airplane flying at three hundred feet could knock it down, but stranger things have happened in war. The attack seemed to be over just after it began. We fired at planes for only a few minutes. Our losses were light compared to those of Wheeler and Pearl Harbor. The regiment motor pool was shot up pretty bad, but the number of men killed or injured was low.

After the attack, we were able to regroup and form some sort of organization expected from a military unit on alert status. We were ordered to go to Fort Shafter to protect against a possible invasion of the island. It was about 10:45 when we began to move out in the trucks salvaged from our motor pool. On our way, we were able to get a view of Pearl Harbor as we passed by Pearl City and Aiea. Numerous ships were sunk or capsized, and the center of the harbor was covered with smoke and with a mist from the water that was being sprayed. Nobody said a word as we passed by the harbor. Everyone moved about to get the best view possible and just stared at the sight with a bewildered and dazed look.

By the time we got to Fort Shafter, things had settled down quite a bit. Company commanders were busy putting together guard detachments and preparing defensive positions for rumored invasion. As night began to settle on the island, everyone seemed to get a little more nervous with each passing second. By the time it got completely dark, fingers were tightly wrapped around the rifles and lightly tapping the triggers. That night while on guard duty, M Company killed some of the ninety-millimeter antiaircraft men of Fort Shafter who were changing guard. They had put on a light that was not blacked out. Orders were to shoot lights out if they were not blackened. At the time, I was in the basement of the command building getting my situation man up to date. When the firing began, I froze for a couple of seconds wondering if the Japanese invasion had begun. For the few minutes afterward, there was a lot of heavy sweating and breathing by everyone at the fort. There was kind of an eerie silence when everyone was afraid to move, speak, or make any kind of sound for fear of giving away his position. Later that night, some men from M Company killed a cow from a nearby pasture that had wandered into the perimeter of the weapons section. All in all, it was a tense night. There was a collective sigh of relief when day started to break over the eastern horizon. For some men, I was sure that turning to see the sunrise was the first time they had moved a muscle all night long. Finally, on the day before Christmas 1941, we went back to Schofield Barracks to clean up and have Christmas dinner. Things now had quieted down. We were all thankful to be alive and I, for one, wondered what happened to "peace on earth, goodwill toward men," which was supposed to have filled the earth from end to end. When we returned, rumor had it that a search of the base laundry turned up several shortwave radios. At the time, the laundry for all personnel was done by about twenty Japanese civilians. To the best of my knowledge, the question remained unanswered whether they were sending information to the other side or just using the radios to listen to broadcasts from their homeland.

After the Christmas break, we went to the western side of Oahu at the Waianae Mountain Range and spent the rest of December and January stringing up barbed wire and building gun emplacements along the shoreline and up in the foothills of the mountains. By the end of January, our unit was coming up to full strength with addition of recruits from the States. In May 1942, I was promoted to staff sergeant without having been a buck sergeant. As the war went on, I became the old man of the outfit in age and time in service.

Albert Glenn served with the Third Battalion, 35th Regiment, as the 25th Infantry Division, nicknamed the "Tropic Lightning Division," made its way through the Pacific, with stopovers at Guadalcanal, Russell Islands, New Caledonia, and Luzon. On 29 June 1945, Glenn was discharged for the convenience of the government after serving over five years.

Hickam Field

NICHOLAS GAYNOS AND WILLIAM ROLFE

At approximately 7:49 a.m. on 7 December, Lieutenant Commander Kakwichi Takashashi broke away from the first attack wave and steered his group of fighter bombers toward Ford Island and Hickam Field. At 7:55, Japanese bombers made their first appearance over Hickam Field, strafing men and aircraft with machine-gun fire and dive-bombing hangars, bar racks, and other buildings. To prevent sabotage attempts, planes were grouped in parallel rows outside their hangars. Among the fifty-six bombers parked on the runway and concrete aprons were a number of the new B-17 Flying Fortresses. The planes were so concentrated that the distance between wing tips was ten feet or less.

On this Sunday, Hickam Field was busy with normal work activity. Many officers and enlisted men were present for the arrival of a new group of twelve B-17 bombers, for which Hickam Field was the first stop from the West Coast. The bombers arrived over Pearl Harbor in the middle of the first attack. Japanese pilots were as surprised as their American counterparts. The American bombers were ignored by Japanese planes and drew fire only when attempting to land. The B-17s, which were unarmed to lighten their load, were low on fuel after a fourteen-hour flight and flew in no recognizable formation. Japanese Zeros attacked the B-17s when they broke through the light cloud coverage on their approach to Hickam Field. Despite the attack, all the B-17s were able to land:

eight at Hickam Field, two at Haleiwa Field, one at Bellows Field, and one on the Kahuku Golf Course.

An ironic set of circumstances led to the arrival of Japanese and American planes over Oahu during the same time span. At 7:02, the radar operators at the army's Opana radar station near Kahuku Point at the northern tip of Oahu detected a large mass of planes heading toward the island. The message was promptly relayed to the Information Center at Fort Shafter. The officer on duty there believed that the planes were the B-17s.

Due to its strategic importance and convenient location on the southeast side of the harbor entrance halfway between Pearl Harbor and Honolulu, Hickam Field was subject to three attacks. Although the airfield was neutralized within minutes by the first attack wave, Japanese fighter bombers continued to inflict more damage and casualties while making their sweeping passes over Pearl Harbor. At approximately 8:54, thirty-six Japanese Zeros, under the leadership of Lieutenant Commander Shigekazu Shimazaki, made a final run over Hickam Field. The planes were part of the fighter coverage for the second wave of attack bombers. When the Zeros encountered little or no air resistance over Oahu, they were free to break formation and attack targets of opportunity. The remaining aircraft on the ground at Hickam Field were easy targets for the Zeros.

The final attack decimated Hickam Field. Barracks were in flames, and the hangars were blown apart by Japanese bombs. More than eighteen bombers were reduced to burned-out shells or mounds of smoldering metal surrounded by debris. One curiosity was the excessive strafing of the ball field. Outdated Japanese maps showed the presence of an underground tank farm at the site. Although no underground tanks existed, they had been considered during the late 1930s and had been depicted in a number of maps used for presentations. The Hickam Field survivors were faced with the grim responsibility of counting their dead and salvaging the few remaining aircraft, but their spirits were lifted by the sight of the bullet-torn American flag still flying near the barracks complex.

The following letter of Private First Class Nicholas Gaynos was typical of the efforts that thousands of servicemen made to notify their families and friends of their well-being. After the attack of 7 December, Oahu was cut off from the outside world by military commanders who readied the island defenses for another Japanese assault. Telephone and telegraph communications between the Hawaiian Islands and the mainland were nonexistent except for priority military transmissions. Back on the mainland, newspaper stories and radio reports could only supply secondhand accounts of the attack and partial lists of the dead and wounded. Letters sent from Hawaii to the mainland after the attack arrived after a two- to three-week delay. Families anxiously awaited any news about the fate of their loved ones. Mothers and fathers kept a lonely vigil in their homes, dreading an official military visit.

Gaynos's letter is of special interest because it contains an uncensored account of the Pearl Harbor attack. The army censored numerous letters thought to contain sensitive information. Many letters that arrived home resembled cookie cutouts, with more gaps than words.

After more than sixty hours of battle, Gaynos, a battle-worn and bone-weary army radio operator from Fairfield, Connecticut, was able to find temporary reprieve on the wooden floor of a barracks. Using a flashlight to pierce the barracks' darkness, Gaynos wrote a dramatic account of the attack on Hickam Field.

---

9 December 1941

Dear Folks,

Well, I'm okay and feeling fine. We sure had a hot time here for a while and I thought that my end had come—God, was it hell. I'll give you an eyewitness account of the Japanese air raid on Pearl Harbor and Hickam Field on Sunday, 7 December 1941. This ought to make a good news copy for the *Bridgeport Post*.

Well, Sunday as usual, all of the men were sleeping late because we had no work to do. I was sound asleep, having gone to bed at

4:30 a.m. after being relieved of duty. It was exactly 7:55 when I was almost tossed out of bed by a terrific roar and the ensuing concussion. Most of the fellows also got up and, on looking out the window, we could see flames about five hundred feet high and huge clouds of smoke coming from Pearl Harbor.

No one thought it was war until we looked out of our eastern windows and saw some of our hangars in flames. Somebody yelled, "They are Japanese planes," but nobody believed it. We all ran out of the barracks and looked skyward. It was plain to see then. They were only from fifty to one hundred feet off the ground, and the huge red circle under their wings proved their identity. Some of them had huge torpedoes under the fuselage almost as long as the ship itself.

The thunder of bombs and the staccato of machine guns made such a deafening roar you had to yell to be heard a few feet away. The splintering of wood as fifty-caliber bullets ripped through the wooden barracks was mixed with screams of men as they ran from one shelter to another. We soon collected our senses and the full realization that war was here.

Some men cried, some laughed, others were terrified, some just couldn't seem to understand what it was all about. I soon had my senses under control and jumped in a car headed for my post. With a hail of bullets and with the planes roaring right over our heads, we raced down the street. I arrived at my transmitters and dove into a hole caused by an exploded bomb. One young fellow was dead, and his legs stuck out of the hole. It reminded me of a book I once read back home. I stayed here until things had quieted down and then scurried for safety in my flimsy office. We all knew they would be back soon so we hurriedly made preparations for their return. It was at 10:20 when the second attack came.

I was busy removing a radio truck to safety. Three men and I kept working as they dived into the big barracks and dropped load after load of bombs. The very ground shook, and my ears were ringing. By this time they spotted my equipment and headed straight for my men and me. I was lying in a small hole about ten feet to the right of my trucks. As the planes dove down at us, I could peek out under the brim of my tin helmet and see them spitting fire at us. The ground in front of me was spraying up and I could see the bombs leave the planes and head straight down at us. One of them was a one-thousand-pound bomb and landed fifty feet on my right. Three kids with a machine gun were shooting at the plane and the bomb landed almost on them. It blew them sky high—gun and all.

The dirt and stones fell all over us and I ached all over. I emptied my forty-five pistol time after time into the planes, but it was futile. I thumbed my nose as they roared right over my head. We all swore like hell.

The planes were still roaring around staffing us unmercifully as those of us that were alive got into cars and started to pick up the dead and wounded. One of the kids who was blown up with the machine gun was lying about fifty feet away. I tried to pick him up and he fell apart in my arms. He was covered with dirt and smiling. We rushed as many as we could to the hospital and gave first aid to those lying near us. Things were now getting quiet and then ambulances, nurses, and trucks came to pick up the men. Some of the things were so ghastly I cannot write of them.

All I can say is that my baptism under fire sure was hell on earth and I saw my Maker on Sunday, 7 December 1941.

Well, after the raid I took about ten men and rounded up a dozen cars and started to gather gasoline, and supplies for my equipment. I kept the best car for myself and kept things moving. Later I found out I was using the general's car and I was wondering why everyone was saluting me. I had everything under control at 2:00 p.m. and sat down and had a good smoke. We had rescued two drums of gas from a blazing yard, and I thought that any moment we would be blown to bits. I worked straight through until Tuesday night. Boy, was I tired! I slept on the floor in front of my radio transmitters and fell sound asleep. I was awakened about 2:00 a.m. by rifle shots. Someone said that saboteurs were in the woods. I hunted all night with a cocked forty-five pistol and a thirty-thirty rifle. My hunt wasn't in vain, for I shot about thirty rounds of ammunition and perhaps I did hit some Jap.

Since the war, I have confiscated about $500 worth of radio equipment, soda, beer, cigarettes, and seventeen cars. Some fun! I conked a Jap in the Sears-Roebuck in Honolulu and had him turn over a short-wave receiver. Boy, was he scared. I hadn't shaved, changed clothes, or washed since Sunday. I had two revolvers, one huge bolo knife—about twenty-six inches long—and a mean look on my face. I was sure having fun scaring hell out of these civilians. Everything is under control now. We will have a good welcome for them next time. I was starting to enjoy this excitement now and I have a twenty-shot Browning automatic rifle now and if I even spot a Japanese I am going to hold that trigger until the magazine is empty. Outside of a few bruises and sore bones, I feel as good as if it had never happened.

So, I shall say good-bye now and don't worry about me as I can see now that if I keep my head I shall be okay. Hope you are all okay back home and wish you all the best of holidays, Merry Christmas to all my friends and say hello to anyone who asks for me and tell them I shall write as soon as I have more time as I am very busy now and I should be sleeping right now. I am writing this by flashlight on the floor and so excuse the pencil and writing.

Aloha,
Son, Brother, Soldier,
Nick

P.S. I won't be a private very long.
P.P.S. I was to have become a corporal on 8 December, only those Japs have disrupted our office and I have to wait now.

*   *   *

In the 1930s, a young man's interest and imagination were easily captured by "those magnificent men in their flying machines." During air battles fought high above the trenches of World War I, the airplane proved a weapon with unlimited potential. The pioneers who operated these frail and flimsy crafts became the first generation of fighter pilots. The "flying aces," who had colorful names, fought legendary battles and became international heroes. In just a few years, aviation had evolved from a hobby into a science and an industry. Careers were waiting for those willing to join this great adventure.

For Private First Class William Rolfe, who had grown up during the Great Depression, the airplane offered an escape. Aviation meant an opportunity for success.

———

My mother died in 1937 just after I quit school in the tenth grade. While working as a warehouse manager in Richmond, Virginia, my thoughts were with the future as I was alone in the world with no living relative.

My thought turned to the future in aviation. If I could enlist in the army air corps and get those years of experience as an airplane mechanic, I could then apply for a job with the Federal Aviation Administration as an apprentice airplane mechanic and my future would be assured.

I enlisted in the army air corps on 3 June 1940. The very next day I and a group of other men left the Main Street station bound for Fort Slocum in New York to wait for a ship to Oahu, Hawaii, and Hickam Field.

We sailed from New York on the USS *Hunto Ligette*, moving through the sea to Panama, then Panama to San Francisco and then on to Honolulu. It took us about thirty days to make the trip. God, was I seasick. I and others slept above deck for most of the trip. The food smells from the galley were unexplainable. I had thought of falling overboard and I never wanted to set foot on another ship. The trip from Frisco to Oahu wasn't near as bad as going through the Windward Passage.

On arrival at Hickam Field, I was assigned as a clerk in Headquarters and Headquarter Squadron, Fifth Bombardment Group. After working this area for six months, I requested to attend the Airplane and Engine Mechanic School. Upon graduating from the class, I was given a rating of aircraft and engine mechanic, first class, and assigned to B-18s under the watchful eye of a crew chief.

A few weeks before 7 December 1941, I was assigned to an anti-sabotage squad. They issued us steel helmets, ammo, 1903 Springfield rifles, and gas masks. On weekends we were taken to strategic points to guard for possible sabotage in downtown Honolulu.

The week before 7 December, we were all restricted to the base. We knew something was up, but did not know just what. On 7 December, the restriction was lifted, so most of us were going to leave the base and a lot had already gone.

The time was 7:15 a.m., 7 December. While sitting on the side of my bunk getting dressed in my civilian clothes, I heard a bomb go off, another, another, and another. I pulled on my pants, ran to the windows just as a Jap Zero came flying low over my barracks with machine gun going. I could see his fixed landing gear and the big red circle under each wing. I yelled "Great God! The Japs are here!" The other guys at the time laughed at me. Looking over at Pearl Harbor, I could see our ships at anchor with smoke pouring from them and Jap planes over them like hornets. Airmen, running out of the barracks onto the parade ground to get a better look, most of them in their underwear, were machine-gunned by the Jap planes winging over Hickam after dropping their bombs on the navy ships that couldn't seem to get out of their way.

I grabbed my rifle, helmet, and ammo after changing into blue denim dungarees and went down to the first floor of the barracks. The only person I could see in charge was a corporal, who was telling everyone to go to their station.

I went to the hangar line. Crews were trying to start the B-18s as the ordnance men were trying to load bombs in the bomb-bay doors. A lot of these brave men, like many others, died on the spot without the planes getting off the ground. I fired several times at Jap planes, but I'll never know if I hit any. Antiaircraft were shooting with their coast artillery. We saw a couple of B-17s trying to land with Japs on their tail, and they couldn't. High-flying planes came over the hangar line dropping bombs; how I didn't get killed, I'll never know.

Orders were passed around that the Japs were wearing blue coveralls and that if any of us had on blue denim to change immediately because any person wearing blue would probably be shot on sight, with no questions asked. I changed into my other uniform quickly and never knew what happened to my blues from that date on.

That Sunday night on 7 December, most of us had an idea that the Japs would try to land on the island. At some time I can't remember, all hell broke loose. It seems that a pilot was coming in for a landing at Pearl Harbor after having been out on a search mission, but he used the wrong required approach. Every gun in the area let loose on him; the tracer bullets lit up the sky. I heard later that he had been shot down, but made it to shore safely.

Monday, 8 December, was spent trying to piece together airplanes so they would fly, and getting organized.

In January 1942, William Rolfe was transferred to the 72nd Bomb Squadron at Bellows Field as a B-17 mechanic. In June 1942, the squadron participated in the Battle of Midway. In 1943, his commission as a second lieutenant resulted in a billet at Patterson Field in Dayton, Ohio. His aviation career ended in 1945 with a discharge from active service and a promotion in the army reserves.

Ford Island

HARRY MEAD

Conveniently located in the center of Pearl Harbor, Ford Island was the geographical hub for the air and sea traffic of the US Pacific Fleet. The island, which was large enough to accommodate an airfield, primarily served to receive aircraft carrier planes and to operate and maintain them while they were in port. The air base was also headquarters for PBY navy patrol planes and Utility Squadron One. The latter was responsible for miscellaneous duties, such as delivering mail, towing targets, and aerial photography.

Ford Island proved an ideal location for both planes and ships. Being in almost direct alignment with the channel entrance to Pearl Harbor, it offered easily accessible berthing space to larger ships, which had limited mobility and maneuverability. Just offshore of Ford Island, quays, or tiny concrete islands, provided much-needed deep-water anchorage. The docking arrangements called for battleships to the northeast of Ford Island, and carriers to its northwest side. Even with the carrier force away from Pearl Harbor on the weekend of 7 December, space was at a premium. On Ford Island's northwest side, the cruisers *Detroit* and *Raleigh*, the former battleship turned target ship *Utah*, and the seaplane tender *Tangier* took up temporary residence. On the island's northeast side stood the pride of the US Pacific Fleet: Battleship Row. Lined up in a tight formation side by side were the *Nevada, Arizona, Tennessee, West Virginia, Maryland, Oklahoma*, and *California*. Also in or near this group of battleships were the *Vestal, Neosho*, and *Avocet*.

Like other airfields on Oahu, Ford Island was one of the first targets for the original wave of Japanese dive-bombers. Within minutes of the first round of bombs, the capacity of the air base at Ford Island to mount an aerial counterattack was destroyed. Those planes not destroyed by bombs and secondary explosions were chopped to pieces by continued strafing from enemy planes that swept over the island and dropped their payloads. Ford Island was even subject to attack by torpedo bombers. Numerous torpedoes that passed under their floating targets ended stuck in the muddy banks along the island's perimeter.

During and after the first wave of attack planes, men on the island prepared for what they thought would be a continued attack to finish off the rest of the fleet. Salvaging anything useful from the debris of the planes and hangars, they quickly worked to set up makeshift machine-gun emplacements and antiaircraft fortifications. The lull between attacks was a chance to catch their breath and appraise the fate of the fleet. The view from Ford Island was anything but encouraging. Around the island was a panorama of sinking and burning ships against a background of fire and smoke. Because the backbone of the US Pacific Fleet had been crushed and shattered, many on the island concluded that the rest of the fleet suffered a similar fate. Many had thought that Ford Island would be the last stronghold against a Japanese invasion force.

Immediately after the second attack, forces throughout the island regrouped for another air attack and a possible invasion by an amphibious assault force. Priorities were to assess the damage to the fleet and the ground forces and to locate and chart the movement of the Japanese attack fleet. The few remaining operational aircraft were pressed into service for aerial patrol and reconnaissance. On Ford Island, the only available planes were a few unarmed amphibians. Due to the large number of casualties suffered at the larger airfields, crews to fly the planes were as scarce as the planes themselves. Therefore, personnel were grouped together to get the planes airborne. For Radioman Second Class Harry Mead, being assigned to fly on a search mission offered the chance to see the devastation of Pearl Harbor from the ground and the air.

———

Seven December 1941 was a "duty day" for me. I was scheduled to relieve the supervisor of the watch in our utility wing base radio station that morning. I had showered and shaved the evening before. After I rolled out of the sack, I proceeded to the combination washroom and head to complete the usual morning ablutions. After dressing, I went down to the mess hall on the first deck of our barracks building and ate breakfast. (I really have no positive recall of this, but it was my usual routine before going to the hangar.) Finishing breakfast, I strolled leisurely down to our corrugated-sheet-steel hangar and mustered with the Duty Section.

I was twenty years old and finishing up a minority enlistment. I had joined the navy on 25 January 1939, six months after graduating from high school. My main reason for joining was to circumvent what I thought was harsh parental rule. And to go to radio school so I could learn to copy Morse code well enough to pass the Federal Communications Commission amateur radio license exam. Upon graduating from "boot camp" at Newport, Rhode Island, Naval Training Center, I was retained on board to help train two successive companies of recruits. In June 1939, after receiving an interview for suitability, I was transferred to the Naval Training Command, Norfolk, Virginia, as an applicant for Anticipher School (Radio). Graduation from this school in October 1939 found me scanning the "new assignments" (transfer) list. Before I knew it, I was bound for an old World War I, flush-deck, four-piper tin can in red-lead row in the Philly Navy Yard. Subsequently, the ship to which I was assigned was traded to the British and became the HMS *Churchill* (previously, USS *Herndon*). Through a fluke of fate, I was transferred to the West Coast to another destroyer (USS *Cushing*) in September 1940. By this time I had advanced in rating to radioman third class. Shortly after reporting aboard the *Cushing*, we departed for Pearl Harbor. My life aboard destroyers was miserable—the one feature of navy life I failed to consider before joining was seasickness. And I had a chronic case of it. In July 1941, I was transferred to Utility Squadron One (USS *Rigel*), based at Ford Island. I had to agree to extend my enlistment for two years to get this new assignment. It was worth it. No more seasickness, and I've never been bothered with airsickness.

The duty section mustered at 7:30 a.m. on the hangar deck. After mustering, my watch-stander and I walked over to the "radio shack" to relieve the watch. I had been promoted to radioman second class while aboard the *Cushing* and thus qualified for supervisor of the watch in the Ut Wing Base Radio Station. We relieved the watch at precisely 7:45 and were "briefed" on the previous night's messages, etc. As I recall, it had been a "dead evening" for the off-going watch.

Our base radio station was located in the southwest corner of the hangar that was closest to the new, concrete-reinforced operations building. We had an old National HRO receiver, on which we monitored the international distress frequency of five hundred kilohertz, and some other equipment used to communicate with our own aircraft, plus a teletype hooked up with CinCPac headquarters and an old wire telegraph system that was also linked to CinCPac and, I believe, to our sister squadron, VJ-2 across the field.

Prior to 7 December, CinCPac had issued an order that made it mandatory to tune in on nine hundred kilohertz in the event of an air raid in order to receive modulated continuous wave broadcasts in Morse code from CinCPac headquarters. It was customary for us to undergo periodic mock air attacks by some of the army aviation units stationed on Oahu in those days.

At 7:55 a.m. on 7 December, I heard a plane starting a power dive and immediately thought, "Oh shit! Another mock air raid. Well, I'll go outside and have a look." I opened the door leading out to the tarmac, where our planes sat in two rows, and gazed skyward towards the northwest. A plane resembling a P40 was in a dive and headed straight for the PBY hangars at the south end of Ford Island. I saw something drop off the plane and thought, "Hell! He's dropped a piece of cowling off his plane. Some mech is gonna catch hell for that." All of a sudden there was a tremendous explosion and water spewed upward like a geyser. It slowly dawned on me that the pilot had dropped a live bomb. "Boy! Now somebody's really gonna get it," I thought. The second plane corrected his dive and dropped his bomb in the middle of a row of parked PBYs. The hangar was at a sufficient distance from me and the blast so deflected that I felt no concussion. Fortunately for the personnel in that area, a new drainage ditch was being dug around the perimeter of the airfield. The hangar doors were only open about five feet, but it seemed as though forty or fifty men came running through them in less than a minute and dove into the ditch. A chief petty officer standing near me uttered on oath and said, "Those planes have the Japanese insignia. Them ——— bastards are bombing us!"

With that, I dashed back into the radio room and immediately set up nine hundred kilohertz on one of the available receivers. I remember portions of a message being sent concerning reports "that Japanese paratroopers are landing on Barber's Point." Later it was learned that it was one Jap pilot who had bailed out of his damaged plane.

By this time dense clouds of black smoke from burning oil in the harbor were drifting up into the sky. The noise of the bombs and torpedoes was terrible. To say that I was scared would be an understatement. I was terrified. Soon, the duty messenger came in and said, "The officer of the day says for everyone to take cover in the Operations Building."

I turned to my watch-stander, "Come on, let's get the hell outta here."

We ran over to the Operations Building with a group of other men and crouched in a stairwell, fearing the worst. I had no sooner found a spot than the messenger came by and said, "The officer of the day wants you in the radio room right away. He didn't mean for you to leave."

I got up, made my way past all the guys in the stairwell, and made a mad dash for the hangar. About halfway there, I looked up and saw a Jap plane making a pass on Battleship Row. His machine guns were winking at me, and I could see little chips of cement flying up in the air. They appeared to be heading straight for me as I ran. Just as I figured I had run out of luck, I came abreast of a four-by-four weapons carrier (truck) parked nose-in toward the hangar. Crouching down by the front bumper, I waited for the plane to pass overhead. Once it was gone, I continued to the radio room.

Inside, the officer of the day was waiting and told me, "Send a message to Maui [our other squadron, VJ-3, was located there] and tell them we're under attack. Tell 'em to take evasive action by rolling some gasoline drums out on the runway."

"Aye, Aye, Sir," I replied and set to the task. All the time I was transmitting the message (in Morse code), I could hear the rat-a-tat-tat of the bullets strafing the hangar. Apparently most of them could not penetrate the walls and roof, because of the corrugated exterior and flew off into space.

By this time our leading chief of the radio gang had returned from shore leave and had gathered most of the radiomen in the radio room.

"I want three volunteers. You, you, and you!" he said, pointing to me and two others.

"But Chief—I've got the duty. I'm supervisor of the watch," I replied.

"I'll relieve you! Get out there and man your plane."

So that's how I got airborne that day. Our planes were rather old, Sikorsky JRS-1s. A twin-engine, parasol-wing amphibian—it was a noncombatant type of aircraft used for photographing fleet battle practice, towing targets, and carrying mail personnel. Some one gave us three Springfield rifles for defensive weapons, and we proceeded to get airborne. Our takeoff coincided with the lull between the first and second waves of attacking Jap planes.

Our pilot set a course to the south of Oahu, as ordered, and we flew a typical pre-sector search pattern looking for the Japanese fleet. Our sector was three hundred miles out, fifty miles across, and three hundred miles back to base. We didn't see a darn thing, but halfway through the mission I intercepted a message from "Benny" Benefield, in one of the other planes: "Under attack by Japanese Zero X Posn

Lat (?) Long (?)." I figured, "There goes my ole liberty buddy." As luck would have it, Benny's plane emerged unscathed. Apparently the Jap was out of ammo or his guns were jammed. Upon our return to base, as we flew over Pearl Harbor in the landing pattern, the view of the harbor was horrendous. Billowing clouds of dense black smoke climbed high into the sky. Firefighters and damage-control parties swarmed over the burning ships trying to establish order out of utter chaos. It was the most heartbreaking sight I've ever seen: our navy a shambles! The decks of the *Arizona* were awash, and Old Glory hung limp and bedraggled just barely above the water at her stern.

We landed (I don't recall the time) in the late afternoon. Almost immediately, we were put to work belting ammunition. During my absence on the search mission, machine-gun tripods had been fashioned from angle iron, sandbag emplacements had sprung up around the perimeter of the landing field, and there was a rather hushed sense of urgency and dogged determination in the air. Everyone expected another attack. We all believed that the rumor of troopships was valid and we were bent on preparing for the worst. Invasion!

Just after dusk I was standing near one of the machine-gun emplacements. Heel-and-toe watches were in force around the perimeter of the airfield. Everyone just seemed to be waiting for the inevitable: another attack. Suddenly, in the distance came the drone of planes. We all strained to determine from which direction the sound was coming. In a very short time we made out a single plane, in the normal landing pattern, coming in for a landing. Without warning, a gunner opened up with a machine gun; tracer bullets arced toward the plane. Before you could bat an eyelash, every gun in the harbor was firing. Tracers were going every which way. Our officer of the day was having a fit running up and down the area yelling, "Cease-fire! Cease-fire! They're friendlies. Ceasefire!" All to no avail. No one could hear him for the noise of the guns. I understand one of the planes crashed near the Pearl City Tavern—a favorite hangout of some of our crew. It was learned later that they had shot down three F-4Fs from the USS *Enterprise*.

I was still wearing the enlisted white working uniform that I had donned that morning. It would be three days before I was to receive permission to leave the area and go to the barracks for a shower, shave, and fresh clothing.

Our water mains to Ford Island had been ruptured during the bombings and torpedo attacks on the battleships. Somehow they brought potable water over from the mainland in a small tank trailer for drinking purposes.

From here on my memory is not nearly so vivid. I only remember vignettes: the *Nevada* being run aground in the edge of channel to prevent her sinking and blocking the channel; an antiaircraft battery of the USS *Curtis* getting a direct hit on a Jap torpedo plane; the USS *Solace* being towed away from over a Japanese midget two-man sub hovering neath her hull; a barge crane dropping steel netting over the sub and then raising her with the grappling hooks by the tail like a big fish; sleeping anywhere as time permitted. These things all have a tendency to run together in my mind, with no cognizance as to time of day or whether it was 7, 8, or 9 December. The passage of time dims the past. The other day I happened across the postcard we were issued to send to our families right after the attack. It was pre-printed with a place for check marks and room for two or three lines of text. I wrote: "Am okay, unhurt, will write when I can." I'm glad I was there, but I hope I never go through another similar incident.

On 21 March 1942, at mail call, I received a letter from my dad with a news clipping from our hometown paper (the *Bucyrus Telegraph Forum*). He kind of admonished me for not telling him about the news item in the clipping. It seems I had been awarded the Navy Cross for my actions during the attack on Pearl Harbor.

"Boy! What a joke," I thought. Apparently the public information officer of the Navy Department released the information before it became known officially in CinCPac headquarters in Pearl Harbor. I treated the entire incident as a hilarious joke, never realizing it would come true several weeks later.

On 7 April 1942, I was up on the wing of my assigned aircraft in the hangar, restringing an antenna. We were going through a routine

120-hour check. One of the yeoman came out of the personnel office and yelled up at me.

"Hey, Mead, you gotta clean suit of whites in your locker?"

"Yeah," I replied. "Why, do they want me to go into town and buy some parts?"

"No," he answered, "they want you over on the *Nevada* at 2:00 p.m. Admiral Nimitz is gonna pin the Navy Cross on you!" He then proceeded to tell me that our commissioned officer would like to ride over to the Navy Yard in my car with me. Our commissioned officer at that time was Commander Paul B. Tuzo, a tall, sparse gentleman, whom I knew by name only.

We rode the officer's motor launch from the Naval Air Station landing to the hospital landing. My car was parked in the hospital parking lot. On our drive over to the Navy Yard, the commissioned officer began relating how I should stand at attention, and after the presentation shake hands with the admiral, back step one pace, salute, then about-face, and return to ranks.

The award recipients gathered on the quarterdeck of the USS *Nevada* and assembled in two ranks of twelve individuals. Directly, Admiral Nimitz and his retinue arrived and the ceremony commenced. The sun shone brightly, and a slight breeze furled and unfurled the signal flags hanging from the yardarms in a lazy, lackadaisical manner. When it came my turn, I approached the admiral, saluted smartly, and stood at rigid attention. He pinned the Navy Cross on the left breast of my jumper and grasped my hand. As we shook hands, I stared straight ahead, my eyes riveted to a distant cloud formation. I heard the admiral say, "Look at me, boy!" I shifted my gaze to those cool, pale-blue, penetrating eyes, and the twinkle there seemed to say, "Well done, lad, well done!" I thought later that the commissioned officer had coached me well, except for telling me where to look.

CinCPac Headquarters

WALTER HOFFLAND

For the latter half of 1941, weekend duty at CinCPac headquarters at the submarine base tucked away in the eastern corner of the Southeast Loch was anything but routine. Dispatches from the War and Navy Departments updated Hawaii on the deterioration of diplomatic relations with Japan throughout October and November. The first sentence of the final warning sent from Washington, D.C., to Pacific outposts on 27 November 1941 read: "This dispatch is to be considered a war warning." As early as February 1941, the secretary of the navy advised the secretary of war of the possibility of an air attack on Pearl Harbor. Copies of this memorandum were sent to army and navy headquarters on Oahu.

By the end of August 1940, the highest security code of the Japanese had been broken under the cover name "Purple." The operation name for monitoring and deciphering the "Purple" code was appropriately titled "Magic."

On the morning of 7 December 1941, CinCPac radio traffic at the sub-base administration building was normal. The situation changed dramatically at approximately 7:20 when a message arrived reporting a Japanese submarine had been sunk by the destroyer USS *Ward*, near the Pearl Harbor channel entrance. By the time the message was verified and attempts made to notify Admiral Husband E. Kimmel, Japanese bombers were making their first pass over Pearl Harbor.

Throughout the morning, CinCPac headquarters received and transmitted reports of Japanese military action. The reports reflected the confusion, panic, and uncertainty that prevailed throughout Oahu after the attack. Japanese paratroopers (who turned out to be downed American pilots), Japanese carriers thirty miles offshore of Oahu, and amphibious landings on the northern shores of the island were reported to CinCPac headquarters throughout the next couple of days.

Walter Hoffland, a radioman striker from Cleveland, Ohio, was relieved that he was at CinCPac headquarters, away from the ill-fated USS *Arizona*.

My first ship was the USS *Arizona*, going on board as a radio-man striker after completing the course in communications at the Naval Training Center in San Diego. By April 1941, I had reached the rating of radioman second class. There was one other radioman second class on board, a reserve who recently had been called to active duty. CinCPac had established his headquarters at the Submarine Base, Pearl Harbor, for convenience in communications. In order to handle the additional communication load, since he was also designated CinCUS (commander of the three fleets—Atlantic, Pacific, and Asiatic), radiomen second class from four battleships were ordered to be transferred to CinCPac flag allowance.

The *Arizona* had the two radiomen second class, and the division officer tried to pass off the recently mobilized reserve. However, the reserve couldn't copy the code well enough, so he was sent back to the ship, and I was transferred instead. I took over the reserve's bunk and his place on the watch list. His lack of proficiency was his death warrant; eight months later he was dead and I was still alive.

On the morning of 7 December, I had gotten up early from my bunk at the submarine base barracks and gone down for breakfast. As I was coming back from the mess hall, I saw the crew assigned to raise the colors standing by the flagpole outside the barracks. From the direction of the Naval Air Station on Ford Island, I could see several planes diving and the "crump-crump" sound of explosions. My thought was that there was some early-morning maneuvers going on.

As I went up to my quarters on the second deck, I could see smoke and flame arising from the Naval Air Station, so I and some others ran up a ladder to the roof so we could see what was happening. Our first thought was that there was a big fire and that the planes had taken off to avoid it. Then a plane painted dark gray with a red ball on the side went by us a short distance away. We were horrified to see it drop a torpedo in the harbor and a tall, thin spout of water rise up from the side of one of the battleships. We finally realized that we were under attack by Japanese planes and that we were an open target to machine gunners, so we got off the roof and ran through our part of the barracks, yelling to the men that we were being bombed, to get up and get out.

A chief petty officer from the base told us to get out of the building in case it was bombed and so I led a small group of men out onto the ball diamond, where we sought refuge behind the padded backstop. At the nearby oil tank farm, a marine sentry walked his post, rifle on shoulder, seemingly oblivious to the attack. Most ships were firing back by then, some PT boats and submarines moored at the base were blasting away with fifty-caliber machine guns. A torpedo plane, apparently hit by the fish's warhead, blew up like a thunderclap near the base's diving tower. Three white-painted bombers flew low over a sugar mill; suddenly, one burst into flames and plunged to the ground, the other two continued on.

Several high-level bombers in a vee formation came in from the south, with antiaircraft shells bursting all around them. It appeared that they were too high for our guns to reach them. At least one burst appeared to be right in the middle of the formation, but was actually lower. These planes dropped armor-piercing bombs, one of which blew up the *Arizona* in a blinding flash. We ran back into the barracks to escape the shower of shrapnel that was coming down. I gave a bedraggled survivor my extra suit of dungarees; he had lost his clothing in the water, all except his shorts. The *Pelias*, a nearby sub tender, started blasting away with her bow gun; an air corps B-17, one of twelve that arrived from the mainland during the attack, was the target. The bewildered fliers were trying to escape; everyone was shooting at them.

All these events happened much quicker than it takes to tell about them. A funny thing, here we were CinCPac's flag allowance, and no one had ever drawn up a watch, quarter, and station bill that included a general-quarters station. In other words, I was under no orders to go anywhere in the case of an attack. The place for a radio-man in an emergency was in the radio room, so I reported there. The place was crowded, so several of us went to the roof with rifles. Radioman First Class Joe Hallett and others were with me. One lone Jap plane flew by and everybody on our side of the harbor had a shot at him, before he turned away toward the hospital trailing smoke.

I was ordered to get some men together to eat lunch and come back to relieve the men on watch; there were a lot of extra positions to man. Coming back, I took over from Radioman Second Class Spur-way. He was just getting a new circuit going, as we were taking over (Oahu) NPM's Fox schedule. This was a fleet-wide broadcast with messages sent by a powerful transmitter on a very low frequency. All ships from Manila to San Diego had to copy these messages, which were sent consecutively "blind." In addition, through a radio relay, we were going to key the transmitter of NPL at San Diego, which covered the West Coast of the United States. There was a small transmitter, gasoline powered, on the roof and this was controlling both the NPM and NPL. Normally, the Fox Broadcast was sent by a tape keying machine, but this day there wasn't time to punch tape. I sent all the messages by hand key. For hours, I sent messages direct to the fleet. Some of the stuff I was sending out scared even me, let alone the people that were copying it.

I don't remember the exact wording, but one message concerned paratroops landing. They supposedly wore blue uniforms with a red ball on the back. Another concerned enemy transports that were supposedly approaching Oahu. Both messages were incorrect, as it turned out.

It was a good thing that I had been practicing sending for a federal licensing examination and that I had been playing a lot of tennis at the base courts. This gave me a strong right arm for replacing the machine for about five hours. As sunset approached, the amount of messages died down, and finally the operator back in San Diego got to send some of his messages on NPL. Every time he had tried, I had to break in on him and use his transmitter as I was handed another urgent message.

I often wondered why the Japs didn't drop a couple of bombs on the administration building where our radio room was. There would have been no communications from CinCPac if they had. Perhaps, the Japs didn't know we were there, or they were more interested in the ships. They didn't hit the Navy Yard or the oil tank farm either, both targets would have kept us out of the war for months if destroyed.

In April 1944, Walter Hoffland was commissioned an ensign. After the war, he applied and was accepted for a permanent commission. He remained on active duty for over twenty years before retiring as a lieutenant commander on 1 August 1958. His last duty station was executive officer of the USS *Lyman K. Swenson* in the US Pacific Fleet.

Coastal Artillery

ROY BLICK AND ALEX COBB

Like the other defensive installations and fortifications that dotted the coastline of Oahu at strategic points, Fort Kamehameha was ineffective in defending Pearl Harbor from Japanese bombers. Named after Kamehameha I, the legendary king who united the islands of Hawaii under his rule with a victory at the Battle of Nuuanu Pali in April 1795, the fort was the largest coastal artillery fortification guarding the entrance to Pearl Harbor. Many military analysts considered the fort the pillar of inland defense. Although the fort, located on the southeast peninsula at the harbor entrance just below Hickam Field, appeared a formidable sentinel guarding the "gates to the harbor," it contained outdated weaponry and represented military tactics and thinking of a past era. Military brass could boast of the island's fortifications and claim to the world that they had made Oahu an impenetrable fortress. This claim was justifiable for military preparations in the early 1900s, when battle plans for an invasion centered on an amphibious assault force. However, the utilization of the airplane as a weapon of war revolutionized military tactics after World War I. The airplane was the constant element of surprise, which could link continents in a matter of hours and deliver a payload of death and destruction greater than any assault force. Although large invasion forces supported by offshore naval fleets were not obsolete, military brass were gradually turning their attention to the use of large strike forces employing a number of aircraft carriers.

While it was not impossible that the Japanese would anchor their armada off the coast of Oahu and attempt to seize the island by establishing a number of strategic beachheads, it was unlikely when all the circumstances were considered and studied. If such an offensive was undertaken, the sixteen-inch guns of Fort Kamehameha and other coastal artillery installations would prove insurmountable barriers. Despite their drawbacks, coastal fortifications for military bases such as Pearl Harbor were a necessity in the early 1940s. However, on 7 December these concrete sentinels and their personnel could only bear eyewitness to the attack on the fleet. Private Roy Blick was guarding the sentinel at Fort Kamehameha during the attack.

I had a southern heritage with both grandparents serving in the Civil War with the Confederacy, an uncle who volunteered and lost his life in the Spanish-American War in Cuba, and other relatives who served in World War I. I was proud of those who had served and realized that we were drawing closer to another war every day.

I had joined the Civil Conservation Corps in 1940 and was stationed at Camp William Tell at Tell City, Indiana. On 3 February 1941, I left camp to go home to Lyon County, Kentucky, for the weekend. I had an hour wait for another bus in Evansville, so while I was waiting I took a walk that delayed my trip to Kentucky and home for almost four years. My walk took me past the post office, where I saw a recruiting sign. I went in to talk with the recruiting sergeant and enlisted for two years of overseas service as a replacement and was to get credit for a three-year enlistment. By 11:00 p.m., I was in Fort Benjamin Harrison in Indianapolis, Indiana. By 6 February, I was in Fort Slocum, New York, to await overseas shipment. On 2 April, I left Fort Slocum for the Brooklyn Army and Navy Overseas Replacement Depot. On 8 April, I sailed on the USS *Washington* for Pearl Harbor, by way of the Panama Canal and San Francisco. On board we had twenty-five-hundred troops and a cargo of war bandages for the Chinese.

On 26 April, I arrived in Hawaii and went into training camp for six weeks. When the training was completed, I was assigned to A Battery, Fifteenth Coast Artillery, Fort Kamehameha, Territory of Hawaii, Pearl Harbor Defense. For a time, I was assigned to Fort Weaver, across the Pearl Harbor channel from Fort Kamehameha. By late summer, I had made the rating of first and fourth and was gun mechanic on the number-one sixteen-inch gun. I lived in the gun emplacement, with bunks in the toolshed.

On 7 December 1941, I awoke about 7:30 a.m. and was alone that morning at the sixteen-inch gun battery, except for the guards in the gun emplacement. One off-duty guard was asleep on an army cot under a tree, and the guard on duty was walking post and waiting for his relief, who had gone to chow. I told the guard that I would take his post if he wanted to go to chow before they threw everything out. He took me up on the offer, and I took his post to wait for his relief.

It was a beautiful Sunday morning with a good breeze. I was on the post only a few minutes when I heard a flight of planes coming in from the seaward side of our gun position. When the planes came over our position and flew over the Japanese salt beds into the harbor, they were very low and I could plainly see the Japanese pilots. The large red circles under the wings were easy to identify. I called to Private Parsons, who was sleeping on the cot, that the Japanese were bombing the harbor. By this time, the guard had come back from chow, so I locked the gates to the gun position and divided the hundred rounds of ammo for the 1903 Springfields that we were armed with. By now, the woods in Fort Weaver were full of smoke with shrapnel from the antiaircraft fire and strafing planes. The gun crew was trying to make it to the gun position from the A Battery campsite near the marine barracks. The crew was using the woods for cover and yelling for me to open the gates. As I was moving toward the gate, a large object hit the sand nearby and sent a shower of sand and dust in the air. I hit the ground and waited, but whatever it was it didn't explode. I never went back to dig in the sand and find out what exactly it was.

When the gun crew made it to the gun emplacement, we took our battle stations. After someone shot the lock off of the magazine entrance, we were able to get out ammo by the case. We had plenty of targets and fired a lot of rounds, but we never knew if we hit anything. Being gun mechanic, I had to check the pressure on the recoil cylinders and the recuperators on the sixteen-inch gun. We had by that time gotten orders to be ready to fire, if we could get a target for the sixteen-inch gun. We never did get a target for the big gun, and we never fired a round from it during the attack. After checking the sixteen-inch gun, I took my position again, firing my Springfield at passing Japanese planes. When a Japanese strafer ripped the sand within five feet of me, I took a position under the sixteen-inch gun that was depressed to about three feet off the ground. The gun finally found some use.

After the attack, we had no way of knowing what was next. From our position, we could see the smoke and fire in the harbor and hear explosions as they echoed across the water. We remained at our gun position for the day, and weeks and months following that. We dug trenches and built pillboxes by day and waited for the invasion by night. We had orders to defend the battery to the last man. The invasion never came, and in time the war moved across the Pacific. Most of us remained with the sixteen-inch guns, A Battery Fifteenth Coast Artillery, for the defense of Pearl Harbor. We always remarked how fortunate we were that we never had to fire the sixteen-inch guns in actual defense of the harbor. If it ever did come to that, we knew we were in deep trouble and would most likely be fighting for our lives until the last man fell.

*   *   *

Roy Blick remained at the sixteen-inch gun at Fort Weaver for the duration of the war and was promoted to sergeant and gun commander. In August 1945, he departed for the mainland and on 9 September 1945 was discharged at Camp Atterbury, Indiana. He then returned home to Kentucky.

In the island-hopping campaign that lasted until the last days of the war in the Pacific, Americans would learn at a costly price the advantages of fortified coastal positions to defend strategic locations. Battles for Pacific islands such as Guadalcanal, Tarawa, and Pelelieu resulted in some of the fiercest combat witnessed in any war. "The smaller the island, the higher the casualties," a saying of many infantrymen, proved true. Japanese defenders were able to inflict heavy losses on American amphibious assault forces by constructing small, relatively lightly armed, well-fortified positions, which guarded the only avenues of approach to their location.

Many guns from the coastal fortifications on Oahu were melted down for scrap in the early days of the war. Although many fortifications continued to be manned, they were tigers without teeth. During the war, Fort Kamehameha was used as a clearance center for thousands of men departing for battle areas or returning for furlough, rotation, and discharge.

*   *   *

Another vital link in the chain of coastal artillery units was Fort Ruger. Built behind Diamond Head crater, Hawaii's most famous and distinguishable natural landmark, the installation provided air and sea defense for the Oahu's southeast portion. Any attackers traveling to the southern portions of Oahu by way of its eastern coast placed themselves in jeopardy. Just east of Waikiki Beach, the crater was also the strategic piece of high terrain that dominated the southeast portions of the coast as far west as Pearl Harbor. Whoever had control of this position could easily control Oahu. In a ground war resulting from an invasion of Oahu, Fort Ruger and Diamond Head crater most likely could have been the site of one of the bloodiest and most bitterly contested battles in American history. With each passing hour after the attack on Pearl Harbor, the possibilities for such a battle diminished. Although Fort Ruger was bypassed by Japanese bombers, it did participate in the defense of Oahu. Alex Cobb was one serviceman who witnessed the attack from the fringes of the target area and felt its devastating effects radiate across the island.

———

I was born 1 December 1917 in Richmond, Indiana, but at age one moved to the East. I was really brought up in Newark, Delaware, where I attended public schools and graduated from the University of Delaware in 1940, with a Reserve Officers' Training Corps commission as a second lieutenant in the Coast Artillery Corps.

In April 1941, I was called on active duty at Fort DuPont, Delaware, where I was assigned as plotting-room officer in a submarine mine battery. Several months later, I responded to an officers' call asking for volunteers in the first and second lieutenant grade (Coast Artillery Corps) for the Hawaiian Department. Several of my close buddies joined me, and by July 1941 we had arrived in Honolulu by the *President Line* from San Francisco.

I was assigned to Fort Ruger, up behind Diamond Head crater, and became junior officer in an eighty-man antiaircraft detachment. The unit was part of C Battery, Sixteenth Coast Artillery, with gun emplacements at Black Point, on the east side of Diamond Head. My battery commander was First Lieutenant Elvin T. Wayment, from *Utah*. There were just two of us running the battery. He was battery commander and I was everything else (executive officer, range officer, mess officer, motor pool officer, chemical officer, and, after radar arrived in 1942, I became radar officer).

Elvin Wayment was an excellent officer to train under, although at the time I probably didn't appreciate it. Being a Mormon, he was a real taskmaster. He took his job very seriously and wanted the officers to work twice as hard as the enlisted men. He had attended Utah State on a basketball scholarship and ended up playing varsity football, earning all-conference honors at center for his last two years. We nicknamed him "Tarzan." He was very athletic and had a most competitive spirit about everything we did, whether it was training the battery, running the obstacle course, or playing volleyball.

When I reported for duty, First Lieutenant Wayment immediately had me jump down in a crater and learn how to run a jackhammer, which he had scrounged up from somewhere along with some dynamite and blasting caps. We were making ammunition and personnel shelters alongside the three three-inch fixed-mount antiaircraft guns. They had to be blasted out of lava rock. Later, we covered them with wooden beams and several layers of sandbags. I would say we were well ahead of most of the other fixed-mount antiaircraft batteries on Oahu in this respect when the attack came.

On 6 December, we had a morning parade at Fort Ruger, and in the afternoon I attended the Shrine football game between University of Hawaii and Williamette University (Washington). That evening I put in a brief appearance at a reception at the officers' club, then picked up my girlfriend and took her out to a party given by some mutual friends in the Hickam housing area. We didn't leave until the wee hours of the morning, and I was just lucky we didn't decide to spend the night, or otherwise I would have had a terrible time trying to get back across town to the battery.

I was rooming with three other officers in a bachelor officers' quarters overlooking the parade ground at Fort Ruger, Territory of Hawaii. Shortly after 8:00 a.m., one of the officers, Lieutenant Francis Pallister, who had been at the officers' mess for breakfast, came running up the stairs urging us to wake up and get to our duty stations immediately. He said we were in condition three (battle stations), but he didn't know exactly what was going on. Most of us thought at that point it was just another practice alert.

I stepped onto an upstairs screened porch on the way to the bathroom and, looking out over Honolulu Harbor with Pearl Harbor in the distance, could see strange black (navy) antiaircraft bursts over the island. There was also a large plume of black smoke rising in the distance from the direction of Pearl Harbor. I decided to speed things up!

I dressed rapidly, grabbed my canteen and leggings (you always needed these for alerts), and followed my battery commander, First Lieutenant Elvin T. Wayment, in my car down to our gun site at

Black Point, just to the east of Diamond Head. We had three three-inch fixed-mount antiaircraft guns, which were protecting a seacoast battery consisting of two eight-inch fixed-mount railway guns. This gun emplacement served as the easternmost defense from the sea for Honolulu Harbor.

At the time of the attack, approximately half of our eighty-man antiaircraft detachment was eating breakfast at the permanent battery's mess hall at Fort Ruger. Some of our men were also on pass, although the number of passes had been limited since we went into condition two (man the close-in defense) in early November.

We commenced setting up our fire director and stereoscopic height finder. Normally these units required a crew of eight men to carry them from the storage area, but on this particular morning we made the trip with as few as four or five men, the balance having been assigned to bring ammunition from the seacoast battery's casemate to the antiaircraft gun emplacements.

As I was battery-range officer, we set up the B.C. Scope and began orienting the battery. We tracked several planes bearing large Japanese "meatballs," but they were out of the range of our guns. We were manned and ready to fire, as I recall, about 8:45 to 9:00 a.m.

Finally the post executive officer came down from Fort Ruger and officially informed First Lieutenant Wayment that we were "at war with Japan" and that we should undertake firing on any "enemy places" that came within range of our battery. This must have been about 9:15 to 9:30, and we only spotted one or two planes in our sector after that.

There were some fires set in the Kaimuki section of Honolulu to the north of Fort Ruger, and several spent navy antiaircraft shells landed in Diamond Head crater. A steady stream of confusing, conflicting and, as it later turned out, false messages from higher echelons flowed into our command-post message center. Diamond Head blocked our view of the chaotic situation at Pearl Harbor. It was a confusing time.

We spent the rest of the day "liberating" tools and building materials from nearby construction projects in order to commence construction of a permanent mess hall, a latrine, and, eventually, permanent living quarters adjacent to our gun emplacements. It looked like it was going to be a long war!

Several weeks later our antiaircraft battery received a written commendation from the commanding general for the advanced state of our gun emplacement camouflage and the construction of safe ammunition storage pits at the three guns, which we had excavated from the lavarock foundation which forms Black Point. All of this resulted in an advanced state of readiness on 7 December 1941.

—◦—

Alex Cobb gained his silver bars midway through the war and in 1944 made captain. After attending Advanced Gunnery School at Camp Davis, North Carolina, he returned to the Pacific theater as operations commander of the aircraft warning system for the 53rd Antiaircraft Brigade on Okinawa. In August 1945, Cobb was discharged with the rank of major.

The Punchbowl

W. J. WALKER

Commonly known as the Punchbowl, the extinct volcanic crater overlooking the heart of downtown Honolulu was named Puowaina (Hill of Sacrifice) by ancient Hawaiians. Centuries before the arrival of the white explorers, Polynesian priests made human sacrifices during pagan ceremonies to appease the gods. The flat-topped crater had a panoramic view of Oahu's southern portion. Because of its strategic location, the crater was utilized as a defensive position for the island's defense. By the early 1940s, the military importance of the crater had diminished, and it was used primarily as an observation post. The crater also became a popular day spot for tourists, picnickers, and hikers, as well as a popular nightspot for enchanted couples seeking a romantic refuge overlooking the lights of Honolulu. For Corporal W. J. Walker, the Punchbowl provided a bird's-eye view of the Japanese attack on Pearl Harbor on the morning of 7 December 1941.

My military career began in 1937, when I enlisted in the army. At that time I figured that life in the service had to be better than life on a small farm in Mississippi. For a number of years, my family had operated a sawmill, cutting to size trees brought in by the loggers and those families clearing the land for wood to build their farms. After all the timber in the area had been cut, the sawmill business slowly grinded to a stop. The family then took to a farm so poor that the welfare people wouldn't even help us. In 1937, I realized it was time to see some of the rest of the world and what it had to offer.

In November 1941, after being in Hawaii for over a year, I was assigned to guard detachment responsible for the security of the Punchbowl. Our hours of patrol ran from the early evening to the early morning. On the evening of 6 December, I had been ordered to take three men to the Punchbowl and set up an observation security post. We arrived at the crater at approximately 9:00 p.m. and within no time were taking verbal abuse from the civilians and military personnel who came to the crater with their lovers to enjoy their outdoor open-air parties. It was not hard to see why they were attracted to this spot. The view from our observation post was breathtaking. Directly in front of us was the city of Honolulu. To our left were Waikiki Beach and Diamond Head, which was farther down the coastline. To our right were Pearl Harbor and Hickam Field. With such a view, it was not too hard to miss having weekend liberty and being out on the town ourselves. Hawaiians said that the crater was named Puowaina for the custom of sacrificing human lives to the gods. The men often joked that the only things sacrificed today were virgins under the moon over Hawaii.

Things for the rest of the night were pretty much quiet. At 2:00 a.m. on 7 December, I received a call from a private first class on duty, who was next in command at the post. At the time, I was trying to get a few much-needed winks of sleep while still in uniform. When I heard the call for "corporal of the guard," I immediately grabbed my rifle and ran down to the private first class's post. At this time of the morning, I had no idea what the commotion was all about. By this time, most of civilian and military personnel on the island were calling it a night and making their way home, wherever that was for the night. When I got to the checkpoint, there was an admiral seated in a large touring sedan with about six cars and maybe ten motorcycles lined up behind his sedan waiting to get through the checkpoint. As the admiral got out of the sedan, I saluted him and explained our purpose for being there and stated my orders as they were given to me by my commander. The admiral replied in a sarcastic tone as he pointed toward Pearl Harbor, "Corporal, what in the hell do you foot soldiers think the navy is doing down there?" Without waiting for me to reply, he answered his own question, "We are here to take care of anything the Nips want to start and to protect the army." After some quick deliberation in my own mind, I told the admiral he could pass, but the rest of the party would have to have their credentials checked. The admiral muttered something under his breath about the army, returned to his sedan, and turned around at the checkpoint, leading his entourage back down the crater. It appeared that the admiral wanted to impress his friends and end his Saturday-night party at sunrise in the Punchbowl. Of course, at the time, the admiral and I didn't know that three-quarters of his mighty navy would be sunk or crippled less than six hours later.

The rest of the early Sunday passed without any further incidents. We stayed up on the crater the rest of the morning, enjoying the sunrise out over the ocean and looking forward to coming down off the hill and getting a good hot meal. As with any Sunday morning, things over Honolulu were very quiet. The only people who stirred were the early churchgoers or the late-Saturday-night partiers. It was around 7:50 a.m. that we noticed the sounds of airplanes buzzing over the city and Pearl Harbor. The only thing unusual about this was the fact that it was Sunday morning. Usually, most flying and training exercises were done during the week. We thought it unusual that the army or navy pilots would put in flight time on Sunday morning. We didn't think about the planes again, until we heard explosions coming from the direction of Pearl Harbor. At first I thought that there was an explosion aboard one of the ships, but after repeated explosions and the sight of more airplanes over Pearl, it hit me that we were being attacked. I couldn't believe what my eyes were seeing. I thought I was in some kind of crazy dream.

As the attack increased in force, I called my officer of the day at Fort Ruger and tried to report a picture in his mind of what I was seeing from up on the crater. As I reported what I was seeing, the captain listened for a few moments and then burst out laughing over the phone. I heard him say to someone in his office, "Pour me another cup of coffee; a drunk is trying to tell me something crazy." The captain then said he wanted to speak to the private first class. I heard him ask the private first class, "Private, be honest. Isn't Corporal Walker drunk?" The private first class replied, "Captain, if Corporal Walker is drunk, I'm drunk, too, because I'm seeing the same things he is." I think the captain finally gave up on the conversation. He told us to remain at our post until further word.

From the Punchbowl, we watched the attack over the next two hours. We were helpless to do anything. The whole attack was taking place before our very eyes, yet there wasn't a thing we could do to help. It was like sitting in the top row of a ballpark and watching the action taking place far below on the field. With field glasses, we were able to see what was going on at a closer range, but, when the fires and bombs started to form large smoke clouds over the harbor, our line of vision was partially blocked. By early afternoon of that day, we were able to see that a number of ships had been sunk or capsized. From where we stood, the damage to the fleet looked great, but we had no way of knowing the losses.

Later that morning, I received a call from our captain, who told us not to let any civilians or unauthorized military personnel in our area. We started to worry that Japanese snipers or foreign agents would try to take our position to direct another attack on the harbor or try to pinpoint our losses after the attack. We remained at our position in the Punchbowl for about a week until after the attack. We received a number of reinforcements, but for the most part things were quiet after the attack. With martial law in effect, along with a curfew and a blackout, attempted visits to the Punchbowl were few. Every time we heard a vehicle or something move outside our position, we tightened the grips we had on our rifles and swallowed hard, because we didn't know what to expect next. The days following the attack, we were able to watch the efforts to put the fleet back together. Pearl Harbor seemed to be in a race with the clock to get the ships floating once again. The harbor was always alive with a beehive of activity. Although we were doing our part guarding the Punchbowl, we all felt we could be more useful if we were down in the harbor helping in some other way. After a few days had passed and it was unlikely the Japanese would attack again, we were able to relax a little and start thinking where in the war we would be going. After the second week in December had passed, I was still waiting for that hot home-cooked meal and wondering how the admiral had fared with his party.

———

For W. J. Walker, the attack on Pearl Harbor was the beginning of a forty-four-month tour of duty in the Pacific campaign. World War II was one of the highlights of his thirty-year career, which ended with retirement in 1967.

In 1949, the Punchbowl did indeed become the Hill of Sacrifice. In that year, the 114-acre floor of the Punchbowl became officially known as the National Memorial Cemetery of the Pacific. Today, beneath simple flagstone markers lie more than twenty-six thousand dead from World War I, World War II, the Korean War, and the Vietnam War. Among the servicemen, servicewomen, and dependents are twenty-two recipients of the Medal of Honor. The famous war correspondent Ernie Pyle is buried with the soldiers he immortalized in print. Also located in the Punchbowl is the Garden of the Missing, a marble monument inscribed with thousands of names of servicemen and servicewomen missing in action. Since 1979, the Punchbowl has become Hawaii's leading visitor attraction. Every day, thousands of islanders and visitors bring leis and flowers to honor and remember those who sacrificed their lives for their country. The schedule of ceremonies is highlighted each year with a sunrise Easter service. On this day, thousands of visitors participate in a moving ceremony to honor these and other fallen warriors.

Semper Fidelis

JAMES ARION JENKINS

Because of the navy's tremendous losses in personnel, planes, and ships, the plight of the Marine Corps during the attack is often overlooked and overshadowed. The final body count for the marines listed 109 men killed and 69 wounded. Although the numbers were less than those of the army and navy, the percentage of killed and wounded to the total number of marines on Oahu was greater than that of the other services. Casualties at the marine barracks scattered around Pearl Harbor were minimal because they were not the primary or secondary targets of Japanese bombers. The largest number of losses occurred aboard ship and at air bases. The marine air bases at Kaneohe and Ewa were two of the hardest hit. Japanese bombers took special care to make sure these bases on the eastern and southern coastline of Oahu were completely immobilized. A number of bombers, making their way with the first attack unit on the sweeping approaches over the coast, broke off from the assault wave to attack the airfields away from Pearl Harbor. The plan worked to perfection, and the results were devastating. Of the eighty-two planes parked at these two bases, only one was in shape to fly at the end of the attack.

For air and ground marines, the attack provided a glimpse of the tenacity and fierceness of the Japanese fighting man. These latter-day Samurai warriors had a spirit of total dedication to God and homeland, which took its toll on marine assault forces throughout the war. Even in the face of overwhelming odds, Japanese soldiers, sailors, and aviators were formidable opponents. Oahu was the first place in the Pacific whose soil was saturated with the blood of fallen marines. The island-hopping campaign produced a continuous string of battles that became legendary in Marine Corps and American history. Guadalcanal, Mantanikau, New Georgia, Bougainville, New Britain, Tarawa, the Marshall Islands, Eniwetok, the Mariana Islands, Guam, Tinian, Peleliu, the Philippines, Iwo Jima, and Okinawa were the stepping stones that led from Pearl Harbor to Tokyo Bay. Corporal James Arion Jenkins was one marine who survived the long march to Tokyo.

In 1940, I had lost my sweetheart and was walking down the street feeling blue. I happened to be on the sidewalk in front of the post office in Tulsa, Oklahoma, and saw a sign with a picture pointing at me, saying, "Uncle Sam needs you." Join the marines—travel, education, romance. Little did I know there wouldn't be any romance where I was going. I joined the marines on 18 September 1940.

I was a corporal in the Headquarters Company Second Engineer Battalion, commanded by Lieutenant Colonel Elmer E. Hall during the attack on Pearl Harbor. The Second Engineer Battalion was stationed at Pearl Harbor at the marine barracks. We were quartered in five-man tents on the parade ground. We were building a marine camp about halfway between Pearl Harbor and Honolulu. At that time we called it Salt Lake Camp. I worked at the sawmill under Sergeant K. O. Sears, building rafters for buildings. We were doing just fine in the Hawaiian weather and going on liberty every night that we had the price of a bus ticket and a beer or two. On the night of 6 December, I made such a liberty. Coming back to camp late and being tired and sleepy and knowing the next day was Sunday, I planned on sleeping in, but it didn't happen that way. On 7 December, I was awakened shortly before 8:00 a.m. by the explosions and the earth trembling. At this time I came out of the tent, there was a plane coming down on fire over the Naval Hospital. I went back into the tent to get my rifle and noticed a bullet from the strafing plane had come through my tent and through my bunk, which

I had just gotten out of. The next thing I knew everyone was on the parade ground firing at airplanes. Most of us were in our underwear and had our old World War I helmets on and were firing the old 1903 model bolt-action rifles. Some had the old water-cooled thirty-caliber machine guns. I remember that a marine on the other side of the parade ground firing a machine gun was either hit or dropped it from the tripod, causing a few wild shots to come across the parade ground and resulting in three or four casualties. Also during the excitement, a man was running and came out from behind a barracks, colliding with a truck, which killed him. The planes came in so low you could see the goggles on the pilots' heads.

Later, high-altitude bombers came over, releasing a load of bombs over our heads. It looked like they were going to land on top of us. One of the bombs was short of its target and landed just on the other side of a building, saving us. The planes came in at random, bombing and strafing without opposition. We didn't have anything to fire except rifles and small machine guns. Some of the marines standing guard at the docks were killed, so I was immediately put on guard duty, with no breakfast. The planes would drop their bombs then strafe the docks and warehouses where I was on duty. On two occasions I had to take cover behind some large heavy crates. It was now past noon, and I had not had any relief. With no breakfast or dinner, I had a headache from the old iron kelly rocking back and forth on my head. My rifle with fixed bayonet was getting heavy, and I was getting sick. To make it worse, the navy boats began bringing in burned bodies and throwing them at my feet on the docks. I was standing guard across from the *California*, which was still smoldering, and I could look to the north and see the *Arizona*. The *Oklahoma* had turned over on its side.

Suppertime was now past, and still no relief. Up till now, this was the most miserable day of my life. The next morning, 8 December, they were expecting another invasion, so we were loaded in trucks before dawn and placed around the island at possible landing sites. I was one scared boy. At this time I was wondering how we were at peace one day and the next day we were waiting for an invasion that

I'm glad never came. Now the bombing was over and we were burying our dead. Some of us in the Second Engineer Battalion stood guard over the bodies on what we then called "Red Hill."

About four months passed, and our camp construction was over. We were state-bound and I would get my first furlough in two years. Time passes. I was then in the Third Engineer Battalion getting ready to ship out, when I was on liberty one night in San Diego. I saw two black men kill a Chinese man and then take a shot at me. At about that time two policemen appeared on the scene, and I helped capture one of the killers. This caused me to be a star witness, so they wouldn't let me ship out with my unit. I had to stay until the trial was over. Now I was a sergeant and in charge of a replacement company that went to Numea Caladonia and from there to Guadalcanal, joining the Second Aviation Engineer Battalion, commanded by Lieutenant Colonel Clark. We were boarding ship for our next invasion. We were on board a week and were dirty and smelly, so we stopped off at the Kwajalein Atoll to bathe and to wash clothes. We were then on our way to Saipan. As we were floating reserves, they didn't need us, so I landed on Blue Beach with the Guam invasion. We moved in heavy equipment by day and held the front lines at night for about a week. Then we had to take "Red Hill" every day and pull back to the beach every night.

One night on the front lines on Guam, I dug my foxhole in a low spot. It seemed like it always rained during my invasion, so I built a roof over my foxhole with a piece of tin, but the water ran in one end and out the other. Now we had orders to stay in our foxhole, and anything outside was to be shot. I was tempted to crawl to another foxhole nearby, but I wasn't ready to die just yet, so I spent another miserable night, of which I have spent many during the war. My four-year hitch was up while we were landing on Guam, so I was forced to extend my enlistment two more years. I was now feeling ill and I didn't know why, but it seemed I had to go on.

I was in war four years now without relief. We were to stay on Guam six more months. We were now loading ships for our next invasion. We landed on Blue Beach again, D-1 on Iwo Jima. We received lots of shelling from big guns from Mount Surabachi and from another hill near the center of the island. Lots of equipment couldn't make it ashore in the sand. Boats, equipment, and bodies were rolling together in the surf. We were now back at Guam replacing and training men for the next invasion, which was going to be Japan. Our ship was loaded and ready to land in Japan when the war ended. They shipped home men that had 64 points. I had over 164 points. Because I had to extend my enlistment, I was bound for Japan instead of going home. We landed in Sasebo Harbor on the same day that we had planned to invade Japan. I was one of the first troops in Nagasaki after the atomic bomb. As we entered the harbor, I was so thankful the war was over. They would have picked us off like sitting ducks. I can thank President Truman and the way he handled the atomic bomb for saving my life and the lives of so many others. My illness was getting worse, but I still couldn't go home. About four months passed. I had been to the sick bay and had some tests. I had jangled nerves and bleeding ulcers. They shipped me to the Naval Hospital in San Diego.

James Arion Jenkins remained in the Naval Hospital for four months. He was discharged in November 1946, just a few months short of his six-year enlistment.

Inside the Inferno

JOHN KUZMA

On 7 December 1941, Japanese bombers were not the only enemy to be battled. Within seconds of detonation, bombs and secondary explosions produced many major fires. If allowed to burn out of control, the fires had the potential to be more lethal than the Japanese attackers. For hours after the attack, fires ravaged the airfields, barracks, and ships. The infernos, with their searing heat and suffocating smoke, consumed everything, living and nonliving, in their paths.

From a distance, it appeared that the entire US Pacific Fleet was ablaze in Pearl Harbor. Despite the abundance and proximity of water, the great ships of the fleet caught fire and burned for days in smoldering heaps of steel. Feeding on flammable liquids, as well as combustible materials, including explosives and ammunition, the fires turned the ships into gigantic bombs waiting to detonate at any second. The waters surrounding the ships became a dead zone. The fleet's ruptured tanks leaked fuel oil, setting fire to the surface of the water and raising a wall of flames around the ships.

The courageous and superhuman efforts by sailors and soldiers in fighting these fires often went unnoticed in the chaos following the first bomb. The seemingly endless battle against the flames was an emotional and physical test in which strangers united to save others, despite jeopardy to their own lives. The story of John Kuzma is typical of the stories of those who fought the battles behind the curtains of smoke and fire that engulfed Pearl Harbor. Seaman Kuzma had the opportunity to witness the attack from outside Pearl Harbor, and then inside the Navy Yard and on Ford Island.

—◆—

After high school, I joined the Civilian Conservation Corps in 1937 and was stationed in Hyram, Utah, where I worked with the Army Engineers building dams, bridges, and parks. In 1940, me and my buddy Francis ("Franny") Burke, who lived across the street from me in Binghamton, New York, joined the navy, with orders to report to the training base at Newport, Rhode Island. After boat training from July to September 1940, we went aboard the USS *Pyro*, an ammunition ship at Philadelphia, which took us to Pearl Harbor. I was assigned to the Naval Air Station firehouse on Ford Island and Francis went to one of the yard tug boats.

On the night of 6 December 1941, Franny and I had a date to go dancing with two pretty Hawaiian girls. His date was Victoria, and mine was her cousin (in 1943 Franny married Victoria, and I was best man at their wedding). After the dance, Franny went back to the Navy Yard to his tug, and I stayed the night in Honolulu. The next morning, on the way back to Pearl Harbor and the firehouse, I could see an awful lot of air activity in the direction of Hickam Field. With the explosions and gunfire coming from the Navy Yard, there was no doubt in my mind that we were coming under attack.

The taxi dropped me off near the Naval Gate, which was manned by the marines. Only identified people were allowed to pass the gate. There were all kinds of gunfire as I made my way to the docks. People were shooting at the attacking aircraft with rifles, handguns, machine guns, and antiaircraft guns aboard ships. As I was running through the repair yard, I stopped to give a hand with the large fire hoses that were being used to fight the fires at the large dry dock, which held the USS *Pennsylvania*, the USS *Cassin*, and the USS *Downes*. There was so much smoke and spray from the hoses in the air that it was impossible to tell what had happened to the ships. After they had the hoses directed in the right direction, I continued on my run across the yard. By this time many of the ships had been hit by bombs and torpedoes. Planes continued to strafe the yard, and it was hard to concentrate on making it to the dock without constantly looking over your shoulder to see where the next plane was coming from. As soon as one appeared over the yard, everybody dove for cover under the nearest thing. At this rate, I wondered if I would ever make it to the island and whether we would have enough time in between attacks to put out all the fires. There seemed to be fires everyplace you looked. Everyone was fighting back in the best way they could. Some were fighting fires, some firing back at the enemy, and some were making rescue attempts and helping with the wounded.

I stopped again to help carry some of the wounded and tend to their injuries near the USS *Shaw*, which was in a floating dry dock not too far from the big dry dock which held the *Pennsylvania*, *Cassin*, and *Downes*. Most of the injured appeared to be suffering from severe burns. Even though most of the clothing was tattered and torn from their bodies, they were covered with blood, oil, and grime, and it was difficult to tell the extent of their injuries. Others had mangled arms and legs, which looked like they had been crushed or ripped apart. You could clearly see where others were missing part of their arm or leg. I was bending to help with a bandage near the bow of the USS *Shaw* when the ship blew up. I heard a tremendous explosion and was thrown to the ground with a wallop. I'm not sure how long I was lying on the ground, but when I got to my feet I was dizzy and had a loud ringing and buzzing sound in my ears. For a few minutes, I had trouble clearing my head and remembering where I was.

After I got myself together, I again helped carry some of the badly wounded sailors to the Naval Hospital. Some men were screaming out loud with pain, while others were limp and silent. We didn't have time to tell whether they were dead or alive. All I knew was that these men were hurt badly and needed immediate medical attention. After one of my trips to the hospital, one of the medics began to wipe off my face and told me I was bleeding from my nose and ears. In the excitement of everything going on around me, I thought I was just sweating. I didn't pay any attention to the fact that the moisture running down my face was my own blood. I never even bothered to look at my hands or clothing. I was told to stay there and wait for somebody to look at me and clean me up, but when I saw how badly wounded the men around me were, I quickly left the hospital and ran back to the dock to get a ride across the channel, back to my own station.

When I got back to the dock, I was almost immediately able to get a ride to Ford Island on one of the launches. Launches and the smaller yard craft were coming and going all the time, and if you just hollered out to one you could get a ride to your destination. The ride across the channel took only a few minutes, but we were on the lookout for planes making a strafing run. If any planes would have made a run over the harbor, we would have been sitting ducks. As we made our way, it was hard to believe what I was seeing. Already numerous ships were slowly sinking and a couple of others appeared ready to roll over. It looked as if every ship along Battleship Row was on fire. Everywhere boats were directing hoses at the burning ships and pulling men out of the water. When I finally got back to the firehouse, many of the men from Battleship Row, who had to abandon ship, were receiving medical attention or being organized into work parties. Many of the men were wet, oil-soaked, and half-clothed. They all had a kind of dazed and confused look, and looked as if they were physically exhausted from the ordeal. Their faces seemed to say, "This can't be happening to us, not on a Sunday morning in Hawaii." As I changed my oily and bloody clothes, I opened my locker and had the sailors that needed clothing help themselves to whatever I had.

After changing clothes and waiting for a detail, I remembered that there were a couple of fire trucks that were brought over from the States sitting at the dock waiting to be delivered. I grabbed a few firehouse boys and went down to the dock to put the fire trucks in service to help fight the nearby fires. We first went over to our airfield and helped put out the planes burning inside and outside the hangars. It seemed almost senseless since the planes were damaged beyond repair, but the fires had to be contained. We also helped the men out of the burning oil when they came ashore from their burning. We tried to break up the burning oil slicks by using the hoses to create little areas in the slicks that weren't on fire. Mostly we just aimed the hoses at the men as they were making their way to shore and covered them with a shower of water as they made their way through burning oil. For those who made it ashore in flames, we quickly diverted our hoses to extinguish them. Late in the morning or early afternoon, we went over to the bachelor officers' quarters to keep water on the building. The building was in danger of catching on fire from the heat of the burning USS *Arizona*. The amount of heat coming from the direction of the ship and the amount of burning debris in the air were unbelievable. At intervals, we had to hose down everything near the building, including ourselves. In between fighting fires, we were kept busy by recharging all types of fire extinguishers that were used to fight the fires aboard the USS *California*. It was a long, hard day with no rest or food, but we were on our feet and able to help out. We were the lucky ones. There were many around us who were not as fortunate. There were a lot of brave men on this day who did their job and more under fire from the air and ground.

Late that night, there were all kinds of rumors that the Japs had invaded the island of Oahu with a large force and that we on Ford Island would probably be the last stronghold to fight the invaders. There were a lot of shots being fired that night, but the worst came later when some aircraft came flying over us. It seemed like every gun on the island opened fire at once. For a split second, the whole night was lit by the gunfire. We later found out that we had shot down some of our own aircraft that were coming in for a landing. We all agreed that this was the longest night we would ever live through.

John Kuzma returned to the States in 1943 to attend Advanced Aviation School, but spent the rest of the war in the Pacific theater. Active throughout the years in the Pearl Harbor Survivors Association, he has appeared on a number of television and radio shows as a result of his war experience and affiliation with the association. For two years, Kuzma worked with Twentieth Century Fox Studios during the filming of the movie *Tora, Tora, Tora*. As a result of his association with its producers, production staff, and consultants, he had the opportunity to spend the day at the home of Admiral Husband E. Kimmel, who had been fleet commander on 7 December. Kuzma attended the admiral's funeral and burial at the US Naval Academy in May 1968.

An Outpatient

DON JONES

Pearl Harbor Naval Hospital, like the other civilian and military medical facilities on the island, was a well-equipped professionally staffed, but small unit. A lack of space limited its medical services. Within minutes of the first attack, an endless procession of injured passed through the hospital's doors. Teams of doctors, nurses, and other medical personnel worked around the clock for ten days following the attack. The situation was similar at the Army Tripler Hospital. Honolulu hospitals were quickly filled to overflowing with military and civilian personnel. Schools were converted into temporary hospitals. Vehicles of every type and vintage transported the wounded to vacant beds. A well-organized civilian defense program resulted in the immediate mobilization of civilian medical personnel and the procurement of urgently needed blood supplies.

Don Jones, a marine private first class from central Kansas, found out the hard way that being in a hospital did not qualify for exemption from the Japanese attack. Unlike the hospital ship USS *Solace*, the land hospitals did not indicate their noncombat status with painted red crosses.

———

Being in Pearl Harbor almost two years by December 1941, and having advanced all the way to private first class, I, of course, was counting the months and weeks till when I would be going home. Well, my story really started about two weeks before 7 December, when I was admitted to the Pearl Harbor Naval Hospital for minor surgery, so I was told. My problem was a cyst near my rectum that required surgery. After the good navy doc checked me over, I was informed that I also had hemorrhoids. Even though they had probably not given me any problems they should be removed, and that now would be as good a time as any, since I was there and the doc had the time and could use the practice. It would be of mutual benefit for both of us.

So, after the usual preparation for an operation of this type, I was given a spinal anesthesia to deaden my lower body. The doc arrived and was assured that I had no feeling below my waist and proceeded with the help of four or five corpsmen, who kidded me all the time as to what they were doing to a poor defenseless marine, and how sore I would be tomorrow. Finally, the doc announced that he had finished with that project and wondered out loud what else he might attend to. Well, one of my good buddies, a corpsman, said that I had never been circumcised. I was assured that this should be taken care of, and now was as good a time as any. Besides, the doc had the time and could use the practice, and it was something that should have been done about twenty years earlier.

Well, guess what? Came 7 December and I was able to walk around a little, but I sure had to be careful as I had many stitches in tender places. The first we in our ward knew of the raid, I was lying on my bunk reading the Sunday paper, when we heard some loud explosions. We thought they were blasting for some construction project, when a guy ran into the ward shouting that we were being attacked by the Japs. Well, we all ran out the back door of the ward, and, sure enough, there were planes all over the place with the rising sun on the wings.

Talk about pandemonium! No one seemed to be in charge or to really know what to do. When one plane flew over real low, and the dirt kicked up around us, someone said, "What's that?" and someone else said, "Stupid, they're shooting at us." Well, this got us to thinking about a place to hide in case he came back. There was some new construction taking place close by, and there was a newly dug ditch some three feet deep, and two- or three-feet wide, so we stayed close just in case. In the meantime, we had spotted some bombers dropping bombs that looked like long silver cigars, headed in our direction. We were about ready to get in the ditch when someone shouted, "Here he comes again!" We think it was the same plane that had strafed us earlier, but this time he was on fire and headed right at us. The pilot was standing up and seemed to be ready to jump. Well, we dove for the ditch, and the plane crashed right on top of us. I slid in on my stomach and landed on top of a big sailor, who was really crying and cussing and praying, all at the same time. Well, after what seemed forever, but was probably less than a minute, I scrambled out and everyone seemed to be okay except the Jap pilot, who must have gone through the propeller, as the biggest part of him that was left was a leg. One fellow had it and was beating it on the ground and screaming that he would kill him. When he seemed to realize what he was doing, he stopped, pulled the boot off, and announced that he had the first souvenir of the war. He may have; I don't know.

By this time, I realized that sliding into a ditch on my stomach in my condition was a very bad thing. So I went back in the ward, looking for a doctor. Well, he took a quick look at it and said I was walking, and was in good condition compared to the people who were starting to come in by then, and, as long as I was up and about, to start helping out by giving everyone that wanted water all they wished to drink, which I did for about an hour. Most of the fellows were badly burned. I would try to talk to the ones who would talk by asking them where they were from and what ship they were on. I found one fellow who was from a town near where I was raised, who remembered me, as we had competed in sports in high school. I might add, he always beat me in running the 400. After about an hour, the doctor told me to go on back to my barracks and sit in some warm salt water two or three times a day, and I would probably be all right. I spent that night on top of the barracks helping man a machine gun, just in case. Two or three days later, I got a corpsman cornered and we had quite a time removing stitches, but everything turned out okay.

Don Jones had the distinction of witnessing the beginning and the end of the war in the Pacific. On 23 September 1945, Jones was with the first American troops to land in Nagasaki. On 9 August 1945, Nagasaki became the second Japanese city to feel the effects of the atomic bomb. When the Second Marine Division landed, Nagasaki was still reeling from the attack. The death and destruction that Jones had witnessed at Pearl Harbor were dwarfed by the total devastation of Nagasaki. Jones noted that "there were so many dead people floating in the harbor, it looked like the entire population had drowned. I wondered how the bodies got there and what would happen to them. It seemed that the landing craft wouldn't be able to make it to shore. The floating bodies were bulldozed out of the way by the wake of the boats."

An Inpatient

HOWARD WARD

Throughout World War II, combat veterans echoed the saying "It's the one you don't see or hear that will kill you." The cliché was prevalent in early war movies. Such movies often depicted a battle-worn and -weary foot soldier passing on a piece of survival philosophy to the untested replacements who have just joined the unit and are awaiting their baptism by fire. In a deep voice, as coarse as the stubble on his face and as worn as the tattered clothing on his back, the soldier would lament, "If you know where they're coming from, you can go around them. If you can see them coming, you can go beyond them. It's all the others you have to worry about, because they're the ones that will get you."

The cliché came to life when the first Japanese attack planes arrived over Pearl Harbor. There was no warning and no chance to prepare for the rite of passage. Japanese bombers became awesome killing machines. Appearing out of nowhere, they strafed and bombed a path of destruction with no escape. The whirlwind of shrapnel and debris found its way into every corner and hiding place, ripping through flesh and bone. Survivors often had painful and lingering injuries.

A Japanese bombing and strafing run was a nightmare turned into a reality. No matter how fast or what direction servicemen ran, the planes were fast on their heels. They could not run fast enough or far enough. Seconds turned to minutes, and minutes to hours. An overwhelming sense of hopelessness prevailed, as their destruction seemed inevitable. Private First Class Howard Ward was caught in the nightmare on the morning of 7 December.

I joined the Army Air Corps on 17 November 1939 at Fort Crook, Nebraska. I arrived in Hawaii on 22 December 1939 and was assigned to Hickam Field. At that time Hickam Field was only a tent area and a couple of hangars. Over the next couple of years, the base was built up to the point where it became a permanent air base with concrete barracks and additional hangar space.

My first unit was the Headquarters and Headquarters, Seventeenth Air Base Group. My first regular job was day-room orderly. Later, I was assigned to the boiler room, and I was on duty the morning of 7 December. We had been on and off alert for months, so working weekend duty was no real concern. Even though passes were scarce, there were always enough for those who wanted to spend a night on the town. On that Saturday evening, I and about 50 percent of my squadron got passes. I got in at 4:00 a.m. and went on duty at 6:00 a.m., so I was ready for another day of easy Sunday duty.

Sunday was always a good day to relax. It seemed that most of the men slept in as late as they could, so there wasn't too much activity in the morning hours. Most of the men were somewhere in between breakfast and church services. When the first planes were heard overhead, my first thought was, "Why on Sunday morning?" For weeks, a lot of planes had been diving and practice bombing near Pearl Harbor. I never gave it another thought, until Hangar Fifteen was blown apart, and bullets started to ricochet in through my boilers. At that moment, I knew we were under attack. If a bullet had hit right and penetrated one of the boilers, it would have blown up everything for blocks. My boiler room was located in the big cement three-story barracks, just off the kitchen, where food for five thousand men was prepared in big steam kettles. Breakfast was just over, and I was standing in the kitchen, when a bomb hit near the coffee urns located between the kitchen and the dining room. I couldn't tell if the bomb passed through the outside wall and came through the ceiling, or exploded outside the building. There was such an explosion and flash that for a second I almost thought the coffee urns had blown up.

Within a fraction of a second, hundreds of men were scrambling for their lives. When the bombing first started, the mess officer had given orders to keep right on cooking and cleaning, and for me to keep up a full head of steam, because we had no guns, and not even helmets. For the moment we were glad to be busy. When the bomb hit, about 150 men tried to get out the one back door. I was on my way out when one of the cooks said, "In here." It was an empty walk-in refrigerator. I kept on going for the door, because I wanted to see the guy that would get me. After the attack, they found five men dead without a scratch in the refrigerator. The concussion from one of the bombs had killed them quickly and cleanly, without leaving a mark. Some men thought they had suffocated in the closed box.

As I ran out of the back door of the kitchen, planes were bombing the barracks. When they saw the large number of men coming from one building, they dived lower and began to machine-gun us. I ran across the street to a parking lot. It seemed the best thing to do was keep moving and maybe somehow avoid the trail of strafing. Going back into the kitchen didn't seem the best thing to do, since the building was just bombed and everybody was running like mad to get out of the place. As I made it across the street and into the parking lot, bullets suddenly started to kick up all around me. I could hear them "rick-o-shay" off the lot with a zinging sound. If I didn't get hit with a direct shot, I was almost sure to get hit with one bouncing off the parking lot. As bullets started to land everywhere around me, I dove under the back end of a 1936 green Chevy coupe. At the time, it was the only protection available. I laid there with my hands over my head, listening to all the commotion, when I felt a sharp sting, followed by a painful burning sensation in my leg. I wasn't sure what exactly happened, until I reached down with my hand. When I looked it was covered with blood, my blood. I had been hit in the left hip by a ricochet tracer, a bullet which sets things on fire. Within a few seconds, two of my buddies, Harold Zuspan and George Bushey, pulled me out from underneath the coupe. They grabbed me around the shoulders and half-dragged me across the parking lot and an open field to the Hickam Field Hospital. We made the whole trip under fire from more planes strafing the air base. This time I was afraid we'd all be hit and none of us would make it to the hospital.

At the field hospital, they treated the wound and gave me something for the pain. By now the fear and shock were wearing off and the pain was unbearable. The ricochet gave me three fractures of the hip and two of the pelvis bone. The glancing blow put a hole in my hip that I could fit my fist in. After being treated and stabilized at the field hospital, I was transported to Tripler Army Hospital. The attack had been over for hours, and the fleet was beginning to treat the wounded sailors and crippled ships.

Tripler was overflowing with wounded servicemen. Even though I had received a serious injury, I was not taken to surgery until 7:30 p.m. the next day. I couldn't believe the number of men with injuries more serious than mine. For days, doctors were taking off arms and legs that couldn't be saved. When I saw the number of men who lost limbs, I realized that my injury was far from over, and I could be next. Within the next couple of weeks, I had three more operations to repair the damage. After the third one, I was taken to Farrington High, which had been turned into a recovery ward. Four months after the attack on Pearl Harbor, I was still on crutches. Because of my condition, I was offered a medical discharge. I refused, because I was going to make the army my career.

While still on crutches, I received permission from my commanding officer, Captain Howard Cooper, to return to light duty. At the time the war started, I had just made private first class. When I came out of the hospital, I was promoted to corporal. I made sergeant in July 1942. That was the end of the line for my army career. I received no more ratings and was told I was passed over due to my limited service. I remained a sergeant for three years and three months until discharged at the end of the war. The first decorations of World War II took place on 26 April 1942 at Hickam Field. I was decorated with the Purple Heart.

In 1943, the army came up with a readjustment plan. There were thousands of men who had over three years' service overseas and never had a furlough. On 23 May 1943, I arrived in San Francisco. On 4 July 1943 (three years, seven months, and seventeen days after joining up), I got my first furlough.

———

Howard Ward, perhaps the first American to be wounded at Pearl Harbor, finished the war stationed at Pratt Army Air Base in Kansas. After his discharge, he received a 40 percent medical disability.

A Nurse's Station

MYRTLE WATSON

For hundreds of injured survivors, the Battle of Pearl Harbor lasted long after the Japanese dropped their last bombs on Oahu. Although their combat action lasted only a few seconds, minutes, or hours, their struggle to recover and regain their health would last weeks, months, or years. These men had unceremoniously become the first casualties of the war. Commissioned officers and platoon sergeants were replaced by doctors and nurses, foxholes by hospital beds, and military uniforms by hospital gowns. The first step on the "Road to Tokyo" was with the aid of crutches and wheelchairs. Although the new combat zone extended only as far as the manicured hospital lawns, the hell of living out a nightmare rivaled that of the front lines. The fate of the injured was in the skilled hands of the medical personnel on Oahu. The medical corps responded to the call for arms with razor-edged surgical steel. While workers at the Navy Yard labored to cut and weld damaged ships, doctors and nurses labored to cut and stitch the bodies of soldiers and sailors. Doctors were forced to play God with life-and-death decisions, and nurses were pressed into service as makeshift surgeons. They witnessed the darkest side of war, as the procession of human carnage made its way through hospital corridors. Many of the injured suffered traumatic injuries, including severe burns, dismemberment, and evisceration. Many medical and hospital personnel never forgot the sight of the dead and injured.

On the morning of 7 December 1941, Myrtle Watson was an army nurse on duty at the Schofield Barracks hospital. She witnessed the human tragedy of war as the first bombs that fell on Oahu landed on Schofield Barracks and nearby Wheeler Field.

On that Sunday morning, I was working on the orthopedic ward with only a few other nurses. We were busy after breakfast wheeling bedridden men onto the second-story porch so that they could watch a barefoot football game about to begin. I remember it was about 7:45 a.m. As we stood on the porch looking out at the field, we heard the low sound of planes coming overhead. Some people on the ground and the porch began waving at the planes. Our curiosity was aroused because the planes just kept coming. There was no letup.

I was standing in the doorway looking at the planes with an injured GI named Jack. Jack, who called me Chick because of my blond hair, seemed to have a crush on me and followed me around like a shadow. We couldn't quite recognize the planes, and I said to Jack that I didn't think they were our planes. Jack, who was a sergeant and knew planes, said, "Chick, I think we're at war." I said in a rather shaky voice, "We couldn't be at war; someone would tell us." We just stood frozen in our places staring at the sky as the planes made their runs. The effect was almost hypnotic. When we recognized the rising-sun insignia and heard the explosions start to go off, we pushed the beds back into the ward so that they would be under cover. When I went back onto the porch to wheel in the second group of men, the planes were flying so low you could see the goggles and scarves on the pilots. The sound of gunfire and the drone of the plane engines intensified. Jack was still out on the porch and I was standing next to him when suddenly he shoved me aside and to the floor of the porch. A line of bullets was cutting a path from the ground and up the side of the building. Two heavy bullets lodged in the door frame, right where my knees would have been. Just a fraction of a second longer, and the strafing would have cut me off at the knees. I almost became a patient in my own ward. I got up trembling all over and headed for the safety of the ward. I felt a little foolish when I thought of the ideal target that I presented to the diving planes. The only thing I lost in the ordeal was my nurse's cap.

After I got back inside the ward, I began cutting some of the guys out of traction and moving them under their beds. As the strafing was still going on, I piled mattresses around them, then climbed under the bed with them.

Within minutes of the attack, the wounded started to stream in the hospital. For three days, there seemed to be an inexhaustible supply of wounded and dying men. They were bringing men in so quickly that they didn't have time to separate the living from the dead. Bodies were piling up like cordwood wherever there was space. It was unbelievable what I was seeing. Some men were missing arms and legs, while others had limbs hanging by a shred of skin. It was hard to think that these men might be considered lucky since they had an outside chance of pulling through. The saddest and most depressing cases were the burn victims. Some of the men who were brought in were charred to a crisp, while others had their skin burned off, so their bodies resembled strips of fried and partially burnt bacon. It amazed the medical staff that these men were still alive when they were brought in.

Until the doctors had a chance to examine the more severely injured and wounded men, the nurses did their best to comfort them and see to their immediate needs. We were constantly changing dressings and checking vital signs. Basins were placed beneath the beds to catch the blood that soaked through the thin hospital mattresses. Empty whiskey and vodka bottles filled with hot water served as hot-water bottles to men in shock. The first man who died on me was a young, dark, and handsome nineteen-year-old sergeant. When he came to the ward, he was minus two legs and suffering from abdominal wounds. There was another young fellow I was helping who looked up at me, saw my nail polish, and said, "Nail polish . . . on an officer . . . in the middle of a war." Two hours later, he was dead.

The next three days following the attack were a blur of activity: nursing the dying, giving them whiskey and morphine, eating only chocolate bars and coffee, worrying about a Japanese invasion, little sleep, blood, death, and more blood. Red became the prevailing color as blood seemed to work its way into every nook and cranny of the hospital. Although it meant very little to the wounded men at the time, they were fortunate that the island had fully staffed and well-equipped medical facilities. If they had been elsewhere in the Pacific, it is doubtful that many of them would have survived. We were prepared for almost any type of emergency, short of an all-out attack on the island. Despite the suddenness of the attack, the only items we ran low on were blood and space. The shortage of blood was only temporary. Once the call went out for donors, we had hundreds of men lining up to give blood for their comrades and buddies who had just spilled their own. The lack of space was something we had to learn to live with. Until arrangements could be made to move some of the men to other buildings, hallways had to serve as temporary wards.

I think what hurt and stuck with many of us who cared for the wounded was the fact that these young fellows were so spirited and so young and had no chance to protect themselves. It didn't seem fair that these fellows didn't have a fighting chance. Many of the soldiers at Schofield Barracks had gone to bed numb with Saturday-night parties and awoke to an alarm clock of bombs and bullets, signaling the end of something and the beginning of something else. When you picture young men going off to war, you hear bands and you see marching and flags waving. These poor guys had been awakened suddenly. They were hobbling out, trying to get on their packs, pulling up their zippers, and adjusting helmets. It made you wonder what kind of chance they could have. As the men scurried around the base trying to find their units or battle stations, you could see the smoke from Pearl Harbor in the background. It was not an encouraging sight for those who did not know what was happening in the harbor below us.

Myrtle Watson remained at Oahu for the duration of the war. Despite the constant influx of patients from the Pacific front, the island offered enough diversions during the off time to ease the stress. For those who remained behind, Oahu offered the best and worst of a world at war and peace. Watson saved the bullets that had almost claimed her as a casualty. The cold metal is hard evidence for the memories that still bring tears. Although the years have passed and dulled the memories of many survivors, the painful cries of the injured still echo with freshness and intensity.

Taking a Prisoner

IRVIN KNIPP

In the dim gray light and faded shadows before the dawn of 7 December, six Japanese carriers launched 360 planes toward Oahu. Only 29 planes (9 fighter planes, 15 dive-bombers, and 5 torpedo bombers) failed to return to the decks of carriers. Within minutes of their appearance over Pearl Harbor, antiaircraft fire from the fleet succeeded in downing a number of enemy planes. The constant barrage of gunfire not only took a toll on the attacking aircraft but also caused many pilots to miss their designated targets. Downed planes were reported throughout the island, but no prisoners were taken from the wrecks.

A prisoner was almost taken by the crew of the motor launch from the USS *Montgomery*. The launch was dispatched to investigate the report of a downed aircraft in the harbor. The plane was soon spotted in the water, and its pilot was seen treading water near one of the shattered wings. As the launch drew alongside the remains of the fuselage, the pilot was ordered to swim to the launch. The impromptu surrender ceremony produced only an angered look from the pilot. The thought of surrender was out of the question, much less the thought of swimming over to his captors in order to do it. As the launch maneuvered into position to make the pickup, the pilot reached in his jacket and began to slowly draw his pistol. Before the pilot could get the weapon completely out from under his jacket, a shot rang out. The impact of the bullet fired by the coxswain jolted the body of the pilot beneath the surface. By the time he was lifted into the launch, he had died. Sergeant Irvin Knipp started the war at Hickam Field, where he manned the rear guns on a grounded A-20A plane and was credited with shooting down at least one enemy aircraft. He was one of the very few tail gunners who could claim an air kill while his plane was still on the ground. He relates an unusual and memorable event that occurred after the attack on Pearl Harbor.

On the morning of 14 December 1941, an order from Hawaiian Headquarters, Fort Shafter, arrived relating a report about a downed Jap fighter pilot who was terrorizing a group of natives on Niihau Island. Since my pilot was also operations officer, he delegated himself for this reconnaissance mission to verify this report. Since I was part of the plane's crew, I was automatically delegated to go along on the mission.

We departed promptly from Bellows Field and landed on Kauai at Burns Field. There the Hawaiian National Guard was alerted and briefed of our mission. We then flew to Niihau, which was a short distance away. On our arrival, we made a circular sweep at a low altitude of the entire island. Despite the jungle and the sugarcane, we were quickly able to spot the crashed Zero fighter in a cane field. At this point the pilot cautioned me not to fire any weapons (twin thirty-caliber machine guns). He said we would go down low for a good look. Since unofficially we were called "grasscutters," we then hit the deck. We were so low that we appeared to be riding on the top of the field. As we closed in on the crashed Zero, the Jap pilot managed to open fire on us with a single machine gun. For a while, it looked like Pearl Harbor all over again, only this time we were being the ones shot out of the sky. The odd thing was that for a few seconds I had the Jap pilot centered square in my gun sights, but couldn't squeeze the trigger, on orders from the pilot.

It seems the Jap pilot had somehow managed to remove a wing machine gun and attached it to the side of the fuselage in a makeshift manner. A second pass was not necessary. Since positive identification had been made on the one pass, we departed the area for a return flight to Burns Field. After landing at the field, the Hawaiian National Guard was again briefed. The commander decided to go in after the pilot and take a prisoner. A long boat was dispatched to make the capture with a platoon of infantry. I wondered to myself if one platoon would be enough to take him alive. We had all we could handle with an airplane and two thirty--caliber machine guns. We wished them all the luck in the world and returned back to Bellows Field. When we landed back on the island of Oahu, our mission ended.

Weeks later some informal reports came drifting back to Oahu about the fate of the Japanese pilot. Word from the Hawaiian grapevine produced an almost unbelievable story. Seems after we departed from Niihau, a heated argument developed between the head chief of the local tribe and the Jap pilot. Everyone in the nearby village had seen or heard the pilot fire on an American attack plane. This greatly upset the chief and his supporters, who had grown fond of the Americans and the American hospitality shown during brief encounters between the two. It seems the chief decided to take matters into his own hands, literally. Moments after we left the area, the chief confronted the pilot and tried to explain, as best as he could, he didn't want any American airplanes shot down over his island. Neither side was ready to give in to the other's way of thinking. When the Jap pilot made some threatening gestures, the chief reached out, grabbed the pilot, and threw him bodily to the ground. The chief quickly got astride the pilot and pinned him to the ground. In the meantime, the chief's wife had picked up a pumpkin-size rock and proceeded to beat it against the pilot's skull. In all this commotion, the pilot somehow managed to extract his Nambu service revolver and, shoving it into the chief's abdomen, fired a full clip of ammunition into the chief. After a belly full of pistol bullets, the chief was more than annoyed, he was dead. The chief 's wife, still pounding the head of the pilot, finally did him in. In a rage, she kept pounding and pounding, until the head was broken open and beat into the shape of a pancake. Thus ended another attempt to capture a Japanese aviator who participated in the bombing of Pearl Harbor. My pilot and I were never called on to make a return trip to the island and follow up on the story. Word had it that the incident was being handled by Army Intelligence.

During the war in the Pacific, Irvin Knipp had numerous chances to "squeeze the trigger" in the heat of battle. In May 1943, after logging more than three hundred combat hours in the Pacific theater, he was shipped to the mainland. After combat-crew training in the B-24 bomber, Knipp was transferred to the European theater, where he flew in over fifty combat missions.

A Civilian Reports

DAVID THOMPSON

Until 1940, Pearl Harbor was a minor naval base in the Pacific theater of operations. With the decision to base the US Pacific Fleet at Pearl Harbor came an accelerated building program to upgrade and renovate the existing facilities. To augment the existing workforce at the Pearl Harbor Navy Yard, the navy actively recruited thousands of civilian workers for technical and trade positions. By the summer of 1941, the Navy Yard was staffed and equipped to service the fleet. The increase in civilian and military personnel resulted in an expanded schedule of fleet functions. Although major overhauls for the larger ships, such as battleships and aircraft carriers, were performed at the West Coast yards, the Pearl Harbor Navy Yard could now handle limited overhauls and install and test the latest advancements in radar, armament, communications, and damage control.

David Thompson was one of a thousand civilians who came to the Hawaiian Islands to escape the throes of the Great Depression. He quickly found his version of paradise in a good job and a leisurely and idyllic lifestyle. Like most civilians, the twenty-two-year-old technician took up residence in Honolulu, approximately eight miles east of Pearl Harbor. Although the city was not a target during the Japanese attack, its proximity to the bull's-eye at Pearl Harbor did not allow it to escape the death and destruction. Over forty explosions were reported, with sixty-eight civilians killed and thirty-five wounded. Property damage was estimated in excess of $500,000.00. Although city residents reported seeing numerous bombs rain from the sky, only one Japanese bomb was officially recorded as landing in the city. The remaining explosions were the result of errant American gunners or defective antiaircraft fuses. From the edge of the battlefield, Thompson provides a unique account of the attack as seen through the eyes of a civilian, a view which has been overshadowed and overlooked.

In December of 1941, I was living at 14 Panahou Street and working at Pearl Harbor for the Pacific Naval Base Contractors, a group of five large contractors. I was working in a laboratory analyzing aggregate used with cement to make breakwaters for use at Midway.

Early on the Sunday morning of December 7, everyone in the neighborhood heard ack-ack fire but thought it was practice. At 9:00 a.m., I had an appointment to fly at the airport so I got on the bus about 8:30 and proceeded to the airport, which is about five miles from Pearl Harbor on the very outskirts of Honolulu. Now Pearl Harbor is maybe eight to ten miles from Honolulu, so this explains why many of the people did not know about the attack until planes began bombing Honolulu itself. I remarked to the bus driver, a rather rotund Hawaiian, that the ack-ack fire looked very realistic. We in Honolulu were conditioned to constant ack-ack fire and heavy coastal gunfire from the army and navy, who were constantly on maneuvers. Planes with towed sleeve targets were always offshore providing ack-ack practice for the big guns of the island forts. I wondered out loud what was going on as the shrapnel would probably do some minor damage. The driver just grinned at me and said that he could tell it was practice and that he never heard of shrapnel falling on anyone.

We were now passing in front off Iolani Palace, home of the governor of Hawaii, and saw a car on fire with a small group of people standing around it. We all craned our necks as we passed, little knowing that we were gazing at the first damage to the city. Later it was reported that one incendiary bomb, apparently aimed at the palace, missed its mark by a few feet and landed in the street, killing one lone Chinese and igniting the car. In a few minutes, the bus was out on the open highway, and I could see a big pall of smoke hanging over Pearl Harbor. No excitement was aroused, only a few curious remarks about where the smoke was coming from. After a few minutes on the road, the bus ground to a halt for another bus that was stopped in front of us. The driver of the bus that was in the middle of the road frantically waving his arms up and down. "Whattsa matta? Whattsa matta you?" asked our driver. "J-J-Japs bombing Pearl Harbor, get the hell out of here," he cried. I jumped out of my seat and dashed for the sidewalk.

Many of the passengers simply sat in the bus, too stunned to move or speak. One Hawaiian woman burst into tears while her husband tried to comfort her. After collecting my wits by the side of the road, I decided to get out for the remaining few miles to Pearl Harbor and see what was going on. I stuck out my thumb and tried to get a ride for over an hour, but no soap. Cars were passing me at 90 mph and not stopping for anyone. They were headed toward Pearl Harbor jammed to the roofs with passengers. Soldiers and sailors were pounding on the shoulders of taxi drivers to get them to go faster. One seven-passenger cab had at least fifteen people in the rear seat and five more in the front. Later, a convoy of army trucks passed by me, going like hell away from Pearl Harbor, possibly to Diamond Head. The trucks were crowded with soldiers who had the most scared faces I had ever seen. There were a few civilian cars ambling along the highway, but this line of army trucks had them off the road in a few seconds. The soldiers were gesturing wildly and pointing to the curb to get them over to the side.

With all the traffic on the road, I still couldn't get a ride. I didn't know what the hell to do. I still wanted to get out to Pearl, but everybody was in too much of a hurry to stop, especially for a civilian. I turned around and went back to town to tell everyone what I had seen. By the time I got back, news of the attack was all over the radio. One announcer was so damn excited all he could say was "This is it folks. This is it. The island is under attack . . . Enemy tentatively identified as Japs." He would then scream, "Don't get excited. Don't get excited. Take it easy. Take it calm, folks. Stay by your radios and listen for instructions." All of a sudden, the studio, maybe afraid of scaring the public, put on a program of cello music in the midst of the attack. After the cello program, the announcer came back on the air with instructions on how to protect against bombs with such things as buckets full of water, sand, and wet sacks. One of the fellows in my house who had gone to a couple of air warden classes suggested that we go out in the vicinity and tell people what to do in case of attack. For about the next hour-and-a-half, I went around giving frightened householders a few rudimentary precautions on getting ready for incendiary bombs. After covering about three square miles, we figured we had covered our district, so we quit. I then went down to the police station to offer my services at anything. When told they didn't need any help and everything was well-in-hand, I got mad and decided I would find somebody who could use me.

After leaving the station, I headed for the yacht harbor to see if any boats were being taken over by the navy or the Coast Guard. As I looked up to the sky, wondering where the Jap planes were coming from, I heard a bomb fall. It was not a screaming variety but more of a swishing, like the sound of water being thrown out of a bucket. The swishing lasted about ten seconds then stopped. About a block behind me, right where I had been about four minutes earlier, the bomb exploded.—I jumped, to say the least, then ran back to the smoke. The bomb hit a drugstore, which was now on fire. I joined in with a whole mess of people to help put out the fire. After a fire truck arrived, I once again turned around and headed for the yacht harbor. As I was walking along, some babe stopped her car and asked me if I wanted a ride. "Sure," I said and got in the car. I looked at her and could tell that she had been crying. When I asked her what was the matter, she said that she felt so awfully bad because she had been out to a party the night before and was with a couple of navy officers who had been stinking drunk. She was worried that they wouldn't be sober enough to help out on their ships. She was all in pieces but had enough control to ask me where I wanted to go. "Yacht harbor," I said. "Let's go have a drink first. I need it," she replied. "Okay, I guess I do, too," I said, but I didn't guess. So we stopped at a swanky bar in Waikiki and had a shot of scotch. I'll always remember sitting there with this good-looking babe with tears running down her cheeks, drinking scotch in the middle of the attack. What I didn't know was that the attack was already over. We finished our drinks and headed to yacht harbor.

When we got to the harbor, I thanked the gal and got out. Just as I arrived, a small fishing boat was pulling up to the dock. A mess of fellows got out carrying one fellow who had his back grazed by a Jap machine gun. As they were standing in the stern of their boat watching the attack, a Jap bomber strafed them from such an angle that they didn't know it until this one fellow had been hit. The owner of the boat was excited, to say the least. He really got excited when, a few minutes later, a Coast Guard officer requisitioned his boat. A fellow was needed to help take the boat a mile or so down the beach, so I volunteered. As soon as we tied up to the dock, some Coast Guard people began mounting a machine gun on the boat. I told the Coast Guard officer that I had a license and asked him if he could use me. He sent me up to the district Coast Guard office, where I was sworn in as a volunteer at 11:00 a.m. I was assigned to a small patrol boat whose job was to look for any mines, sabotage, or anything suspicious.

During this first patrol, I saw one of the most unforgettable sights of the war. Immediately after the attack, local FBI, police, and Naval Intelligence rounded up all Japs, Germans, and Italians whom they had been keeping an eye on and put them in an internment camp on Sand Island. All that Sunday afternoon and for days afterward, these spies, potential spies, and just plain enemy aliens were packed on barges and sent across to their new home. The barges were covered with hastily erected wooden benches that were surrounded by soldiers acting as guards. God! What a sight! There were about fifty Japs and Heinies on a barge and about forty guards. The soldiers were mostly kids, but they were fierce-looking. With fixed bayonets, they were pointing their rifles at the heads and throats of the prisoners. They were holding those rifles in the ready position as if they were going to charge. There were some doggies with Thompson submachine guns whose expressions indicated they were waiting for just one twitch so they could let someone have it. From the faces of the two groups, you could see that the doggies were itching to let the Japs have a taste of cold steel and lead, while the Japs were just as determined to live a bit longer. Just one sneeze and someone would have had a bayonet in his throat in seconds.

That night after patrolling all day, I got a few hours of liberty and finally made my way to Pearl Harbor. When I got there, the *Arizona* was still burning fiercely. It was then and there that I decided that I was damned if I was going to stay on a fat defense job when all of this was going on. I couldn't see myself being a civilian shirker and missing out on a fight. I was a volunteer from December 7th until the 27th when I joined the Coast Guard Reserve as a seaman. I was immediately called to active duty.

Only a couple of months before the attack, I had to register for the draft in Hawaii and, in due course of time, was called up for my physical examination. Two old guys doing the examination took one look at my leg and said I was 4-F.

—◆—

David Thompson's reaction to the Japanese attack was similar to that of other civilians on the island. On the morning of 8 December, army and navy recruiting offices were jammed with hundreds of potential recruits who were anxious to carry the war to the steps of the emperor's palace. Thompson first went to sea aboard the cutter *Taney.* He later became a radio technician and served on a number of cutters along the West Coast. He later attended Officers Candidate School, flunking out just as the war ended. Immediately following the war, he went to work for the navy as a field engineer.

The *Taney,* a 327-foot steam-driven cruiser christened on 3 June 1936 at the Philadelphia Navy Yard, served in World War II as an antisubmarine escort and amphibious flagship, and in Korea as a support ship. In the 1970s and early 1980s, the ship was tasked with offshore law enforcement, search and rescue, drug interdiction, and training cruises. On 7 December 1986, the last active survivor was decommissioned and the ship given to the city of Baltimore, Maryland.

Battleship Row

The USS *Neosho*

EARL ALLEN

Since July 1941, the *Neosho* had been engaged in the vital task of ferrying aviation fuel from the West Coast to Pearl Harbor. On 6 December, she arrived in Pearl Harbor, discharged her cargo of fuel to the Naval Air Station on Ford Island, and prepared for return passage to the West Coast, where she was to pick up another shipment of her precious cargo. Despite being anchored between three battleships (the *Maryland* and *Oklahoma* to her stern, and the *California* to her bow), the *Neosho* escaped the attack without any damage. Within minutes of the attack, the ship opened fire on swooping dive-bombers, splashing one and driving off others. Realizing that his ship was blocking the possible exit for the *Maryland* and *Oklahoma*, Commander John S. Phillips, captain of the *Neosho*, got underway and maneuvered her to a safer area in the harbor. When her mooring lines were chopped away, the *Neosho* backed away from the fuel pier, just barely clearing the *Oklahoma*, which had rolled over bottom up in the harbor. During the heavy gunfire and bombing runs of the Japanese, the ship slowly cleared the carnage at Battleship Row. Only three of her men were wounded in the ordeal. Although the *Neosho* had delivered almost a half-million gallons of fuel to the Naval Air Station, she still had a number of gallons in her cargo tanks. If the ship had waited one more day to unload or if the Japanese had pushed up their attack date to 6 December, a successful attack on the USS *Neosho* could have produced an explosion capable of obliterating the eastern section of the harbor along Ford Island and Battleship Row.

Earl Allen witnessed the attack on Pearl Harbor from the decks of the USS *Neosho*, as a passenger rather than as a crew member. His ship, the heavy cruiser USS *Northhampton*, was out at sea operating with one of the task forces.

I was born 30 September 1915 on a homestead northwest of Billings, Montana. My family moved to Salt Lake City, Utah, when I was eight years old. I attended school in Salt Lake City until 20 October 1932, when I enlisted in the navy at age seventeen. After boot training, I spent the rest of my first enlistment aboard the USS *Detroit*. After reenlisting, I went to the US Pacific Fleet. I returned to the United States in 1940 and, after reenlisting once again, was assigned to the USS *Northhampton*.

On 7 December 1941, I was a passenger on the USS *Neosho*. I was returning to Pearl Harbor to catch the USS *Northhampton* after my reenlistment leave. We had sailed from San Pedro on 1 December and arrived at Pearl on 6 December. After off-loading some fuel at Hickam Field, we moored that evening at Ford Island. The USS *Oklahoma* and the USS *Maryland* were astern, and the USS *California* was ahead of us.

I had just finished breakfast and was topside on the fantail when I noticed a plane drop a bomb on Ford Island. The plane had pulled out of his dive, and I didn't recognize the silhouette. My first thought was that it was a strange place for practice bombing. Within seconds the next plane came into sight, and I recognized the Jap insignia. When the first bomb exploded, I knew then it wasn't practice, but a Japanese attack. Along with some of the crew and passengers, I was wondering what was taking so long to get underway. Although the ship was sitting much higher out of water, we didn't know how much of the highly combustible and flammable fuel was still aboard. Everyone was asking everyone else the same question, "How much fuel is still in the tanks?" We had very little firepower and could only watch the attack and hope we didn't get hit. Any type of hit could have blown us across the Pacific in a million pieces.

General quarters sounded for all passengers to muster in the mess hall. We had a gunner's mate as mustering petty officer. Before all passengers were present, a seaman came running up to the gunner and asked if he had the keys to the magazine. His answer was, "Yes, do you want it opened?" The muster was delayed, and a detail was sent forward to break out ammo. I helped carry a box of five-inch aft on the catwalk. Then one of the engineering chiefs got me to go below to light off the boilers.

While I was forward, the USS *California* called away the "fire and rescue party," but immediately changed it to general quarters. When I got aft with the ammo, the USS *Oklahoma* was listing over twenty-five or thirty degrees. I could see the torpedo planes flying low down the channel from Merry Point Landing then turn off to drop their torpedoes aimed at the wagons. I saw the USS *Oklahoma* and USS *West Virginia* take hits. Just before I went below, one of the destroyers in dry dock with the USS *Pennsylvania* blew, and we all thought it was the flagship of the fleet being hit.

I wasn't in the fire room very long until they collected the regular crew. I was then sent back topside. I remember seeing the USS *Nevada* steaming by, and everyone topside cheered. The USS *Neosho* backed out of our berth and passed the USS *Oklahoma*. She was capsized by this time, and as we were alongside a man came to the surface. He had done the impossible and somehow escaped from below one of the decks. He was really screaming for help. We hailed a passing motor launch to pick him up. Our ship kept moving astern past the USS *West Virginia*, which was afire in the midship section. We then went alongside the dock at Merry Point Landing, astern of the ammo supply ship, the USS *Pyro*. The passenger working party began hand-carrying the three-inch, twenty-three-caliber anti-aircraft ammo to resupply what we had used. One Jap reconnaissance plane flew by so low that we could see the photographer with his camera. It seemed like everything in the harbor was firing at him, but

An aerial view of the attack from the cockpit of a Japanese bomber. In the center, the USS *West Virginia* takes a torpedo hit. Other warplanes are visible in the right-hand corner.

An aerial view of Battleship Row from the cockpit of a Japanese bomber. The view from lower left to upper right shows the USS *Nevada*, USS *Vestal* outboard from the USS *Arizona*, USS *West Virginia* outboard from the USS *Tennessee*, USS *Oklahoma* outboard from the USS *Maryland*, USS *Neosho*, and USS *California*. The *West Virginia* and *Oklahoma* are listing from torpedo hits. In the center, smoke is visible from the dry dock holding the *Cassin*, *Downes*, and *Pennsylvania*. In the background, smoke from Hickam Field obscures the harbor entrance.

An aerial view of Pearl Harbor looking southwest in October of 1941. The photo highlights the harbor's geographical features and dimensions. Ford Island is in the center; Navy Yard is across the channel opposite the upper-left portion of the island.

The first wave of Japanese warplanes prepares for takeoff from a carrier deck, 230 miles north of Oahu.

Army airplanes reduced to piles of scrap metal. The first wave of Japanese bombers immobilized the island's airfields, thereby ensuring Japanese air superiority.

A motor launch plucks a survivor from the water near the *West Virginia*. Abandoning ship was a perilous and often deadly swim through fiery, oil-coated waters.

The burned and sunken hulk of the USS *Arizona*. The force of the magazine explosion, which literally lifted the ship and broke it in half, is evidenced by the bent and twisted shape of the superstructure.

The USS *Nevada*, beached and burning after her run for the open sea. Fearing the ship might block the entrance to the harbor, High Command ordered her to run aground. Damage to armor plating is seen at the waterline forward of the main gun turret.

The USS *Utah* lists to port side just before capsizing. To escape, sailors slid down the starboard side and bottom of the ship.

Sailors survey wreckage on Ford Island. The fireball in the background is the exploding USS *Shaw*.

A sweeping view of destruction from Ten-Ten Dock. The USS *Oglala* is capsized in the foreground. The USS *Helena* is tied up along the dock. Forward of the *Helena*, the mast of the *Pennsylvania* and smoke from the *Cassin* and *Downes* are visible. Across from the *Helena*, smoke billows from the dry-docked *Shaw*. To the right of the *Shaw*, fire aboard the *Nevada* is visible.

The USS *Cassin* rests against the burned, sunken hulk of the USS *Downes*. The USS *Pennsylvania* in the background escaped serious damage. The dry dock was flooded as a precautionary measure after the attack. Note the stripeless Stars and Stripes on the bow of the *Pennsylvania*.

The USS *Shaw* in Floating Dry Dock Number Two burns after the explosion that severed her bow. The dry dock sank after the same explosion.

Marines fire a volley over a grave site near Kanahoe Naval Air Station. Many of the dead were reinterred at the Punchbowl, the National Memorial Cemetery of the Pacific.

A Japanese midget sub beached near Oahu. A midget sub was detected near the harbor entrance at 3:45 a.m. on 7 December. By the time the information was forwarded to the proper authorities, the attack was underway.

he just kept on taking pictures. I don't believe he was ever hit. Later that day, we moored in the back channel and anchored opposite the capsized USS *Utah*.

I was transferred back aboard the USS *Northhampton* just after Christmas 1941. I remained on her until she was torpedoed and sunk on 30 November 1942 at the Battle of Tassafaronga.

After the sinking of the USS *Northhampton*, Earl Allen returned to the mainland and was assigned to the newly commissioned cruiser USS *Mobile* at Newport News, Virginia. After a shakedown cruise, he returned to the Pacific theater aboard the ship and remained there until September 1944, when he was transferred to shore duty at Newport, Rhode Island. He retired from the navy in 1954 as chief boilerman.

The USS *Maryland*

CARL WHITAKER

On the morning of 7 December, the *Maryland* was berthed inboard of the *Oklahoma*, forward of the *Tennessee*, and astern of the *Neosho*. The wall of ships served as an armored shield for the *Maryland* and resulted in her suffering the least damage of any of the eight battleships. Despite the added protection, the ship received two hits from armor-piercing bombs, but the low detonation of the bombs saved her from serious damage. The first bomb struck the forecastle awning, tearing a twelve-by-twenty-two-foot hole and penetrating the compartments below deck, but causing relatively minor damage. The second bomb resulted in more serious damage, entering the hull at the twenty-two-foot water level and causing heavy but limited flooding, which dropped the bow five feet in the water.

A gunner's mate striker, who was writing a letter near his battle station at the beginning of the attack, brought the first of the ship's machine guns into action. He shot down one of the two attacking torpedo planes. Within minutes, the crew managed to bring all the ship's antiaircraft batteries into operation. In the midst of tending to her bomb hits and directing her firepower against enemy aircraft, the crew of the *Maryland* sent fire and rescue parties to aid her sister ships along Battleship Row. After the attack, the Japanese imperial command announced to the world that the *Maryland* had been sunk. Although a large number of bombs had been hurled in her vicinity, very few found their desired mark. The USS *Oklahoma* felt the full impact of the attack, taking five torpedo hits before capsizing.

Carl Whitaker was a teenage sailor aboard the *Maryland* at the time of the attack. Like many other young servicemen, he made the transition from boyhood into manhood by the day's end. His narrative provides not only an account of the attack but also a view of life in the battleship fleet.

My childhood and early youth were spent in a small town in central California during the 1930s. Within the shadows of World War II, I enlisted in the navy at age eighteen and was assigned to a battleship. At some point during the bombing of Pearl Harbor, I grew up. I was then privileged to participate in eight major engagements against the Empire of the Rising Sun, and I arrived in Tokyo Bay in time for V-J Day, 2 September 1945.

In May 1941, I was assigned to the USS *Maryland*, and, for the first time in history, following the war games, the US Fleet was retained in Hawaii. This was a shocking experience for the personnel involved, many of whom were married and had families in their home ports. The admiral of the US Fleet, J. O. Richardson, affectionately known as "Uncle Joe" Richardson, was violently opposed to retaining the fleet at Pearl Harbor. He had suggested twice on visits to Washington that the fleet be either returned to the West Coast or placed on a rotating schedule. That would have placed one third of the ships at Pearl, one third enroute to the West Coast, and one third on the West Coast. This was known as the "love cruise" method. The admiral felt that the ships were inadequately manned for war, the Hawaiian area was too exposed for fleet training during such a period of international tension, and the defenses against both air and submarine attack were far from adequate. In January 1941, he was unexpectedly relieved of fleet command and succeeded by Admiral Husband E. Kimmel. It was known that the fleet, as then constituted, was too far from Eastern Asia to have a deterrent on Japan; plus the fact we did not have enough supply, tankers, and other support ships to support the fleet that far from a permanent base. Furthermore, the already inadequate fleet was weakened by the detachment in March 1941 of three battleships, one aircraft carrier, four light cruisers, and eighteen destroyers for duty in the Atlantic.

It must be remembered that the Japanese secret code had been broken about four months prior to the start of the war, and Washington was fully informed of Japan's interest in Pearl Harbor, especially the twice-weekly ship movements in and out of Pearl that Tokyo requested. Yet in the face of unmistakable evidence that an attack might be made on Pearl, there was complacency. After all, everyone knew that the Japanese had bad eyes and that they were generally inferior; this was exemplified by the cheaply made goods imported to the United States. But I personally was not sure of all this. I had been raised in Lindsay, California, where many Japanese were truck farmers. I had gone to school with many Nisei children. They were bright, alert students. Because of the difference in their culture, they were often misunderstood, but they were always respected. As a minority group, they knew only two ways to attain equality: through hard work and education. They applied themselves to both tasks with unbelievable perseverance.

A week prior to 7 December, the fleet had been at sea on maneuvers. It was an unforgettable sight to see the ships of the line with battle flags flying and foamy seas breaking over their forecastles. However, this was an illusion of strength. Against enemy capital ships, their large main battery could have been most effective, but against enemy aircraft they were pitifully unprepared. The *Maryland* had slow-firing five-inch antiaircraft guns that found it difficult to hit a sleeve towed at slow speeds—let alone a dive-bomber or torpedo bomber. We also had several tubs of automatic weapons, but they were largely experimental in nature. So at this time the ships returned to Pearl Harbor, several of them having put to sea for the last time. Although negotiations with Japan were breaking down, the commanders (both army and navy) in the Hawaiian area were never fully informed or advised to put their forces on a wartime-alert status. Lieutenant General Short deducted from communiqués from Washington that his greatest danger was subversion by the Japanese elements in Hawaii. Therefore, he prepared for sabotage by grouping his air force units closely together so that they would be more easily guarded. No attempt had been made to implement the Joint Army-Navy Hawaiian Defense Plan, which had been widely acclaimed by Admiral Stark, chief of naval operations.

So dawned 7 December. At 6:00 a.m., Admiral Nagumo, the commander of the Pearl Harbor strike force, launched forty torpedo planes, fifty-one dive-bombers, and forty-nine high-level bombers from the decks of his six carriers. At this point, they were 250 miles from Pearl Harbor and completely undetected. Of all the military airplanes in the area, only seven navy PBYs were on patrol and were many miles to the southwest. Of the 780 antiaircraft guns on ships in Pearl, only a fourth were manned, and, of the army's thirty-one anti-aircraft batteries, only four were in position, having no ammunition. They had been returned to depot to avoid getting rusty. The Japanese plan was simple but effective. Their first strikes were the navy bases at Kaneohe and Ford Island; the army bases, Wheeler, Bellows, and Hickam, and the marine base at Ewa were almost completely wiped out. The planes, closely grouped for security against sabotage, were perfect targets. Three minutes later, at 7:58, the message heard around the world was "Air raid Pearl Harbor—this is no drill."

A battleship is much like a modern city, providing its own electricity, water converted from seawater, its own hospital facility, laundry, machine shop, and all of the facilities to support the activities of fourteen hundred men. We were observing a typical Sunday routine. Breakfast had been served at 7:00. I was writing a letter to a friend in Long Beach when I happened to look out of one of the portholes and saw several airplanes. My first reaction was "Damn the army," practicing on Sunday, and they have even gone to the trouble of painting the rising sun on the wings. Just then general quarters sounded, and all hands went to their battle stations. I immediately reported to main engine control, which was the nerve center for the engineering department. This was located twenty-five feet below the waterline. Almost immediately, the news from the bridge was unbelievable. Within one minute after the attack, the *Oklahoma*, which had come alongside and moored the previous morning, was hit with four torpedoes and almost immediately listed to port and turned over, trapping four hundred of her ship's company inside. Seven battleships were tied up in Battleship Row—first was the *California*, next the *Maryland* and the *Oklahoma*, the *Tennessee* and *West Virginia*, then the *Arizona*. The *Arizona* was hit by a torpedo, and a moment later she was attacked by high-level bombers. Five bombs were dropped, some going through the forecastle and starting a fire, which quickly spread to 1,600 pounds of black powder. This is the most dangerous of all explosives and should have been stored in magazines below the armor-plated deck. As soon as the powder exploded, the ship literally leaped out of the water amidst a blast of smoke and debris; then the 32,600-pound ship broke in two and quickly settled to the bottom. This murdered over eleven hundred men, and no war had yet been declared.

Ironically, many of the company I originally started with in boot camp were shipped to the *Arizona*, and only the fact that I contacted "cat fever" and was held back a month kept me from being on this ill-fated ship. In fact, a friend of mine from Lindsay, California, is still down there. He and some other musicians were playing in a combo ashore just the night before—a friend I will always remember.

Next in line was the *Nevada*, which sustained a torpedo and a bomb hit, but succeeded in getting underway. However, as she headed out of the harbor she became the target of planes from a second raid—eighty dive-bombers, fifty-four high-level bombers, and thirty-six fighters. She was immediately hit by six bombs and was forced to run aground to keep from blocking the entrance to the channel. The other battleship in the harbor was the *Pennsylvania*, which was in dry dock. She was also damaged, as was the target ship *Utah*. She was sunk when the Japs mistook her for an aircraft carrier.

As suddenly as it started, the attack ended. The state of shock on the *Maryland* was unbelievable. This was particularly true of the older officers and chiefs who had been raised in the navy on the legend of our superiority over the Japanese and of the indestructibility of the battleship. I believe the results would have been even more catastrophic if we had had sufficient warning to put to sea.

Our land-based planes might have been destroyed, and the only two aircraft carriers in operation were more than five hundred miles from Pearl. I feel sure that, without air support, the entire fleet would have been sunk, as were the *Prince of Wales* and the battle cruiser *Repulse*—sunk off the coast of Malaya when they were left to defend themselves against enemy aircraft. Many of the battleships at Pearl returned to the war—the *Maryland, Tennessee, West Virginia, Nevada,* and *Pennsylvania*—and served for bombardment purposes in the long journey through the island chain that led to Tokyo Bay on surrender day.

Carl Whitaker remained in the navy and retired at age thirty-eight with twenty years of service. Whitaker found the solution to the problem facing many retired servicemen by developing new skills and improving on old ones at colleges and universities near his home in Long Beach, California. At age fifty-nine, he retired from a position with the Los Angeles Board of Education.

The USS *Oklahoma*

WILLIAM M. HOBBY

On the morning of 7 December, the *Oklahoma* was moored in Battleship Row outboard alongside the *Maryland* and forward of the *West Virginia*. The *Oklahoma*'s outside position would be fatal. Shortly after the first bomb fell over Ford Island, the *Oklahoma* took three torpedo hits in rapid succession. The torpedo hits ripped gaping holes in her side and caused severe flooding, which caused her to list almost immediately. As the ship began to list to her port side, two more torpedoes scored direct hits. Within twenty minutes of the first appearance of Japanese bombers, the *Oklahoma* rolled over on her side.

The roll of the ship was stopped when the masts and the superstructure hit the harbor bottom and imbedded themselves in the mud. Crew members, who had begun to abandon ship after the first series of torpedo hits, found themselves prey to strafers as they attempted to make their way to shore or another ship. Many of the survivors made their way through the fire and oil on the water to the decks of the *Maryland*, where they assisted with the antiaircraft batteries. Of the 1,354 men aboard the *Oklahoma*, 415 lost their lives. Twenty officers and 395 enlisted men were listed as killed or missing in action. Sailors and civilian workers, who worked throughout the attack in the heat of the searing oil fires, rescued 32 men who had been trapped in the overturned hull. The rescue operation paralleled similar undertakings aboard the *Utah*, which was on the other side of Ford Island. Julio Decastro, a civilian yard worker, was credited with having organized the rescue team that saved those lucky few from becoming entombed in the hull of the *Oklahoma*.

The men trapped inside the *Oklahoma* and the *Utah* were rescued through similar methods. They made their presence known by banging hammers, wrenches, or other tools on the steel structures in the lower compartments. Rescue workers on the outside of the ship heard them and answered with banging sounds in Morse code.

Chances appeared good for successfully rescuing the trapped crew of the overturned *Oklahoma*. The battleship had capsized through 170 degrees, and its bottom was nearest the surface and visible above the water. It seemed that the rescue operations would involve cutting holes in the ship's bottom and pulling out survivors from various compartments. The first holes were cut with acetylene torches. This method was stopped when it was learned that the fumes from the oil both in the water and in the ship, combined with the burning cork used for insulation, could produce a toxic gas capable of killing crew members trapped in the vicinity of the operation. The Navy Yard and nearby ships furnished tools and equipment using compressed air, as well as submersible pumps, sound-powered telephones, and air ducts and fans for ventilating rescue compartments. As trapped men were located and freed, they alerted rescue workers about additional personnel who were trapped in various sections or frames along the ship's entire length and width. The last man climbed out of a makeshift hole at 2:30 a.m. on 9 December. All survivors emerged in good condition. A watch was maintained on the hull of the *Oklahoma* until 11 December, but no further signs of any survivors were detected.

On 7 December, Lieutenant Commander William M. Hobby Jr. was aboard the USS *Oklahoma* as second in command. His narrative details the quick death dealt to the mighty battleship by Japanese bombers.

On the morning of Sunday, 7 December, the *Oklahoma* was secured at berth F-5, Pearl Harbor, outboard of the *Maryland* and starboard of her. Commander J. L. Kenworthy was senior officer on board, and I was second in command. At about 8:00 a.m., I heard the word over the loudspeaker to man the antiaircraft battery, then shots from an indeterminate direction, then a second time the word to man the antiaircraft battery for a real attack. As I was going topside, the word was passed to man all battle stations. I ran up the starboard side out to the main deck aft, by the break of the deck. Before I reached the main deck aft, there was a din of gunfire and explosions from all directions.

I started up the ladder from the main deck aft to the antiaircraft gun platform on the starboard side; at this point I felt what I believe was the first torpedo hit—a dull thud and a powerful reverberation on the port side, and the ship began listing to port. I started back down with the idea of getting to Central and directing the flooding of the starboard blisters, but almost immediately there was a second torpedo hit and then a third, and the ship listed more; at this time streams of men were pouring up through hatches to the topside. A second or so later, at about the time I was back down to the main deck aft again, came the fourth torpedo hit, and the ship continued to list to port at least a twenty-degree list at this time, I estimate, and still listing. I directed petty officers near me to spread out over the length of the ship and keep the men as orderly and calm as possible. I sighted Commander Kenworthy on the starboard catwalk and made my way to him and told him that I thought the best now was to save as many men as possible, and that it was now impossible to make further watertight closures and establish any further watertight integrity. He agreed, and we both passed the word to abandon ship. I called to men on main deck aft to attempt to get to work on the loudspeaker.

Although there were now hundreds of men on the starboard side, the general conduct of all hands was quiet and calm. There was an explosion around the port side of the forecastle, which I thought was a bomb hit. I worked my way forward, and Commander Kenworthy worked his way aft. There was another shock and concussion and vibration, and fuel oil splashed in streams over everything topside. This was either another torpedo hit or a large bomb hit close aboard. The ship continued to list over to port, now about thirty degrees, or more, I thought. I entered the number-one casemate to see about the escape of men from below to topside. Men were still coming out through casemates and thence out through gun ports to the catwalk and onto the side. When no more men were to be seen in casemates, I climbed up through a gun port and out over the side; the ship was capsizing and the angle was about ninety degrees. I pulled myself along the side and bottom as the vessel keeled over; the ship finally settled when the mast and stack apparently hit bottom, with an angle of approximately 145 degrees, starboard side uppermost.

I sat on the bottom at about frame sixty, as hundreds of men were along the hull making their way to the water's edge. Keenum C. W., Chief Boatswain's mate, joined me and rendered much aid in steadying the men and directing them to swim to the *Maryland*, to the Ford Island landing, or to a motor launch, depending on their location. The air attack continued and bombs were dropping nearby, but none struck the *Oklahoma* after she capsized. All men who reached the topside were apparently saved, swimming to either the *Maryland*, the shore, or a motor launch. There were many cases of men aiding others to swim, and in some cases actually towing them to shore or the *Maryland* or a boat. The general conduct of the crew continued to be excellent.

I saw the *Oklahoma* officers and men who had boarded the *Maryland* go to her antiaircraft battery and aid in her antiaircraft fire. I saw Boatswain Bothne acting as coxswain of a motor launch and picking up men and taking them to Ford Island landing. After all others had cleared the hull of the ship, as far as we could see, Keenum and I made our way out to the bow. I discarded shoes and uniform, expecting to swim in, and at this juncture Boatswain Bothne approached in a motor launch, having already landed one load of men. There were about fifty men in this second load. Keenum and I entered the motor launch. The boat made the dock and unloaded all but Boatswain Bothne, four other men, and myself. The *Oklahoma* men on the dock were handling lines of a tanker that was getting underway, and some of them boarded the tanker upon being told that she needed more men to go out on her. Other men on the dock were asking where they could go to aid in antiaircraft fire; all seemed to be thinking of how to fight rather than seeking safety.

I remained in the motor launch, and with Boatswain Bothne and four other men patrolled up and down the line facing the *Oklahoma*, *West Virginia*, and *Arizona*, looking for survivors to pick up from the water. By this time it appeared that all men had reached shore and the water was clear of men. We patrolled for about twenty minutes, until it seemed that the attack was over, or at least that no more bombs were being dropped that we could see, and we could see no more enemy planes. Then we took the motor launch across the harbor to the mine-dock landing. Here were survivors, other boards, and Navy Yard personnel along the dock. A truck driver volunteered to drive those of us without clothes to the receiving station for clothes. We drove there, and I obtained dungarees, shoes, and a white sailor's hat. Then the truck returned me to the landing. I commandeered a motor boat and returned to the hull of the *Oklahoma*. Others were on the *Oklahoma* and still more were coming aboard as I arrived. With several men, I went over the hull, discussing possibilities of salvaging those still alive inside. Commander Kranzelder, Lieutenant Commander Benson, and Lieutenant Commander Henderson were now on the hull. Also Boatswain Bothne and twenty or thirty men from the *Oklahoma* who had returned. I believed that all returned at approximately the same time. Thenceforth we concentrated on salvage work for the rescue of survivors trapped inside. I remained on the hull or inside the hull for the next sixty hours as senior *Oklahoma* officer on salvage work.

Following the attack on Pearl Harbor, Commander Hobby, a 1923 graduate of the US Naval Academy, was assigned to the cruiser USS *Juneau*, which was launched in February 1942. In November 1942, the *Juneau* joined an American attack group in the Solomon Islands to engage a large Japanese surface force. In the early morning on 13 November 1942, the *Juneau* was struck port side by a torpedo, causing a severe list. At 11:00 a.m., while withdrawing from the battle, the ship was struck by another torpedo at the same location of the earlier hit. Following a tremendous explosion, the ship broke in half and sank within twenty seconds. Only ten of the crew survived. Commander Hobby was officially reported as killed in action on 13 November 1941. His eyewitness account was part of the official after action report. The narrative, more technical and less emotional than the other narratives in the book, reflects how the battle unfolded before the eyes of many higher ranking naval officers.

The USS *Tennessee*

JIMMY ANDERS AND
M. JOSEPH MCDONALD

On the morning of 7 December, the battleship *Tennessee* was moored in the center of Battleship Row. Inboard of the *West Virginia* and with the *Maryland* to her bow and the *Arizona* to her stern, she was insulated and partially hidden from the reach of the deadly torpedo bombers that sank a number of outboard ships. Despite repeated attacks by dive-bombers, the *Tennessee* escaped with minor damage. Two bombs from high-level bombers struck the ship and penetrated her armor. Due to a low order of detonation or no detonation, damage was confined to certain areas of the ship. The first bomb hit the centerline of the number-two gun turret, causing the barrel to crack and rendering all three guns inoperable. The second bomb passed through the roof plate of the number-three turret, damaging it and the rammer of the left gun. Bomb fragments from this blast sprayed the forward superstructure of the ship.

The biggest threat to the *Tennessee* came not from Japanese bombers, but from her surrounding sister ships. When the *West Virginia* sank after receiving six torpedoes and two bombs, she wedged the *Tennessee* hard against the forward quay. Oil fires from the *Arizona* engulfed the *Tennessee*'s stern and caused numerous serious fires aft. The explosion of the magazines aboard the *Arizona* showered the *Tennessee* with burning powder and fiery debris. To avoid the fires spreading to the critical areas of the ships, the latter's forward magazines were flooded. Hoses were continuously sprayed over her stern to keep the burning oil on the water at a safe distance. The ship's engines were started to make five knots, and the resulting propeller wash churned out a safe area between the ship and the oil fires. For twenty-four hours, the engines ran at speeds of up to ten knots. The ship was so tightly positioned between the *West Virginia* and the concrete quays that the continuous running of the engines failed to produce any noticeable movement.

After several attempts to free the *Tennessee* during salvaging operations failed, her weight was lightened by pumping out the remaining fuel oil, and the quays were dynamited. Even before the ship was freed, repairs were already underway. Patches were welded to the armor plates that had warped under the intense heat, and hull rivets that had popped and had been pulled out due to the heat and pressure were replaced. When the ship was finally freed, she was taken to the Navy Yard, where temporary repairs to the internal damage and the gun turrets were made. On 20 December, the *Tennessee*, *Maryland*, and *Pennsylvania* departed for Puget Sound Navy Yard, where permanent repairs would be made.

For Seaman Jimmy Anders, the *Tennessee* provided a close-up look at the action along Battleship Row. From dead center of the Japanese primary target, he witnessed the destruction of the mighty battleships of the US Pacific Fleet.

My story starts in McComb, Mississippi, on a very hot day in June 1940. Several of my buddies and I were lying around under the only shade tree anywhere near, and that tree was in the Illinois Central Railroad yards. We were waiting for the next load of scrap wood to come out and be dumped. It was wood that had been stripped from the old wooden boxcars that needed repair. If we hadn't been there, the wood would have been dumped and burned. We usually managed to drag most of it away, and by the end of the day, if we were lucky, we'd have enough to sell for firewood. If we could find a buyer (and sometimes we couldn't), we'd usually get around a dollar for the whole lot. We would then notify the girls and have a weiner roast that night. We would buy a pound of weiners for fifteen cents, a package of buns for ten cents, and a pack of Bull Durham tobacco for five cents. And the local bootlegger would sell us a half-gallon of wine for forty cents. If any pennies were left over, we'd buy some peppermint to hide the smell of wine in case our parents got close enough to smell it. We'd get all the stuff together, get our girls, and head for the gravel pit.

Along this time they were doing a lot of talk about the draft, so several of us decided to beat them to the punch and sign up for the navy. We sold enough chickens to get money for gas to New Orleans, where we would have to sign up. We all drove down one evening and spent the night in the car. The next morning we all pranced down to the courthouse to sign up. Things didn't work out too well. My good buddy Jack was a little too young; his brother Robert was too young; and his older brother, Dub, didn't make it for some reason or another. As luck would have it, I was the only one to pass. After my pals didn't make it, I wasn't caring much about going in by myself. We all returned home and the trip was more or less forgotten until about a month later, when I received a letter telling me to report for induction.

So finally came the day when I was to leave for New Orleans. It was a very sad day for me. I hated leaving everyone behind, my family and friends. But I took my little duffel bag with a couple of changes of clothes, my train ticket, and no money. I did have a couple of peanut butter and jelly sandwiches in my bag. I walked down to the house of Jack's mother, where the biggest part of our gang hung out most of the time, and said tearful good-byes, with talk of my friends coming to join up with me. Most of the gang stayed together much of the time. We thought of one another as brothers. No one had a job, and much of the time was spent at someone's house. A couple of my buddies walked me to the train station. When it came time for me to board, Jack pressed some change into my hand and said, "It ain't much, but maybe you'll need it."

I arrived in New Orleans and spent the night at my aunt's. The next morning I reported to the courthouse, and by noon I had enlisted in the navy for a six-year hitch, beginning 30 September 1940. I was soon on my way to San Diego for boot training. After six weeks of training, some of the fellows came into the barracks and said a list of ships we'd be going to had been posted. The rest of us dashed down to the bulletin board to see the lists. Some of us went to the *Oklahoma*, some to the *California*, and some to the *Tennessee*. My name was on the list for the *Tennessee*. There was a note attached to the effect that the *Tennessee* would be waiting for us at Long Beach and that the *Oklahoma* would furnish us transportation. My, what a ship the *Oklahoma* was! I didn't think that something that big could float on water. After we got underway, I started really feeling like I was part of the navy, and I loved it. When I went aboard the *Tennessee*, I fell in love with her. She was such a good ship that I never changed my mind about her. After some briefing, I was placed in one of the deck divisions, which I didn't really like. Fortunately for me, the Ordnance Division needed some men to bring it up to full strength, and I was lucky enough to be selected. I always liked guns and thought I'd be working on guns. Instead, we had charge of the storerooms, spare parts, conveyors, ammunition rooms, and the responsibility for the ship's two planes and launch ramps. My job was to keep records of parts issued to all guns and to have the storerooms ready at all times for the captain's inspection. I became good friends with our petty officer, Bob Rassmussen. We had many good times on shore. The only thing I didn't like about Bob was the fact that he was much better-looking than me, and he always had his choice of the better-looking girls, or at least the first choice.

Shortly after I came aboard, we made our first trip to Pearl Harbor. At Pearl, we were put through some very rigorous training. After several weeks, we headed back to the States and stayed in dry dock, where we got a taste of how it was to scrape and paint the complete bottom of the *Tennessee*. Once out of dry dock, we headed for the Bremerton Navy Yard. Seattle was a good liberty port for sailors. Yard workmen would often invite different sailors home for a home-cooked meal. After some good times in port and exercises off the coast of San Francisco, we were on our way back to Pearl Harbor for patrol duty with some of the other battle wagons. December had come, and there was a lot of talk that things were near a breaking point with Japan. Just how near we didn't realize, until the morning of 7 December.

That morning I was up early, had a good breakfast, then went to the upper deck, where they sold newspapers. I bought one and headed back to a small room on the third deck used by the Ordnance Division petty officers. It had a coffeepot and a hot plate, so if someone missed a meal he could fry something up real quick. I had started down to this small lounge room and was just going through a hatchway when the first torpedo struck the outboard side of the *West Virginia*. The force of the explosion heaved the *Tennessee* several feet in the air. Several other torpedo blasts followed, sending the *West Virginia* to the bottom of the shallow harbor. Lucky for us and unlucky for the *West Virginia*, there had been some kind of mix-up in scheduling the arrival of the battle wagons. We had come in a little ahead of the *West Virginia* and tied up on the inside berth. The *West Virginia*, arriving a little later, tied up on the outside. I was told that the *West Virginia* was supposed to arrive ahead of us and take the inside berth.

I was knocked to my feet by the first blast and quickly got to my feet unhurt. A minute or so later, the word was blaring over the loudspeakers to "Man your battle stations; this is no drill." I remember that our bugler first started off with the breakfast call or some other one before he blew "All hands man your battle stations." Word was passed for all ordnance personnel not assigned to gun stations to muster in the armory. When we first gathered in the armory, I made a somewhat foolish remark and said, "I guess we'll go to war over this." Some fellow named Carroll replied, "Hell, we're at war right now." Hewitt, the gunner's mate in charge of the armory, spoke up, "You bet your ass we are." I quickly agreed with him when another bomb rocked the *Tennessee*. We were hit with two bombs and strafed several times. Up on deck, sailors were diving everywhere under the fourteen-inch turrets for shelter. I'm not sure how many casualties we suffered, but we were spared when compared to the other ships.

The two bombs hitting the *Tennessee* were actually sixteen-inch projectiles converted and armed to explode on contact. We certainly felt fortunate that they were faulty and turned out to be duds. They did rip through the steel plating of the ship and cause damage. There were anxious moments before we were able to get such a large projectile out of the small opening of the gun turret. The projectile had penetrated completely through the heavy top armor of the turret and came to a resting place inside the turret.

As the attack continued and problems arose, we would hustle out to take care of them the best we could. Most of the time, we had to improvise. The *Arizona* was so close to our fantail and was burning so intensely that she set fires on our fantail. Men trying to put out these fires sprayed water over electrical wires that had the insulation burned off, allowing the current to run up the fire hoses, knocking many unconscious. Other men were busy pulling sailors out of the water who had been blown over the sides of their ships into the burning oil on top of the water. Most of these survivors looked terrible. Many had their hair burned off, and their faces were burned and swollen to twice their normal size. We gave towels to wipe the oil off for those not so severely burned. We even pulled out several soldiers from the water. Didn't know where they came from, but we gave them some clothing and something to eat.

Because I carried the keys to the spare-parts rooms, I was called out to go below and retrieve a part needed for one of the deck guns. Since watertight integrity had been set as much as possible below decks, no one was allowed to open a hatch or watertight door without permission. Getting special permission in all that confusion wasn't easy. Finally, permission was granted and I went two and three decks below the waterline of the ship. I came to where a good friend was at his battle station. His post was located between three ammunition storage rooms, one where black powder for the signal guns was stored and the other two where explosives were stored. He sure looked frightened, as well as he should have been. It had to be scary being locked up all by yourself without anyone to talk to. He had a phone with a headset, with which he was able to talk to the topside. All the information he had heard was bad. He asked me if it was all true, and I told him that the *Arizona* had been blown up, the *West Virginia* sunk, and the *Oklahoma* capsized. I talked to him for only a few seconds, for truthfully, I was glad to get back above the decks, where one seemed a little safer. At least topside, you could see what was happening.

All this time, our cooks had been busy preparing sandwiches, nice big thick ham sandwiches. Hot coffee and crates of apples had been set out at different compartments, so you could pick something up and keep on the move. In times like this, I was amazed how so much attention was paid to eating. We were pretty hungry, but somehow our thoughts hadn't been on food.

My after-dark battle station was on the searchlights located high up on the cage mast, at least seventy-five feet up in the air. We had taken our places when I received word to stand by to illuminate, for there were reports of approaching planes. Our gun crews had been alerted, but cautioned not to fire until the planes had been identified. We kept getting word to stand by when I heard planes approaching. At this time an additional fear hit me: What if they dropped a bomb and the concussion blew us off the platform onto the deck below? Before I could answer that question, small-caliber automatic fire opened up from the shore, and things really broke loose. It looked like every ship in the harbor opened up with everything she had. For a couple of minutes, the sky was lit up with tracer rounds. I saw one, two, and maybe three planes go down. I couldn't imagine how anything could get through such a hail of fire. Later, we found out they were our own planes, which had flown from one of the carriers headed toward Hawaii.

Something that has remained a mystery to me up to this very day was the fact that I saw several of our undamaged ships go rushing out of the harbor at high speeds and saw them return later with the paint burnt off their barrels, indicating that the guns had been fired a great deal and at a rapid rate of fire

After we managed to get free of the *West Virginia* by blasting away at the concrete mooring bits, we had a tugboat assist us in moving to another anchorage. We removed all surplus equipment, flammables, and explosives from the ship. After the initial repairs, we received a new battleship-gray paint job with camouflage down to the waterline.

Being ready for duty, we soon headed out to sea, where several Japanese submarines were rumored to be in the area. Destroyers were needed for more pressing jobs, and we were without an escort. The second day out at sea, we sighted a ship in the distance that turned out all her lights and went directly away at top speed. We gave chase. As we approached at a high speed, our engines seemed to strain, and there was fear that a boiler might blow. Word was flashed to the ship to heave to, or we would commence firing. This warning brought the ship to a dead stop in the water. As we closed the distance between ships, our searchlights turned upon the ship for an identification. Her crew was running up and down the decks in panic, not knowing what to expect. They had assumed we might be Japanese, and we assumed they might be Japanese. It was a friendly ship, and we were on our way. Excitement picked up after we entered Puget Sound Straits. A Jap submarine was laying in wait for a good target, and we seemed to fill the bill. In the meantime, one of our destroyers had come to escort and, after picking up the sub, rushed out and dropped a depth charge. For a moment, it appeared that the destroyer was too late. A torpedo was coming right for us. Fortunately, the torpedo missed us and exploded on the high, rocky shoreline behind us.

—◦—

A promotion for Seaman Jimmy Anders, while the ship was in dry dock at Bremerton, Washington, meant a transfer to Gunnery School in Washington, D.C. Over the years, his affection for the USS *Tennessee* continued to grow with the recounting of memories above and below her decks. Anders again saw action when he was called up during the Korean War to serve aboard the USS *Amycus*.

*　*　*

Of the many heroic acts performed on 7 December, none was more inspiring and symbolic than that by M. Joseph McDonald. The "raising of the colors" by McDonald and another sailor, Oscar Knoor, helped the spirits of sailors trapped in the hell of Battleship Row. The nation's colors, flying briskly in the tropical breezes against a background of blackened smoke, caught the attention of soldiers and sailors at nearby Ford Island and across the harbor at the Navy Yard. Numerous flags, some which were already raised and some which were in the process of being raised at the time of the attack, were shredded or burned by smoke and fire. The flag that McDonald and Knoor raised was not the only one flying at the time, but undoubtedly was one of the most visible. Many claim this incident to be the first flag raising of World War II.

Unlike other flag raising and sightings in American history, this one did not become a part of legend and folklore. While not as obvious as the flag sighted over Fort McHenry during the War of 1812 (in response to which Francis Scott Key wrote the poem upon which "The Star-Spangled Banner," the national anthem, was based), it was just as stirring to those who saw it. Although not as publicized as the flag raising on Iwo Jima in February 1945, it was just as symbolic. For McDonald, the spontaneous flag ceremony aboard the *Tennessee* earned him the title "patriot."

———

I, Millard Joseph McDonald, on the Day of Infamy, 7 December 1941, did raise the nation's colors on the battleship USS *Tennessee* during the attack on Pearl Harbor by the Japanese. Shortly after the initial attack, I noticed that all the ships in Battleship Row were without our nation's colors. The USS *Arizona* had blown up astern of the *Tennessee*, which was moored inboard of the USS *West Virginia*. The explosion of the *Arizona* wreaked havoc to both battleships ahead of her, and the burning oil blazed around the *Tennessee* and the *West Virginia*, placing both ships in danger. Both battleships caught a number of high-level aerial bombs, causing substantial damage and killing many servicemen. Oil fires from the sinking battleships were slowly making their way to the rest of the battleship fleet.

It was during this time, when the oil fires were threatening a number of ships, that Oscar Knoor, quartermaster first class from the *West Virginia*, leaped into the blazing water and swam to the *Tennessee*. The *West Virginia* was sinking against the *Tennessee*, apparently from a torpedo hit. Those of us on the decks of the *Tennessee* who were not manning battle stations or fire hoses were busy pulling survivors from the other ships out of the water. Oscar Knoor was one of the lucky ones to make the swim through the burning oil and to be pulled to safety.

Fate allowed both Oscar and I, who had the same rating of quartermaster first class, to meet on the quarterdeck of the *Tennessee*. With a large number of sailors being pulled from the water, the *Tennessee* quickly became a shelter for those forced to abandon their battleship homes. When one of these refugees inquired about what he could do to help, the thought of raising the colors aboard the *Tennessee* came immediately to mind. Raising the colors was certainly not planned. I suppose that someplace in my subconsciousness, I noted that no colors were visible along Battleship Row, but not until I bumped into Oscar did the thought come to surface. At the moment we met, it was as if a switch had been triggered in my mind. I looked quickly around at the visible masts and knew it was the right thing to do. I knew that Oscar, thankful for being rescued and eager to repay the debt of kindness, would be the ideal partner for this caper.

I told Oscar to wait for me on the quarterdeck, and I dashed to the storeroom, where extra flags were kept. I secured a set and returned to the deck and asked Oscar to assist me in raising Old Glory to show that the "rebel ship" was underway. At the time, my thoughts were to make an act of defiance to show the enemy that, although we were badly battered, we were not defeated. We ran over to the after mast and began the climb in order to rig the halyards. We climbed as fast as we could, for the steel of the mast was hot from the nearby fires and beginning to burn our hands. We climbed through a thick smoke cloud, and Oscar then climbed to the yard in order to put the new halyard through. The moment he signaled everything was ready, I attached the nation's colors and hoisted them along the mast. We only had a few moments to enjoy our handiwork and observe the colors weaving their way through the smoke-filled breeze. At the very moment we completed our task, general quarters once again sounded. We turned to look at the sky and saw another wave of Japanese planes strafing its way to our position. Being up on the mast, we certainly had to be a couple of the most visible targets to the Japanese pilots. We descended as quickly as we had ascended, if not quicker, until we reached a point where we could jump to the deck without risking considerable injury. I was up higher than I realized. When I made the jump, I hit the deck with such force that I sustained some kind of injury to my knee. I was in considerable pain. Oscar turned to assist me, and, by the time he helped me limp down to the quarterdeck, the watertight hatch was battened down. We were locked out of the ship and at the mercy of enemy strafers. My battle station was deep down in the lower handling room, as the helmsman for manual steering. This information was conveyed to the Combat Division 2 admiral and the captain of the *Tennessee*, who was on the bridge. The decision was rendered that only one of us could proceed through the watertight hatch maze. In shipmate protocol, I allowed Oscar to proceed first. I waited anxiously on the outside for an eternity, until the hatchway was finally opened once again.

M. Joseph McDonald participated in the Pacific campaign until 1943. After the USS *Navajo* was torpedoed and sunk, McDonald floated in the ocean for over seven hours before being rescued by another ship. Badly wounded during his ordeal, McDonald was taken to US Advanced Hospital Espiritu Santos in New Hebrides. While recovering from his wounds, McDonald was awarded the Purple Heart by Mrs. Roosevelt. Of the incident, he writes: "She came to my bedside and, shaking and patting my hand, said, 'You'll be all right, my son.'"

The USS *Arizona*

JOHN RAMPLEY

On the morning of 7 December, the *Arizona* was moored off the northeast corner of Ford Island, inboard of the *Vestal*, astern of the *Tennessee*, and forward of the *Nevada*. Within minutes of sighting Japanese planes over Pearl Harbor, antiaircraft batteries aboard the *Arizona* began taking aim at them. Surviving crewmen reported that at least two enemy planes were downed, but it remains debatable whether the hits were from the *Arizona* or from other ships in the harbor. After the attack, it was reported that fuses on the rounds had not been properly set and that many had failed to burst while in the air.

The battleship weathered the first fifteen minutes of the attack, and then disaster struck. At about 8:20 a.m., as a torpedo passed underneath the *Vestal* and detonated against the underside of the *Arizona*, a bomb penetrated her upper deck, after glancing off the faceplate of the number-two turret. The resulting explosion and concussion touched off the main forward magazine, which was located in the battleship's hull, below the number-one and -two turrets. In the volcanic-like eruption, the *Arizona*'s forward part exploded, sending burning debris and hot shrapnel in a deadly shower over the harbor. The explosion generated so much force that the concussion from it literally cleared the decks of nearby ships of their crews. The number-one and -two turrets, which had fourteen-inch guns and a combined weight of over six hundred tons, were dislodged from their base. The forward conning was dropped forward at a forty-five-degree angle. The explosion broke the ship in two. In less than ten minutes after the initial blast, she was resting on the harbor's bottom. Although the ship was partially submerged, oil fires from ruptured fuel tanks burned for hours on and around her, endangering rescue operations aboard her and her nearby sister ships. During the attack, the *Arizona* received hits from eight bombs and at least one torpedo. Contrary to a popular belief after the attack, the "killing blow" was not from a bomb entering the ship through the smokestack. A check made after the attack revealed that the screen across the opening of the funnel was intact.

The losses aboard the *Arizona* were staggering. Almost 80 percent of her complement perished. Only 289 survived, whereas 1,104 were reported as missing or killed in action. Both Rear Admiral I. C. Kidd and Captain F. Van Valkenburgh were posthumously awarded the Medal of Honor for courageously discharging their duties while on board the *Arizona*. Lieutenant Commander S. G. Fuqua, the senior surviving officer on board, was also a recipient of the Congressional Medal of Honor. In most cases, the difference between life and death was a margin of only a few feet or seconds. On the morning of 7 December, the battle station of John Rampley was inside the number-three turret, the only gun turret unscathed by the enemy's bombs.

— —

I was born on 27 August 1917 in a little town in South Carolina named Inman. When I was three years old, my father died and the family moved to Arcadia, a community near Spartanburg, South Carolina. This is where I grew up and spent all of my school years. Arcadia was a textile community, and, during my senior year of high school, I was able to get employment on the second shift at the mill. After the thrill of earning my first real money, $12.50 per week (big money in 1935), boredom set in, and I longed to see the western part of the United States. I thought the navy was the answer, but in those days there were quotas, and so it wasn't so easy to join. So I continued working in the mill until 1939, and then, in November of that year, I was off to the navy.

After boot camp in Norfolk, Virginia, I went to San Diego, California, for assignment to the US Pacific Fleet. We had a great trip across country by train, seeing much of the United States that I had never seen before. Along with about fifteen men from my boot platoon, I was assigned to the battleship USS *Arizona* in February 1940. After months of deck-force duty, I worked my way into the number-three turret crew, main battery. Its walls are still visible today, just aft of the USS *Arizona* Memorial.

The day was 6 December 1941. Our captain was presenting athletic awards and, towards the end of the presentation, said, "I think I know what all of you want for Christmas. Expect good news on Monday." The scuttlebutt was that we were leaving for Long Beach, California, on Monday for the holiday season. Christmas in Hawaii was nice, but, as far as most of the crew was concerned, there was no place like home for the holidays.

On 7 December, a beautiful, clear, typical island day dawned. Being Sunday, the entire ship would be on "holiday routine." Sunrise over the harbor on Sunday was in itself a religious experience. With the stillness and quietness that surrounded the water, it was as if every Sunday was an Easter sunrise service. Certainly, this Sunday was to be no exception.

I was a gunner's mate third class on the main battery of the number-three turret, part of the third division. Morning chow was over, and we were just loafing around in our living quarters, down in the base of the turret. Some of the men went topside to enjoy a bit of fresh air after breakfast. Without a doubt, loafing and lounging around were the most popular Sunday activities aboard the battleship. It was almost 8:00 a.m., nearly time for colors, when the men in the turret were notified that something unusual was going on. A seaman from the deck unit rushed into our quarters to inform us that ships in the dry dock were being bombed. We thought he was kidding because he was a character, but the strange expression on his face convinced us he might be serious.

At this point, I think a bit of explanation is in order. A few days prior, the *Arizona* had been in dry dock for repairs and was probably in that location during the final Japanese photo recording of the fleet positions in Pearl Harbor. Between that time and the time of the attack, the USS *Pennsylvania*, identical sister ship of the *Arizona*, changed places with the *Arizona*. The *Pennsylvania* was the flagship of the US Pacific Fleet, so this might explain the force of the attack upon the *Arizona*.

Within moments, general quarters were sounded. "This is no drill. I repeat, this is no drill," echoed down the steel corridors of the ship. The words sent a cold, shuttering chill down my spine. At our battle stations on the fourteen-inch guns, there was little to do but pray. In the space of a few seconds, some men made up for twenty and more years of tardy prayers. Inside the turret, there was an eerie silence. Everyone seemed afraid to breathe, much less speak, as if that would somehow give away our position to the enemy or attract the attention of one of the bombs. We waited anxiously for some word from topside. Even though we were protected by the heavy plating of the turret, we felt helpless and defenseless, not being able to take any kind of action to defend ourselves and our fellow sailors. We could hear the thunder and feel the ship shudder as the bombs fell upon her. At one point in time, we felt a tremendous jolt, as if the ship had been lifted up in the air and slammed back down. Little did we realize that this was the fatal blow for the *Arizona*. Rivets popped from the steel walls and flew about the place. It wasn't until sometime later that we realized the number-three turret was the only one spared from the bombs. The number-four turret had a hit, but damage was minor. Being shut away at battle stations within the turret, little did we know the extent of damage to our ship and the chaos taking place on the decks around us.

After what seemed like an eternity, the order came over the speakers, "All hands abandon ship." I looked around for some comfort, but all my shipmates seemed to have the same awareness as myself. Our life together aboard the old *Arizona* was over. I climbed down the ladder on the outside of the turret. Everywhere I touched or grabbed onto the ship, I felt the effects of the fires and explosions. The ship had become a piece of molten steel, a kind of giant tea kettle, where heat was being transferred to all metal and steel parts. The deck was covered with oil, and my first impulse was to return to the turret. I can't explain why, but I did not want to step in the oil. Perhaps it was because I thought the oil would be boiling hot. Finally being outside the turret, it looked as if the rest of the ship was a blazing inferno, encircled by a wall of fire that was quickly closing in. I remember looking around the deck and seeing my shipmates from the deck division with their bodies burned black or lying on the deck bleeding from open wounds. Some men were screaming and jumping over the side of the ship. Others were spread about the deck in various positions, crying and moaning in agony. Charred and mutilated bodies were scattered everywhere in the wreckage of the ship. They lay crumpled like broken dolls who had been picked up in the air by some giant hand and slammed against the structures of the ship. With all the smoke and fire on the decks, it seemed difficult to catch one's breath. I don't know if it was from the elements, or just the excitement. All around, the air was filled with the smell of burning oil and burning flesh. It was a smell that lingered in the air like a heavy fog, saturating one's clothes and body.

I walked, then crawled, very calmly and carefully to the side of the ship and looked down into the water. The water was partially covered with oil, most of which was burning. There was a raft directly below, and men were climbing aboard frantically. From where I stood, all I could see forward was a crumbling mass of twisted metal that had only minutes before been the proud superstructure. The command to abandon ship was being repeated over and over again. Enemy planes were still strafing the ship when I made the decision to jump. The warm water was certainly a refresher. When I came to the surface, I was hoping that the whole thing was a bad dream, some sort of hellish nightmare. I swam a few strokes over to the raft and grabbed hold. The raft was too slow and seemed to take forever to move. I decided to take my chances alone in the water, so I began swimming toward Ford Island. The swim wasn't far, but it was very exhausting swimming an obstacle course filled with oil, debris, and bodies. I reached the island in relatively good shape, considering the ordeal that I had been through. After a short rest and a couple of mouthfuls of water, I got my second wind and was ready to help whenever needed.

It wasn't until many hours later that I learned so many of my shipmates were dead. Of the fifteen from my boot platoon that I went aboard with, I was the only one who survived. This is one thing that has stayed with me to this day, and I think about it often. After a short period on Ford Island, we were taken ashore to the main base at Pearl Harbor. It was here that I learned that all of our turret crew had survived without any injuries. We were without a doubt the most luckiest men on the face of the earth for this one day.

<hr />

After the attack, John Rampley was reassigned to the destroyer USS *Mugford*. In February 1942, he was transferred to the destroyer USS *Drayton*, where he remained until June 1944. Upon completion of Gunnery School in Washington, D.C., he was assigned to the attack transport USS *Stokes*. He finished six years of service aboard her and was discharged in December 1945 as gunner's mate first class.

Navy divers investigated the wreck of the USS *Arizona* to see if anything of value could be removed from the ship. The central part of the ship suffered severe damage, while the stern was reasonably intact. A possible plan to disconnect the after part and raise or float it to the surface was abandoned when the time and labor factors were considered. At the time, the navy could not afford to expend time and personnel on a ship that had no military value. Most of the ordnance was removed from the ship, and the oil, which fouled the harbor's clear waters, was gradually removed from the fuel tanks. The fourteen-inch guns from all turrets except for number two were removed and offered to the army. Naval brass decided that no further salvage work should be attempted and that the ship should remain as a memorial to the men who lost their lives in her defense. The superstructure and the deck and hull projections were later removed.

The USS *Vestal*

BILL STEEDLY

Of all the ships anchored at Pearl Harbor on the morning of 7 December, the fleet-repair ship *Vestal* was in the worst position. She was moored outboard alongside of the ill-fated *Arizona*. Due to her proximity to the *Arizona*, the *Vestal* received numerous hits intended for the *Arizona* and the other battleships. Within minutes of the first attack, the *Vestal* sounded general quarters and opened fire with her five-inch, three-inch, and thirty-caliber guns. For the lightly armed ship, this was maximum firepower in a minimum response time. Crew members on the deck of the *Vestal* during the attack witnessed a number of torpedoes passing underneath her and striking the *Arizona* broadside.

During the first attack, Japanese dive-bombers directly hit the USS *Vestal* twice. The first bomb struck the port side, passed through three decks (including a crew's space), and exploded in a metal storeroom. Tools, supplies, equipment, and a lot of metal junk deadened the explosion and prevented the bomb from passing to the lower decks. However, the resulting fires necessitated flooding the forward magazines. The second bomb hit the starboard side and passed through the entire ship before exploding. The result was an irregular hole about five feet in diameter in the ship's bottom. The hole caused serious flooding and lowered the stern about ten feet, with a port list of six degrees. At the time of the attack, the USS *Vestal*, which had been converted from a collier to a fleet-repair ship in 1913, was thirty-three years old, and, due to age and natural wear, the watertight integrity was flawed and the entire bulkhead was flooded.

When the *Arizona* was struck in her powder magazine, blowing apart her forward section, the explosion cleared the *Vestal*'s decks. Cassin Young, her captain, was among the men blown off the decks into the water. However, he swam back to her, countermanded an order to abandon ship, and gave the order to get underway. The explosion also knocked the gun crew, working on the three-inch gun that had jammed after firing only three rounds, overboard.

The *Vestal* remained alongside the *Arizona* until oil from the ruptured tanks of the stricken battleship caused fires on board the *Vestal*'s aft and amidships.

At 8:30 a.m., two small tugboats got the *Vestal* underway. Bomb and flood damage had rendered her steering inoperable. After she was anchored a safe distance away from Battleship Row at McGrew's Point, a damage assessment was made, and it was decided to beach her. At 9:50, the USS *Vestal* again got underway, and then she beached herself on Aiea Shoal.

On 31 March 1941, Chief Petty Officer Bill Steedly arrived at Pearl Harbor aboard the USS *Vestal*. Her mission was to do the maintenance and repair work that the battleships could not perform. After enlisting in the navy in 1929, Steedly served on a number of ships, advanced in his craft, and became chief metalsmith aboard the USS *Vestal*. On 6 December 1941, she docked alongside the *Arizona* for a scheduled repair period. The battleship was to have a final inspection that day, and repair work was to begin the following Monday. For the *Arizona* and the crew of the *Vestal*, it was a job never to be completed. For Steedly, 7 December was a test of his combat skills. The repairs he made during the months following the Pearl Harbor attack were the ultimate test of his skills as a craftsman.

On the morning of 7 December, I got out of my bunk in the chief petty officers' quarters and went to the washroom. I had already shaved and was under the shower when I heard a tremendous blast.

Our ship lurched up, and I lost my footing and fell in the shower room. I learned later that we had a bomb hit in the crew's mess hall. I ran to my clothes locker and hurriedly put on my clothes. General quarters was sounding to man the battle stations. Then we took another bomb hit in the compartment forward of the chief petty officers' quarters, where I had been a few minutes earlier. After that hit, we took another bomb hit in the carpenter shop. This bomb went through the carpenter shop, then through an oil tank and out the bottom of the ship. A chief storekeeper and I were the last ones to get up the ladder from below. The reason was that we were also hit by incendiary bombs. There was a fire blocking our only exit. We tried to go forward, but all we could see was water leaking around the door. We looked through the glass built into the door, and we could see that the compartment was almost completely flooded. We tightened the dogs (latches) holding the door and at the same time heard the word passed to abandon ship. At that time I learned that our captain had been blown overboard. After about twenty-five minutes of waiting for the fire to cool down, we started up the exit ladder again. I ran to the side of the ship as quick as I could and dove into the water. I didn't remember seeing anything but fire and smoke, when I finally made it on deck. The water was kind of a rude awakening. But after being stuck below deck in the middle of a fire, it felt refreshing.

Then all of a sudden, we had fire on the water between the stern of the *Vestal* and the battleship *Maryland*. We quickly realized we were swimming in a sea of gasoline and of oil from the ruptured fuel tanks. All at once, the fire blazed up and burned the shirt off my back. A lot of men were swimming around in the water, screaming and hollering for help. It was a sad sight to see those men who were struggling in the water disappear in a wall of fire that completely surrounded them. They tried to move away from the fire, but couldn't get away in time. The burning oil and burning flesh made a sickening, hard-to-describe smell. After my shirt was burned off, I swam out of the fire and saw a piece of timber floating by. I swam over and got my arm around it and, with the other arm, paddled away from the burning oil that covered the water next to the ships. Now that we were away from the ships, we had a little better view of what was going on. Even then it was hard to make out what was happening to the battleships. Everything was surrounded by smoke and fire, and by now gun crews had opened up on the Jap planes and filled the sky with black bursts. In the meantime, the Japs were coming in again, dropping their torpedoes and strafing us in the water. The water turned to dots of red when one of the men got hit by the machine-gun fire. Most of us were like ducks on the pond. When we tried to move away from where we thought the bullets were going to strike, it was like we were moving in slow motion in a dream. At one time, I was thinking what would happen to me if I got hit by one of the Jap torpedoes. It was as if, with the fire and the machine guns, I didn't have enough to worry about. I can't remember how long we stayed in the water, but it seemed like hours. After the last attack, our captain swam back to the gangway and called for us to come aboard. A lot of us went back and, once aboard, cut the Manila lines that weren't already burned, so that we could get underway. The ship got underway, and, the way we were riding in the water, it looked like we were going to sink at any minute. Our captain ran the ship aground at Aiea Shoal. The Japs started strafing us again, so our captain had us abandon ship once again. This time we ended up in a cane field a short way from the ship.

Our captain was Commander Cassin C. Young. He was later made four stripes and given the Congressional Medal of Honor by Admiral Chester Nimitz. After the attack, we worked on our ship and at the same time worked on other combat ships. While we were making a patch for the hole in the carpenter ship, we pumped out the compartments flooded by the other bombs. We were one of the last ships to go into dry dock. We were still in Pearl Harbor during the Battle of Midway. Approximately eleven months later in the South Pacific battle area, while repairing damaged ships, we went alongside the USS *San Francisco*. We found out that Commander Young had been killed in a night engagement with the Jap fleet. His ship was shot all to pieces and all the officers were killed, I was told.

——

Bill Steedly finished out the war on a number of repair ships and floating dry docks. In 1943, he was promoted to warrant officer. In 1959, he retired as chief warrant officer. He wrote: "I enjoyed my naval service of thirty years, I am sure we had the best navy in the world."

The USS *Nevada*

JOSEPH TAUSSIG

On 7 December, the *Nevada* was moored by herself along Battleship Row, astern of the *Arizona*. As a result of her fortunate position, which allowed freedom of movement denied the other battleships, the *Nevada* was the only one to get underway during the attack. With the sighting of the first wave of Japanese planes at 8:01 a.m., general quarters was sounded, and, within minutes, forward and aft machine guns and the five-inch gun opened fire. Gun crews downed a couple of Japanese dive-bombers before the ship was hit by a torpedo at approximately 8:10. The flooding problem was corrected by counterflooding, and the ship, which had been readying her engine rooms since general quarters, was able to get underway at 8:40. As the ship slowly made her way past Battleship Row and the harbor entrance, she became the number-one target of Japanese dive-bombers. At approximately 9:00, five bombs, a few of which had been dropped from only a couple hundred feet, hit the *Nevada* almost simultaneously, causing severe flooding and a number of uncontrollable fires. Rear Admiral William R. Furlong—who, at the time the *Nevada* was passing through the channel, was standing on the deck of his flagship, the USS *Oglala*, at the Ten-Ten Dock— witnessed the attack. Fearing that the *Nevada* would block the exit of the other battleships remaining in the harbor if she sank in the channel, he ordered the *Nevada* to seek refuge in the Middle Loch. Shortly after 9:00, she was beached at Hospital Point, just south of the Shaw in Floating Drydock Number Two. The battleship was later freed and, with the assistance of two tugboats, was grounded at Waipio Point, which was on the west side of the harbor entrance.

Ensign Joseph Taussig was the officer on deck aboard the *Nevada* at the time of the attack. Only ten months earlier, he had graduated from the US Naval Academy's first accelerated prewar class. The Pearl Harbor attack was the only action Taussig saw during World War II. For his heroic actions, he received the Navy Cross, the second-highest naval combat decoration.

———

I was an ensign on the USS *Nevada*, which was a battleship built in 1912. At 7:45 a.m., I went up to relieve the officer on the deck of the ship; we were tied up on what we called the "interrupted keys" off Ford Island. I had the 8:00 a.m. to noon watch on Sunday morning: beautiful weather, bright sunshine.

Our ship was the "band ship," as we called it, for the morning. It was our band that was going to play "The Star-Spangled Banner" and raise the flag. So I assured myself that the band was on what we called the fantail—the stern—and they had the right-size flag. And I had fourteen men about to go on liberty, so I was inspecting them, and I guess it was about 7:55. I saw a plane coming over the harbor, which I identified as a navy torpedo plane, and it dropped a torpedo in the water.

Pearl Harbor is only forty feet deep, and we'd never been able to drop a torpedo from an aircraft that didn't dive at least eighty feet, so I assumed the torpedo would stick in the bottom of the harbor and we'd spend the morning watching the divers pick it up. Instead of that, it ran and hit the *Oklahoma*, I think; it was the ship tied up ahead of us that got hit. I realized then that this was a Japanese plane. My boatswain's mate on the watch grabbed me by the shoulder and told me they were dropping bombs on Hickam Field, which was an air force base right there. And he turned in the general alarm, which got everybody up on the ship who wasn't already up, and shouted over the loudspeaker, "This is no drill!"

My battle station was as the starboard antiaircraft officer (on the ship's director). A director is a very complicated machine up on the mast that sends signals to the antiaircraft guns on where they should fire. And since we were tied up, I could see no reason to stay on the quarterdeck looking at things, so I started up the mast. And by the time I got on the gun deck, which was about four decks up, I knew all my guns were firing already, and I climbed up about another four ladders.

I got into the director, and it was already on an airplane and they were tracking it. It was rather traumatic, because the gun that was located right under the director went off, and it just felt like you had a gun going up your pants leg. I watched through the check sight, and the airplane went down. We had an awful lot of puffs of smoke. Everybody was firing at these high-flying aircraft, and nobody knows who hit it.

But the director started to turn to find another aircraft, and I felt a tremendous blow on my leg and looked down, and my left foot was under my armpit. My reaction was, "That's a hell of a place for a foot to be." I was standing in a little doorway, so I didn't get knocked down, but I realized that whatever had hit me had gone through the leg and had gotten into the mechanism of the director, and the director was totally useless.

So I told the director crew that we might as well go into what we called the sky control, which was a compartment between the two directors—I had the starboard director. And so the crew got behind me, and I eased myself back into the sky control. After the order to head out was received, I got the call that said, since I was the officer on deck, why was I not in the conning tower to take it out. And I told them I couldn't very well because I had a broken leg.

By this time the *Nevada* had been hit on the port side forward by a torpedo, which had torn a hole about twenty feet high and forty feet long along the side, and we'd taken a lot of water forward. Once we started out, all of the Japanese planes tried to hit us. We had about fourteen direct bomb hits and I don't know how many near misses, which are very damaging because they give you a great deal of concussion under the water. And in due course we had fourteen fires on the ship and not quite enough firefighters.

As we were going out, it looked like the *Nevada* was sinking. Admiral Harold Train, who was on the *Maryland* and thought we were sinking, didn't want us to block the channel, so he ordered us to run aground. I really didn't want to do that because I knew we weren't sinking. But we decided he knew something we didn't know, so we ran it aground on Hospital Point in Pearl Harbor.

The whole thing is like a dream to me now. I was nearing the end of my watch and was thinking about going to play tennis at Ford Island. I was directing fire at the outset of the attack when I don't know what hit me, something went completely through my thigh. They ordered a cot for me, and I just continued to control the gun batteries. Some enlisted men brought me a stretcher, and I stayed up there until the whole structure caught fire. They brought me down through the fire. The navy said I was decorated because I refused to leave my post. A launch took me to Hospital Point, where I was placed in a cab and driven to the harbor hospital, bleeding all over this poor man's taxi. About 4:00 p.m., a surgeon came in to see what he could do about my badly torn-up leg and finally gave me enough morphine, so I went to sleep. That was about the whole show, as far as I was concerned.

After V-J Day in 1945, I knew the knee was going to be stiff for the rest of my life, and I knew the leg was going to be short. And since there was no more war going on, I lost all interest in getting the leg fixed. I started agitating to get the leg taken off, and, in April 1946, I had it done. I was so glad to get rid of it, I went back to duty two days later.

Joseph Taussig retired from the navy in 1954. He spent the next twenty-five years working as a military consultant to private industry and was involved in the design and manufacture of military equipment and hardware. In July 1981, he was appointed deputy assistant secretary of the navy for civilian personnel policy and equal-opportunity employment. Also in that year, he was named Secretary of Defense Caspar Weinberger's official representative for the December memorial services commemorating the fortieth anniversary of the attack on Pearl Harbor.

THE NAVY YARD

The USS *Shaw*

WILLIAM LECKEMBY

On 7 December, the destroyer *Shaw* was high and dry in Floating Drydock Number Two, which was on the east side of the harbor above the main channel entrance. The destroyer took three bomb hits from the same dive-bombers that had attacked the battleship *Nevada*. The first and second bombs tore through the *Shaw*'s forward machine-gun platform, penetrated the main decks, and exploded in the crew's mess, which was on the first platform deck. The third bomb passed through the port wing of the bridge and exploded in the wardroom pantry, rupturing fuel-oil tanks and scattering burning oil throughout this section of the ship. Fires quickly spread throughout the ship, and by 9:25 a.m. all firefighting facilities were exhausted and the order to abandon ship was given. The flooding of the dry dock only partially controlled the fires. At 9:30, heat from the fires reached the forward magazine and touched off the day's most spectacular explosion. From across the harbor at Ford Island and Battleship Row, it appeared that the entire Navy Yard was detonated at the same moment. The force of the explosion severed the bow and demolished the ship just forward of the bridge. Japanese bombers also attacked Floating Drydock Number Two. Although the dry dock was submerged for protection, it suffered fragment damage from a number of near misses, in addition to the damage caused by the fires and by the explosion of the *Shaw*.

Third-Class Electrician's Mate William Leckemby, who joined the *Shaw* in 1939 when she was assigned to the West Coast, remembers the tense drama aboard her during the attack and prior to the explosion, which set her off like a giant Roman candle.

～

The general alarm began to sound at approximately 8:00 a.m. aboard the destroyer *Shaw*. The alarm meant there was an emergency of some kind, but, without an intercommunication system, there was no way of knowing what it might be. The late sleepers who were taking advantage of a lazy Sunday morning began to roll out of their bunks, dress hurriedly, and rush topside to quarters. From the deck of the *Shaw*, the crew could see the flames of a roaring fire consuming a PBY aircraft on Ford Island, which was a short distance away. While watching the fire and waiting for instructions, the men wondered what may have been the cause of such an accident. The answer was soon to come when an aircraft swooped over the fantail of their ship. The aircraft had a large red ball painted on its side and was so close the pilot could be seen looking at the ship's crew from the open cockpit. Action was fast and furious now, as the men realized they were being attacked. The men rushed to their battle stations. One chief petty officer did so only after shaking his fist at the enemy aircraft.

The destroyer was not an effective fighting ship this day, as she was in a floating dry dock at Hospital Point in Pearl Harbor. A few days earlier, she had been rammed at sea, and she was dry-docked while repairs were being made on her hull. The ship's antiaircraft weapons consisted of four five-inch guns and four fifty-caliber machine guns, and only the machine guns could be fired. Even the machine guns were ineffective, as there were only about 150 rounds of ammunition belted for each gun. As a last resort, 1903 Springfield rifles were used as a means of defense, and these were of almost no use against the fast-moving targets.

I was a sailor aboard the ship, an electrician whose battle station was the thirty-six-inch searchlight. Upon realizing an enemy attack was underway, I rushed to my battle station, which was high above deck. Upon reaching it, I was aware of the incongruity of my action, since the searchlight was useless during the broad daylight. I did have a ringside seat to the battle around me and became an interested observer. Low-flying torpedo planes skimming over the water and dropping their weapons of destruction were of particular interest, since the wake of the torpedoes could be followed to their target. Terrific explosions, sending water many feet into the air, were observed on the hull of the battleship *Oklahoma*. Antiaircraft guns were belching smoke aboard the many ships in the harbor, and the attack was now being met with some resistance. The underwater damage suffered by the *Oklahoma* through torpedo hits was fatal. The ship began to list to one side, and then she picked up momentum and rolled over completely. A thirty-thousand-ton vessel being sunk, almost like a toy, is a sight that will live in my memory forever. As terrible a sight as it was, it made me proud because the antiaircraft guns of the *Oklahoma* were still firing as they sank out of sight. Manning these guns were brave sailors who had given their lives by defending their ship and country.

The surface of the waters around the battleships in Battleship Row were ablaze from flaming fuel oil escaping from the wounded ships. Bombs rained down upon these ships and the surrounding waters, sending tongues of flame and water into the air. Many wounded sailors had to be removed from these ships, and small craft of all kinds were employed for the evacuation. These small boats, risking destruction by bombs, entered the flaming waters and saved the lives of countless men who were trapped aboard the larger ships.

The ping of bullets hitting the aft smokestack of the *Shaw* brought me out of my trance. My immediate reaction was to get back on deck, where I was issued a rifle and a bandolier of ammunition. Targets were many, as Japanese dive-bombers were attacking the battleship *Nevada*, which had now gotten underway. Excitement shook me as I fired my rifle at everything that was flying. There was a moment of extreme exuberance when I thought I hit a plane and, later, a moment of despairing depression as I saw it fly away unharmed.

Suddenly the deck of the ship shook violently after a dull explosion. The *Shaw* received her first bomb hit, and fire broke out in the forward part of the ship. Flying shrapnel broke the stock off the rifle I was using but, miraculously, I was spared any harm. A shipmate who was alongside of me was not quite so lucky. He received a severe head wound. Seeing my shipmate's plight, I placed the palm of my hand over the wound and applied pressure in an attempt to stop the bleeding. A pharmacist's mate arrived shortly and administered first aid to my shipmate. That was the last I ever saw of my companion.

In the meantime, the *Shaw* was hit again by a bomb, and fires were completely out of control in the forward part of the ship. Not having any water pressure aboard the ship, it was impossible to fight the fire, and the order was given to abandon ship. To reach the beach, it was necessary to swim about 150 feet through the oily waters. I removed my shoes and shirt, jumped into the water, and swam as fast as possible to the nearest land. Enemy aircraft were in the area, and the fear of being strafed caused me to seek shelter under a parked dump truck. From under the truck, the *Shaw* was in full view, with flames reaching above the foremast. An earthshaking explosion suddenly erupted, and the forward end of the *Shaw* disappeared in the mist of flame and smoke. The ship's forward magazine had exploded; all that remained visible of the ship was her stern, which did not sink. Now I wondered about my shipmates. Later, it was ascertained that about half the crew was killed that day. Seeing the fate of my ship filled me with emotion, and it was hard to hold back the tears.

I was on my own now and pondered what to do. I knew that I must do something to help, so I proceeded barefoot to the Naval Hospital, which was in the near vicinity. Several wounded men, on litters, were carried into the hospital by myself and other sailors who had no ship now. Two such cases that reflect the horrors of war were a young man with both of his feet blown off and another burned black from head to toe. When his litter was set down, the burn victim said, "Thanks, mate." One cannot understand how this man could possibly talk because he was so badly burned. Seeing the wounded at close range made me feel ambivalent—sad because of the suffering of the wounded, and yet triumphant that I was one of those spared thus far.

During the attack, a Japanese aircraft that received mortal damage crashed upon the hospital grounds. Wreckage and parts of the plane were spread over a wide area, and amidst the wreckage were the bodies of the plane's crew. Spectators viewing the mangled bodies showed no signs of compassion. This was understandable after viewing the suffering and damage that the enemy had bestowed upon the American sailors and ships.

The attack was about over. Few enemy planes were overhead, but evidence of their having been here was all around. Wounded men, men without ships, men without clothing or shoes, clouds of black smoke rising in the sky, burning planes, burning ships, and confusion reigned.

Someone, in trying to help the sailors, opened the Ship's Service Store at the hospital and began to pass out cigarettes and matches. In my frustration, I accepted the gifts, and it was the beginning of a smoking habit that lasted twelve years before it could be broken.

Orders were issued for all men who had lost their ships to report to the Receiving Station at Pearl Harbor. Here the men were issued new dungarees, shoes, and socks. A good meal and shower were the order of the day. The shower really did not help, as most of the sailors were covered with brown, sticky oil, which was almost impossible to remove with soap and water. I, like most of my shipmates, emerged from the shower a golden brown.

Men were assigned to ships—destroyer sailors to destroyers, cruiser sailors to cruisers—and the judgment of what kind of ship a man should go to was left to the individual in many cases. The destroyer *Conyngham*, which was the same class destroyer as the *Shaw*, was to become the habitat for me.

The *Conyngham* had been undergoing an upkeep period at the time the attack began. Machinery had been dismantled, and the fire rooms and engine room were in total disarray. In such a condition, the ship could not get underway. Upon boarding the *Conyngham*, I was asked my rate and qualifications. Being a third class electrician's mate, I was welcomed with open arms, as the ship was in desperate need of an electrician.

Since the ship's regular crew was working feverishly assembling machinery, I was assigned to the main generator distribution center.

Because of my assignment, a man more familiar with the condition of the ship's machinery was freed to help with the repairs. The impossible was accomplished this day by the engineering department of the *Conyngham*. Repairs that ordinarily would have taken two or three days to complete were accomplished in approximately six hours.

Main distribution switchboard watches are boring. Time weighs heavily on a man when he has nothing to do except to watch meters and occasionally parallel generators. Time was now my enemy. It gave me time to think. I wondered what my family would think when they learned that my ship had been sunk. I thought about my less fortunate shipmates. Fear began to replace excitement. I wondered if I would ever see my twenty-first birthday, which was only seven days away. I wondered, too, about the outcome of this war and how many more battles I might experience. With all these thoughts, I was not ashamed to shed a tear, but was thankful I could do so during the solitude of my watch.

William Leckemby finished the war aboard the USS *Shaw*, which was the first severely damaged ship to be put to sea. He remained in the navy and later retired with thirty years of service.

The USS *Oglala*

ROBERT HUDSON

On the morning of 7 December, the minelayer *Oglala* was moored outboard of the light cruiser *Helena* alongside the Navy Yard's Ten-Ten Dock, which was across Ford Island in the East Loch. The berth was usually reserved for the flagship of the US Pacific Fleet, the battleship *Pennsylvania*. At the time of the attack, she and the destroyers *Cassin* and *Downes* were out of the water for repair work in Floating Drydock Number One.

During the first wave of attack planes, an airplane torpedo passed under the *Oglala*'s shallow draft and exploded against the *Helena*'s starboard side. The force of the explosion ruptured the *Oglala*'s lower port side plating and started extensive flooding. Despite her water-tight closures, she continued to flood. Because it was feared that the ship would sink in place and threaten the *Helena*, two commercial tugboats were commandeered to pull the *Oglala* alongside the dock. The ship was secured to the dock, and at 9:45 a.m. she capsized, with her masts and top hamper resting on the dock. Although they suffered no casualties, her crew and that of the USS *Helena* experienced tense moments. Robert Hudson, one of the crew on deck during the attack, witnessed the destruction of the fleet.

~~~

I left high school before I graduated and went up to Canada to help the Canadians fight their war. They were delighted with my proposal and were more than willing to accept my enlistment. I declined the offer after I was told I would lose my American citizenship if I enlisted. Instead, I returned to Saint Cloud, Minnesota, and enlisted in the navy. The year was 1939. Within two weeks, my suitcase was packed and I was on my way to Great Lakes Naval Station for training.

After completing my basic training, I volunteered for duty aboard the USS *Oglala*. The ship was stationed at Pearl Harbor, and I was transported to Hawaii aboard the USS *Antares*. In 1940, I arrived at Pearl and took up my duties aboard the *Oglala*. She had the honor of being the flagship for the mine fleet. She was a marvelous ship with a proud and colorful past. The ship was originally built by the Eastern Steamship Company as a coastal passenger vessel to run between Boston and New York. Under the name *Massachusetts*, the ship routinely carried the elite of Boston and New York social circles. During World War I, the ship was made into a minesweeper and renamed the USS *Shawmut*. After the war, she was used as an aircraft tender. Later, the ship was converted once again to a minesweeper and given the name *Oglala* for a Sioux tribe. When I came on board for service, the *Oglala* was affectionately known in the US Pacific Fleet as the Lollie.

The day of 6 December is important to me, as I could not understand why the navy had me working until 2:00 a.m. unloading mines at the West Loch depot. After all, I was a super classy guy and the navy was lucky to have me! After unloading four hundred mines, we tied up beside the USS *Helena* at the Ten-Ten Dock. I slept on deck, as I had to be up early the next morning to roust out the mess cooks to set up for Sunday breakfast.

On the morning of 7 December, I walked out on the deck to have a cigarette and joined a man named Polard. Polard, a third class cook from Washington State, was enjoying a break from the breakfast routine. As we talked and leaned on the rail of the ship, we gratefully absorbed the morning sunshine and cool breeze. The view of the battleships was magnificent. I was aware of a radio softly playing Hawaiian music somewhere in the background. The morning was sheer bliss. As we continued to talk, we looked at all the ships lined up in the bay and listened to the sounds of them coming to life. We were suddenly interrupted by the approach of planes flying in rather low. We both laughed, as we realized the air corps was in trouble because regulations said no planes were to fly over on Sunday mornings. Any other branch of service that goofed was a delight to us, as we knew that the navy never goofed.

One of the planes dropped something over Ford Island. It hit a hangar and exploded with a roar. Smoke and fire immediately followed. I yelled, "Christ, Polard, is this some kind of drill?" Polard replied, "Must have been some kind of marker bomb that hit something and blew up." Within a few seconds, a plane came directly at us from the direction of Ford Island. It was flying only about fifty feet above the water. Between the plane and the *Oglala* was a motor launch, returning people to their ships from liberty and church services. They looked up at the plane and all dove overboard. The launch raced on madly, without anyone in control. "What's the matter with those bastards?" I yelled. I turned to Polard and said, "Do you believe that?" Polard kept looking ahead at the plane and those in the water.

The plane then dropped a torpedo straight for us. The plane's canopy was open, and the pilot was hanging his head over the side to look at us. On his approach, we saw red flashes from his wings. I thought that it was a drill and that the flashes were from a camera taking pictures of the harbor. When bullets started ricocheting off the bulkhead around us, I knew the plane was not there to take our picture. Polard, who was standing next to me during this time, went down from a hit. I didn't know if it was a direct hit or a ricochet.

In total and absolute horror, I watched the plane raise up swiftly to avoid hitting our superstructure. It was then I realized for the first time what was happening, when I saw the red "meatballs" on the wings of the plane. Instinctively, I ran to my battle station on the forecastle, a round chalk mark where a fifty-caliber machine gun was to be installed sometime in the future. I was nearly knocked off my feet, as the torpedo hit almost directly below me. I had no idea that the fish had passed under the *Lollie* and hit the *Helena*. Poor old *Lollie* seemed to sink from sheer fright, as not one of the bombs or torpedoes made a direct hit on her.

By now I was wearing a ridiculous World War I helmet quickly issued in the mess hall. After some time at my battle station, I heard the command to abandon ship. While manning my post, I heard the command given at least three times. Men dashed about madly, crying and cursing. Planes were dropping torpedoes and bombs, and strafing everything in sight. My world suddenly changed from tranquility to devastation. Black smoke billowed up, with huge flashes of fire from everywhere. Cries for help mixed with the roaring explosions. Debris flew through the air with such force that it was as deadly as the bullets and bombs.

Discipline in those days was such that I did exactly what I had been told to do. I stood on that goddamn chalk mark until ordered to do something else. As I stood in that circle, I watched in absolute disbelief. The *Oklahoma* rolled over with people running down her sides, then across her bottom. Enormous explosions were taking place on the wagons, and the fire and smoke were appalling to behold.

A small untrained crew of volunteers valiantly tried to fire our three-inch gun on the forecastle. The trouble was that they loaded the gun with star shells, normally used at night for illumination. We put on a show like the Fourth of July. We must have amazed the Jap pilots, but we did little or no damage. It was truly a nightmare to see shipmates from both the *Oglala* and *Helena*, in anger and frustration, throwing potatoes and wrenches at low-flying planes. In the middle of all this chaos, Rear Admiral William R. Furlong, commander of the mine force, walked out on the deck of the *Oglala*. He was hatless and had his arms at his sides. As he calmly surveyed the scene, I naturally snapped to attention and saluted. He calmly returned my salute. His demeanor really settled me down. Believe it or not, for a few moments I forgot about being in the middle of a Japanese attack, while the admiral was on deck.

After the attack planes retreated, the *Oglala* started to settle lower and lower in the water. Our watertight compartments weren't able to stop the flooding in the lower decks. Some immensely brave guys came by in launches to take some of the crew off the ship. After the launches, a couple of tugs with a lot of civilians aboard helped us get free of the *Helena* by towing us astern. The *Oglala* finally sank along the dock. Sank really wasn't the right word for it. The ship just kept slowly rolling over until she crashed into the dock. I was still on board after the tugs moved the ship away from the *Helena*. I didn't know which was the best way to get off the ship. I was afraid to jump for the dock, because the *Oglala* was listing desperately and appeared ready at any moment to crash into the dock. Instead, I dove overboard and decided to swim for the pier. Having pride in the fact that I could swim long distances, I felt safe from any strafing while in the water. I was quickly overcome with another fear, as I thought what would happen if a bomb went off near me in the water. Thinking about being deaf for the balance of my life, I shot out of the water and crawled ashore. Immediately had to run for cover under some sheets of construction steel, as a plane strafed my path. Looking out from the steel sheets after the plane had passed, I saw a man dressed only in tennis shorts come running down the dock, yelling for volunteers to man a destroyer. He had a tennis racket in his hand, so I assumed he was a junior officer. I believe I was the first in line to volunteer aboard the destroyer USS *Mugford*.

At the time of the attack, the *Mugford* was in the Navy Yard next to the *Helena*, sandwiched between numerous destroyers that were in the yard for repair or maintenance work. It was a marvelous feeling to board that ship and listen to all her guns firing away at the enemy. Standing on deck, you could feel the vibrations of the guns and the four torpedo mounts as they swung back and forth in the ready position. It was great to be aboard a fighting ship. By the middle of the day, we were able to get free of the dock and get ready to join a number of destroyers on patrol duty to intercept what we suspected would be a large Japanese invasion fleet.

—◦—

Robert Hudson left the navy at the end of the war with the rating of torpedoman second class. Today he lectures about the World War II era. His lectures focus on keeping America strong and on learning from the lessons of the past in order to avoid repeating them in the future.

The USS *Helena*

TED BLAHNIK

On the morning of 7 December, within minutes of the first attack, a lone torpedo plane launched a torpedo that passed under the *Oglala* and hit the *Helena* on the starboard side, almost amidships. Although wiring to the main and five-inch batteries was severed, prompt action and impromptu repair work brought the forward diesel generator to full power within two minutes. With power available to all gun mounts, the crews of both ships were able to sustain a heavy fire that prevented additional damage from the Japanese bombers. Excellent damage-control work and a strict adherence to watertight integrity managed to keep the *Helena* afloat. After temporary repairs at Dry Dock Number Two, the *Helena* steamed to Mare Island Navy Yard in California for permanent repairs and overhaul. For Ted Blahnik, the baptism by fire was a prelude to the final destruction of the USS *Helena* in 1943.

I was recruited in Benton Harbor, Michigan, sworn into military service in Detroit, and trained at the Great Lakes Naval Training Station. I qualified for submarine training, but turned it down because I wanted to get into some branch of naval aviation. I left boot camp on 9 October 1940, with orders for assignment to the USS *Helena*.

On 6 December 1941, I attended a barefoot football game in Honolulu Stadium and spent the day enjoying a little R and R. Sunday, 7 December, started as any other Sunday would have aboard ship, and, after a shower and breakfast, I was hanging around the division compartment when I heard the word passed for a working party from our division. Chuck O'Conner, our boatswain's mate (one of the best, if not the best, boatswain's mates I met during my six-year tour of duty, and he was a "sailor's sailor"), headed in my direction, and I knew that I was going to be asked to go on that working party. He made an error in asking me if I had had my breakfast, and, having been a seaman for a little over a year, I was becoming adept at how to dodge working parties and answered in the negative. I then went directly to my cleaning station, which was located in the forward part of the ship, in officers' quarters. My job there was to clean some passageways in that area.

I was cleaning this area when the general alarm sounded. It seemed rather strange to me that they would be having a drill on Sunday morning; nevertheless, I hurried to my battle station. At this point in time I was a director pointer for Quad 1.1, port side (which happened to be dockside at the Ten-Ten Dock), the second level above the main deck aft. Although I was listed as a director pointer, we still didn't have any directors. Consequently, during any gunnery drills, I would put on my headphones and relay messages down to the gun captain from sky control.

On reaching my battle station and putting on my headphones, I looked towards Ford Island and saw Japanese planes dive-bombing the airfield and installations there. The red "meatball" insignia was plainly visible on their fuselages. I tried contacting sky control, but to no avail. While doing this, I looked down at our gun mount and saw the pointer and trainer in their respective positions, but no one was loading the gun. Feeling quite useless, I put down the headphones and climbed down to the gun mount, where someone started to hand me clips of ammunition and I found myself in the position of a first loader (which I had never done before) and started feeding the clips into the cradles. At times, I recall hearing what I thought were bees, which we later found out were bullets from strafing planes.

Sometime during that first attack, I glanced up just in time to see a Japanese dive-bomber release his bomb as he dove towards our ship. I thought for sure that it was the end of the line for us, but the bomb hit on the starboard side somewhere. I was told later that shrapnel from this bomb killed one of our gunner's mates.

During the lull between attacks, we had some opportunity to survey the damage, and a sight I'll always remember was looking across the water towards Battleship Row, where fires were still raging and the intense smoke almost obscured the area. For just a moment, it seemed that the smoke cleared from one of the wagons and I could see Old Glory still flying. The sight was, at once, chilling yet stirring.

We had many wounded on board as well, as in the surrounding area, and during this lull some of the men were down on the dock taking the doors off of the gedunk stand (snack shop) to be used as stretchers. This, of course, left the stand vulnerable to its store of candy, cigarettes, ice cream, etc. It was soon emptied, and men in the area carried these things to shipmates and friends as we awaited the next attack. I've often wondered if the owner was ever paid for that stuff, or if he even cared.

As I recall, the second attack was by high-level bombers, and it was so frustrating to watch them (unmolested) release their bombs. They performed a graceful arch as they hurtled down toward the eventual devastation.

Dusk turned to darkness, and rumors flooded the ship, such as "Jap paratroopers were landing on the other side of the island" and "Saboteurs were igniting fires in the cane fields to guide more attacks."

By the way, sometime during the attacks we were torpedoed, and I didn't even know it. It was much different than when we were torpedoed and sunk in July 1943, I felt all three of those torpedoes.

That evening some of our carrier planes flew in (wrong thing to do when itchy trigger fingers are nervous and communications poor), and, as our gun was on the opposite side from the firing, I watched. It seemed like every gun in the harbor opened fire on them.

I felt that the Good Lord carried me through that day. The only abrasions I received were cut-up hands, from not knowing how to handle those 1.1 clips properly.

Many days after the attack, we took the place of the USS *Pennsylvania* in dry dock, and one of my most heartrending moments was when I stood alongside the dry dock and watched as they took out the bodies of some of our shipmates through the gaping hole caused by the torpedo hit.

The complete story of the *Helena* has been written, though in places exaggerated, and those of us who served on her until her final demise the night of 5–6 July 1943 will continually regard her as one of the best. I happened to be one of the 165 that ended up on Vella Lavella in the Solomon Islands, and I was told later that I had spent about sixty-nine hours in the water before being rescued by one of "Bishop" Sylvestor's coast watchers. Bless their stout hearts.

———

After the sinking of the *Helena*, Ted Blahnik arrived in San Diego on 4 September 1943. He remained in the States until the end of the war. One of his last assignments was aboard the battleship *Wisconsin* during her commissioning and sea trials in Newport, Rhode Island. He was discharged on 5 March 1946.

The USS *Rigel*

ED SEISER

On 7 December the seaplane tender destroyer *Rigel* was tied up at the Navy Yard, positioned between the dry-dock wall and the *Cummings*, and among the ships in an inside row. The *Rigel* was directly in front of the oiler *Ramapo*. The *Rigel* was still undergoing repairs and was without her armament and superstructure. Unable to fire at attacking planes, her crew turned its skills to rescue and salvage operations. About one hundred men from the ship were sent to the battleship *West Virginia* to help fight fires. Back aboard the *Rigel*, many men were thrown into the oily water from the concussion of a near miss. Whaleboats from their own ship rescued them. One of the whaleboats disintegrated when it suffered a direct bomb hit. The *Rigel* sustained only minor damage from strafing runs and from near misses from errant bombs.

Lieutenant Commander Ed Seiser was aboard the *Rigel* on the morning of the attack. His story includes an account about a different kind of survivor.

I was born on 16 May 1897 in Keytesville, Missouri. My family later moved to San Benito, Texas, where I finished high school. I entered the University of Texas for premedical sciences. When the draft for World War I started, I enlisted in the navy and was sent to Goat Island, in the middle of San Francisco Bay, where I took my boot training and my medical courses as a dental assistant. When the big flu epidemic broke out in 1918, I was loaned to the city of San Francisco for nursing duty, where I spent six months on night duty.

After the war was over, I came back to the University of Texas for a third year in premed training. Then I entered the University of Tennessee at Memphis for dentistry. Because I had credit for all of the required basic sciences, I was given the job of instructor in those courses for the first three years of dental requirements. I started practicing in San Antonio and was getting along fine until the Great Depression started in the 1930s and the bank with my money folded and I was broke. I moved back to San Benito and opened up a new office with $500 I had borrowed from a relative. In 1940, my bank there closed its doors, and I was again broke. I said, "To hell with this," and wrote the Navy Dental Department in Washington, D.C., with my World War I records enclosed, and asked for a commission in the Navy Dental Corps. They wrote back and gave me a commission in the officer corps. I went to San Diego and reported aboard the USS *Rigel* and went to Pearl Harbor in 1941.

When we arrived at Pearl Harbor in the early summer of 1941, we found a beehive of activity in all branches of the military service; a feeling of impending uncertainty or, to put it more concisely, the doom of an uncertain destiny seemed to permeate the air we breathed, but we didn't know just what it would be or when it would happen. Most certainly, not at Pearl Harbor. So we felt rather secure in our enjoyment of the pleasures offered in this piece of paradise so safely isolated on this broad expanse of the Pacific Ocean.

We plunged with vigor into the prescribed work of getting ready for whatever it was that we felt was going to happen someplace, sometime. Life settled into the routine usually found in navy shipyards. Cowboy, a sailor from Texas, had brought along his dog, Brandy, which he offered as a ship's mascot. The dog was accepted as such and was named Captain Brandy. He took off to visit other ships and shore facilities and made many new acquaintances. It took him about two weeks to make the rounds; at least he was gone that long before he returned to his ship. Of course, he was under no obligation to return at all, but he had to come aboard to see how Cowboy was getting along and to check in with his orderly.

Our patrol schedule of the sky was a most methodical arrangement. We sent out observation and search planes every morning at a certain time, to follow a certain pattern and to return to their bases on Oahu at a certain time. The folly of this set practice became apparent at a later date.

The attack on Pearl Harbor changed our complacent world completely. Even the atmosphere, the sky, the sun, the ocean, our feeling of smugness; everything was changed and different. Never before was so much concentrated hell heaped upon one place in so short a time. When we realized it was a real attack and not a "practice run" by what was then the aviation arm of the army, our first reaction was to ask, "Who's attacking us?" Not until we saw the red disks on the underside of their planes did we realize it was the Japanese. And they did an excellent, bang-up job. Catastrophic tragedy, confusion, and death stalked us on every hand. The devastation that was so complete was understandable, because the Japanese that were shot down or otherwise captured had a map of Pearl Harbor strapped across their knees, and on that map was the location of every ship, oil storage tank, and machine shop, and the condition of every installation as of the night before.

The maps revealed the hangars at nearby Hickam Field that had airplanes in them. The ones that were empty were revealed, but only the full ones were bombed. The oil storage tank farms, the machine shops, and other strategic areas were not harmed, which led us to believe that the Japanese intended to come back and take over, which they could have easily done with a couple of shiploads of troops. We certainly had nothing with which to defend ourselves. We sat around for two weeks in a state of jittery anticipation, waiting for the enemy to put in an appearance. The guards were trigger-happy. The Civilian Defense Units were made up of Koreans, and they shot at everything that moved. We didn't dare go out at night. If we had to drive a car after dark, it was quite a tricky maneuver, for the headlights were painted black, with the exception of a round spot in the center of the light about the size of a half dollar, and this was painted a dark blue. We couldn't see where we were going, but anyone in front might see us coming.

All house windows were painted black or blacked out with curtains; we couldn't even have a light showing on a radio dial. Not a light of any kind was permitted. It was claimed that the glow from a lighted cigarette could be seen for two miles. All the beaches, including Waikiki, were covered with barbed wire. With no lights, no air-conditioning, no swimming, rationed food and beer, life was rather dreary, plus there was the prospect of the enemy showing up unannounced. We didn't dare change clothes or even take a bath. Finally, however, after two weeks, we were cheered up a bit with the arrival of some planes that flew over from the mainland, and most of these had British insignia painted on their sides, indicating that they had been prepared for shipment to England, but at the last minute were diverted to Hawaii.

The method the enemy used in planning the attack was simplicity uncompounded, and the Japanese took advantage of our systematic patrol schedule. This made it very easy for them to figure out how close they could approach Pearl Harbor without being observed by our planes over the horizon. Then, when our planes turned homeward on the inbound leg of the triangular pattern, the Japanese launched their planes from their carriers, followed our planes in, and started shooting them down before they could even get into a landing formation. They had no interceptor planes to bother them, for those that were on the ground had been shot to pieces before they could be manned. Our antiaircraft ammunition was locked up and nobody could find the keys, so sledgehammers had to be used to break open the containers. It was a sorry mess. But there was some comedy, too, of a grim and savage nature, in spite of the ghastly situation.

At the height of the attack, we received a call for help from the USS *Solace*, a hospital ship that was anchored in the stream on the far side of Pearl Harbor. The dead and the dying were piling up like cordwood on her decks, and assistance was urgently needed to help with the wounded. The teeth of the dead had to be charted for identification purposes, for the bodies were burned beyond recognition. The skipper of my ship, the USS *Rigel*, gave verbal orders for a medical officer and me to proceed at once, by whatever means were available, and tender our services. We left the ship and started running along the dock area in search of some kind of a small boat, when we happened to look up and saw a Japanese pilot with his guns blazing away, diving toward us between two ships. He was getting our range when we nose-dived under some boiler plate that was leaning against some piling. As he passed overhead, we could hear, above the din of exploding bombs and ships blowing up, his bullets striking the boiler plate over our heads.

We crawled out and continued our run along the docks. Some distance ahead of us, an ammunition truck had pulled off the pavement onto the gravel shoulder, and the driver was unloading some shells for an antiaircraft gun that was being manned by some marines. A Chinese civilian laborer was running ahead of us, and, just as he came alongside the truck, a bomb exploded nearby, whereupon he dived under the truck, covered his head with his arms, and proceeded to bury his face in the gravel. There was so much noise he didn't hear the truck drive off, leaving him completely exposed. But he must have sensed that there was something missing, for he slowly turned his head and when he saw clear sky above, he executed the most extraordinary feat of levitation I ever witnessed. He was making about forty miles per hour before he touched ground.

We finally found a small boat that had been abandoned near where a bomb had gone through the dock. We checked the gas tank and found it to be about half full, which we hoped was enough to get us across the harbor. So away we went into the inferno that lay ahead. How we ever made it I'll never know, with bombs splashing and exploding all around us, ships blowing up and rolling over, strafing planes diving in from all directions, the surface of the water a mass of flames from blazing oil and gas, and the unorganized rescue boats darting about. It was utter chaos and confusion.

We picked up a few bodies along the way and several survivors swimming about blindly—their eyes were so full of oil that they couldn't see and their bodies were so black that we couldn't determine their color or nationality. But among those we gathered up were three whites, two blacks, one Filipino, and one Japanese. They all grabbed the edge of the boat and hung on until we could pull them aboard; under such circumstances, the law of self-preservation speaks a common language. In due time we arrived at the hospital ship, where we worked for three days and nights without stopping, except for a quick sandwich and a cup of coffee.

A catastrophe of any kind always presents interesting incidents that generally go unnoticed. One such incident—which might be termed a grim human-interest story, if such a description could be applied in this case—was that a midget Japanese submarine had been captured in a steel net by one of our destroyers. The one-man contraption was brought in to a dock and made secure. Nobody knew whether or not it was manned, or whether it was a time bomb. Before a decision could be made as to what to do with it, the hatch popped open and out jumped an impeccable Japanese officer. He was not armed, so nobody took a shot at him. He hopped over onto the dock, came to attention and saluted his captors, and, in perfect English, said, "Sir, I had an honorable mission to perform, but I failed. Please shoot me." He was treated as a prisoner of war, but with the respect due his rank. The kind treatment paid off, for a great deal of valuable information was obtained from him.

The Japanese didn't know how badly crippled we were and evidently didn't have any way to find out, mainly because we clamped down on our security and did not release any vital information. In fact, it was exactly one year later that the full report was given to the American public. One of the most amazing circumstances in connection with this phase was the fact that the wives who had been evacuated to the mainland kept the secret so well.

Repair work was made on all the ships not too badly damaged. My ship had about three hundred holes to be plugged up. When I reported back aboard after the trip to the *Solace*, my room boy presented me with a piece of shrapnel he said he had found in my pillow. But what about Captain Brandy? A few days before the attack, one of the smaller ships had to make a run to San Francisco, and Brandy just happened to be aboard at the time of departure. So away he went on a trip to the mainland. The word of Brandy's departure was passed along to Cowboy, so that he wouldn't worry too much.

When his ship arrived in San Francisco, Brandy immediately took off to do some visiting and shopping up and down the Embarcadero. This was shortly after 1 December. Before his ship was made ready for the return trip to Hawaii, the attack took place. Under normal conditions, whenever a ship was about to depart, she would sound her siren and give certain blasts on her whistle to signal what she was going to do. These sounds were a warning to any crew members ashore to hurry aboard and an indication to other ships in the vicinity to watch for a back down from the dock.

But now, with the country at war, all sirens and whistles were silenced, and so Brandy had no way of knowing that his ship was about to get underway. She sailed and left him stranded on the beach. He spent a couple of days wandering up and down the docks before he was recognized by a sailor from another ship, who took him in tow temporarily until he could decide what to do with him. Since there were no navy ships due to leave for Pearl Harbor in the near future, Brandy had no way of getting back to his ship and to Cowboy.

But news of Brandy's plight finally reached the ears of the captain of the *Lurline*, flagship of the Matson Line. With the advent of war, all these ships had been taken over by the navy. So the skipper of the *Lurline* invited Brandy to be his guest and to share his cabin on a run he was preparing to make to Honolulu with a load of marines and a cargo of combat equipment. News of Brandy's arrival preceded him by some unknown means, for all radio communications were silenced. When the *Lurline* arrived in Honolulu, a navy brass band was on hand to head a greeting party. Brandy was mounted on an elevated seat in the stern of a jeep for a parade through the city and out to Pearl Harbor. The dog's picture along with a story about his escapade appeared on the front page of one of the daily newspapers. Even during the stress and strain of a war, it was possible to relax and have a little fun.

— —

Ed Seiser remained aboard the USS *Rigel* until 1943, when he was transferred back to the States. After the war, he served two years in the Philippines. During the Korean War, he served aboard the USS *Boxer* as a senior dental officer. In 1959, he retired from the navy and went into a private dental practice.

The USS *Cummings*

BERT ROGERS

The destroyer *Cummings* was ready to head for open sea and begin patrol of Oahu, but had no way to get there on the morning of 7 December. The ship was docked at the Navy Yard on the inside row between the *Rigel* and the minelayer destroyer USS *Preble.* The *Ramapo* and the heavy cruiser *New Orleans* blocked the *Cummings'* exit to the open waters of the harbor. During the attack, the *Cummings* could only remain in place at the dock and fire her antiaircraft rounds in an attempt to down the aircraft passing overhead. The stationary ship proved an elusive target, for bombs fell ahead and astern without directly hitting their mark. The ship did not incur damage, but some of her crew received minor injuries from flying shrapnel and debris. As soon as the *Ramapo* and the *New Orleans* cleared their berths, the *Cummings* was to head for open sea. The problem of getting out of the dock was compounded by the problems occurring aboard the *New Orleans*. Like the *Honolulu*, the *New Orleans* was receiving power and light from a main power cable running from the ship to the dock. When the cable was accidentally cut, engineers were forced to work by flashlight to raise power in the engine room, which had been undergoing repair. It was probably to the advantage of the *Cummings* that she did not clear the dock until after the attack commenced. As a slow-moving target on the harbor's open water, she would have been an isolated bull's-eye for Japanese bombs.

For Radioman First Class Bert Rogers, the *Cummings* was the vantage point from where he witnessed the Pearl Harbor attack. His story relates events surrounding the attack on Oahu and those out at sea.

—◦—

On 6 December, a fellow shipmate, Radioman First Class Herman Meyers, and I left USS *Cummings* on liberty in order to attend a college football game that was to be played between the University of Hawaii and Willamette University of Oregon. It was an afternoon game and, as I recall, was well-attended. At half time, there was the usual pageantry. One part of the display that I recalled several months after the Japanese attack was this: a simulated army tank moved to the center of the football field. A bomb was shot into the air, and when it exploded the school flag unfurled, fluttering in the breeze as it descended slowly by parachute into the stadium. Another bomb was catapulted into the air, and, upon exploding, the American flag was revealed. Old Glory became entangled in the shrouds of the parachute, which caused a tumbling action and a more rapid descent. A muffled gasp could be detected from the spectators. After the flag had fallen for several feet, it suddenly became disentangled, the parachute opened, and our flag waved in majesty, and, rather than continuing in its natural descent, a light breeze caught it, and it started to rise and float out over the spectators on a much slower descent. A spontaneous cheer rose from the crowd as they applauded the flag as it drifted out over the stadium. In later months, as the war in the Pacific proceeded with its victories and defeats, I felt this incident at the football game was symbolic of our forces being beaten down early in the war and then our slow, but sure, climb back up to victory in the Pacific.

After the football game, Herman Meyers and I had dinner in Honolulu. At approximately 11:00 p.m., we returned to our ship, the USS *Cummings*, the temporary flagship of Commander Destroyer Squadron Three. (The USS *Clark* was the regular flagship but at this time was in the Mare Island Navy Yard in California.) Herman and I were on the staff of Commander Destroyer Squadron Three. The returning liberty party was let off the bus at the Pearl Harbor Navy Yard main gate, and we, along with several others, proceeded to our respective ships in the Navy Yard. The *Cummings* was outboard of a nest of four-pipe destroyers, across from the Ten-Ten Dock. As Herman and I approached our ship, we overheard a conversation between two sailors about some of their experiences of the evening: "You know what that old bastard told me tonight? He said the USS *Pennsylvania* was going to be sunk before the morning." The other sailor replied, "I didn't hear that, but I heard it was going to be sunk before February." Needless to say, Herman and I recalled these comments very vividly after the disastrous attack the following morning.

On 7 December 1941, I arose about 6:30 a.m., had breakfast while reading the local morning newspaper, and went to the radio shack of the *Cummings*. The *Cummings* had been scheduled to be berthed in the dry dock, but the USS *Shaw* replaced the *Cummings* due to some damage the latter had suffered at sea the previous week. I was sitting behind a radio transmitter reading the paper. The time was about 7:50 a.m. The sound of a multimotored airplane brought my attention to a nearby porthole, where I observed a large two-motored airplane go by. I then heard a loud explosion. Someone in the radio shack questioned, "Is the army firing their large shore batteries?" Then there was a series of rat a-tat-tat sounds. Someone remarked, "That sounds like air hammers, but the Navy Yard workers don't work on Sundays." Then another man speculated that it was antiaircraft machine-gun practice on towed sleeve targets. This all transpired in a few minutes. At this time my curiosity brought me to an outside hatch, and the first thing I observed was an airplane with the red-ball insignia of the Japanese, diving in the vicinity of Hickam Field. General quarters sounded. My battle station was the main radio shack. Our radio antennas were down due to yard work to strengthen the mast in order to install radar. We jury-rigged an antenna, and the first message we received was: "Air Raid on Pearl. This Is No Drill." At one time, I saw a Japanese torpedo plane just skimming the water off our stern, coming from the Merry Point Landing area and headed for Battleship Row, near Ford Island.

I observed the USS *Arizona* become engulfed in a huge orange-colored ball of fire as it blew up from a direct hit. I also saw the USS *Oklahoma* as it started to capsize. After the initial attack there was a lull, then came the attack by the high-level bombers. I recall seeing them approach from the northeast. Their bombs, upon release, appeared to be coming directly at us. Then it looked as if they were going to hit the Navy Yard shops. I believe these same bombs were the ones that hit the USS *Pennsylvania*, the USS *Downes*, and the USS *Cassin*. All three ships were in the dry dock. Very minor damage was inflicted on the *Cummings*, as our gun crews fought back with antiaircraft guns. Shrapnel passed through rungs on a ladder to the bridge, through a bulkhead, across a typewriter position, and expended itself on the deck of the storekeeper's office, which was right next door to the radio shack. Navy Yard workers came aboard the *Cummings* and made emergency temporary repairs to the ship's mast by welding guy wires from the mast to the deck. With superhuman effort, engine-room and fire-room personnel got the ship ready and we were able to get underway for sea by about 11:00 a.m. I'll never forget the terrible carnage, the fires, and the boats picking up the oil-saturated sailors, some dead and some alive. Just before the *Cummings* got underway, several sailors from damaged ships came aboard so as to be on a ship that could fight back. Three ships of Commander Destroyer Squadron Three were severely damaged. The *Downes* and the *Cassin* were damaged beyond repair. The bow was blown off of the *Shaw*, which had replaced the *Cummings* in the dry dock.

The flagship *Clark* arrived in Pearl Harbor from the West Coast in the latter part of December. We of Squadron Three flag personnel moved aboard and soon joined a task force, which ultimately arrived at American Samoa. After a time on submarine patrol, we joined up with a task force consisting of the carrier USS *Lexington*, the cruiser USS *San Francisco*, and several destroyers. We were scheduled to make a surprise attack on Japanese-held Rabaul. On the afternoon prior to the scheduled attack, we were sighted by Japanese scout planes. Subsequently, we were attacked by sixteen twin-motored Japanese bombers. Planes from the carrier *Lexington* rose to engage the enemy bombers not far from the main body of the task force. I believe Butch O'Hare, a pilot from the *Lexington*, was credited with four or five kills. One of the bombers managed to penetrate the screen of carrier planes. It appeared to be damaged and was in a steep glide, apparently attempting to crash-dive on the *Lexington*. The *Clark* was astern and to the starboard side of the carrier. About dead ahead of us, the plane exploded and fell into the sea. We passed through the flaming debris. I believe fourteen of the sixteen enemy bombers were shot down.

A short time later, the *Clark* joined up with the two-carrier task force that launched an air attack from off the west coast of New Guinea. They flew over the Owen Stanley Mountain Range and attacked the ports of Salamaua and Lae. I believe that, of the many carrier planes involved in this endeavor, only one failed to return to the carriers.

At this time, we had been at sea for quite a while. Our supplies were getting low. The only replenishment we could get was what we could obtain from the larger ships of the task force. We had depleted our supplies of meat and flour and were subsisting on beans and hardtack three times a day. We received a message from the task force commander stating it was imperative that we remain on station for thirty more days and inquiring about the morale and health of the ship's crew. The *Clark*'s reply was: "Morale of crew is excellent, but, due to shortage of food, the crew had lost on the average of fifteen pounds per man." Apparently, it was decided that the *Clark* should return to Pearl Harbor. Upon arrival, I received orders for transfer to Boston and to report aboard a new destroyer, the USS *Knight*, for duty. I had served five years on the *Clark*.

— —

Bert Rogers ended the war assigned as an instructor in Class-A Radio School at the Naval Training Center in San Diego, California. He retired from the navy in February 1957.

The USS *Honolulu*

CAL FIELDS

On 7 December, the *Honolulu* was one of eighteen ships berthed at the Navy Yard, located on the south bank of the Southeast Loch, across the open water from Battleship Row. These ships were destroyers, cruisers, minesweepers, and auxiliary ships undergoing or awaiting repair or overhaul. They were in double rows at the navy's largest open or wet docking area in the world. If the ships sitting on the open waters of Pearl Harbor were considered "ducks on the pond," then the ships at the docking facilities were "ducks in the pen." For these ships, many of which were without guns, ammunition, or steam power due to repairs, the only way to clear the dock was to back out into the loch's open water. During the attack, only two ships were able to get underway. At 9:30 a.m., the cruiser *St. Louis* began backing out of the dock. Despite the precarious position of the ships, their crews performed well during the battle. Many of the ships promptly sounded general quarters, and their crews manned antiaircraft batteries on nearby ships or assisted in fire and rescue operations on the USS *Pennsylvania* and the *California*. During the first attack and the lull between attacks, numerous machine guns and antiaircraft batteries were disassembled, repaired, reassembled, and remounted for later use. The ships received only minor damage, most of which was inflicted by near misses that landed in the small spaces of water among them. The heavy damage occurred just west of the dock at the Ten-Ten Dock, Floating Drydock Number One, and Floating Drydock Number Two.

The *Honolulu* was docked in the far eastern corner of the yard, on the outside row between the pier and the USS *St. Louis*, and directly behind the minesweeper USS *Grebe*. The USS *Honolulu* was not directly hit, but suffered severe flooding when a near miss passed through the concrete pier and exploded about twenty feet from the hull. This resulted in a five-feet-deep buckle that extended fore and aft about forty feet on the port side. Although the shell of the ship was not completely opened, the flooding damaged the handling room of turret two, several storerooms, and a number of compartments. The main power line to the ship was cut during the excitement and confusion of getting the ship out of the dock. At the time the line was cut, the USS *Honolulu* did not have enough steam to supply her own power and relied on the land line for electricity to operate her lights and gun batteries.

Prior to the near miss, the USS *Honolulu* had sounded general quarters with the first sighting of enemy planes over Hickam Field and passed the word, "Enemy air raid." The ship, credited with downing two torpedo planes, fired 2,000 rounds of thirty caliber, 4,500 of fifty caliber, and 250 three-inch rounds during both attacks.

For many sailors, including Cal Fields, the Navy Yard provided a ringside seat to the action at Hickam Field and Battleship Row.

I was born on 3 December 1921 in Grainola, Oklahoma. I was raised in Kansas and joined the navy in Twin Falls, Idaho, on 4 February 1941. I was at a prime age for the draft. Being a Depression teenager, I had not accomplished a great lot prior to going into the service. I quit the tenth grade in Kansas, then began the tenth grade all over in McCall, Idaho, to completion. These dates were about 1936 and 1937. I started the eleventh grade in McCall High School, but did not finish. I quit and went to work as a stock and delivery boy in a local grocery store. I then went back to Kansas, and, some time later, my parents moved to Twin Falls, Idaho. I joined them there in the summer of 1940. The navy quotas were full during the rest of 1940. In February 1941, I was accepted and went to San

Diego, California, for boot training. In about May 1941, upon the completion of boot camp, I and many more recruits were placed aboard the USS *Enterprise* for transportation to Pearl Harbor. Upon arrival, I went aboard my assigned ship, the USS *Honolulu,* one of the newest ships in the fleet; I believe she had been commissioned in 1938. There were nine light cruisers of her "bobtail class." She had fifteen six-inch, forty-seven-caliber main battery guns mounted on five turrets, three forward and two aft. She had eight five-inch, twenty-five-caliber antiaircraft guns; they were dual-purpose guns—four on each side—amidships. Numerous twenty- and fifty-caliber guns were also part of her armament. We also carried a couple of S.O.C. pontoon biplanes for scouting purposes. War clouds were omnipresent even then, but we were young and, even though Europe was torn up, confident war would not touch us. I was only twenty years old. How I wish I had the optimism of youth again.

I was placed in the Fourth Division Deck Force and assigned to a compartment cleaner till one day the division petty officer caught me playing cribbage during working hours. I was immediately assigned to cleaning the "head."

I qualified on the wheel as helmsman prior to the bombing of Pearl Harbor, which called for two-hour watches at sea. My battle station was in the aft, A.A. Director Control. Here we had control of the five-inch battery.

Our ship was tenderly noted as the Blue Goose, and Pineapple Maru, and unprintable names. She acquitted herself quite well later on, especially when we had run out of heavy cruisers, had no battleships, and the carriers we did have could not maneuver in the Solomon Islands Straits.

On the fateful day in question, I had planned to visit a friend in the base hospital. He had just experienced an appendectomy. I was in the water closet showering when the P. A. system blared out a bugle call. It sounded much like the motorboat call. Being part of the crew and forgetting that I had liberty, I muttered to myself, "Why call away that boat this time of morning?" I started back for my bunk and locker when someone yelled, "That was general quarters." The next time the bugler got his act straight and sounded a decent call to general quarters and then announced, "This is no drill; the Japs are bombing us." I lit out like a scalded cat and reached topside. If it hadn't been so serious, it would have been funny.

The peacetime navy dictated that awnings be rigged. They were and, as a result, hindered what little mobility the five-inch guns had. So, seeing their chance, the boatswain mates and seamen joined in and slashed the canvas and associated parts into many more parts.

Ammo was carried in lockers—small caliber as well as five inch. These lockers were padlocked by normal routine, and no one could find the guy who had the keys. In addition, the fore and after gangways, even though not used at this time, were cast, most haply, loose and allowed to sink out of sight. They were tedious to keep up, especially the fore one, which was the officers' gangway.

All these things were viewed in a trice as I was making my way upwards in the superstructure to my battle station.

We found that the director and the three-inch guns were practically unusable because of the close proximity of the ship. When the five-inch guns could shoot, it was straight up and the bombers were out of reach. So we just sat there and watched our surroundings collapse around us.

I watched the *Pennsylvania* blow up in dry dock, along with the *Cassin* and *Downes*. The *Arizona* and *West Virginia* went up, and, in a blast second to none, the *Oklahoma* was lifted out of the water and turned on her side.

We were tied up port side along the Ten-Ten Dock with the *St. Louis*, our sister ship, tied to our starboard side. We quickly chopped her lines loose and backed out of the slip, whereupon we chopped our stern lines and made an attempt to get out. A bomb dropped and went through the pier on our port bow and exploded in the water. Our seams were ruptured, and we took on water and went down by the head. At this time the old man ordered the ship tied up and said that we were going nowhere. So we sat it out, watching an unopposed systematic destruction of our fleet, air force, and facilities.

The ringside seat we had was not so pretty when we later climbed out on top of the director to better survey the damage. Things had come to a halt by that time. It was then that I noticed the Sunday colors had been hoisted. They hung down to where I could touch them, and a closer look revealed many bullet holes. Whether they came from enemy plans or out of our own ships, I'll never know, but, if they had been a bit lower, some seven or eight more casualties would have been logged in.

We in the director did not participate, and this alone was frustrating, but later, much later, when some of us were allowed to go below decks, the realization of what happened and what could yet happen took hold and not many of us would have given a slug for our lives. We all expected the Japanese troops to follow up with a landing. They did not land, and I was among the fortunate to survive not only 7 December, but also the balance of most of the war.

In about February or March 1942, the patched-up *Blue Goose* left Pearl for Mare Island. There we really were stuck together and given new guns and radars—yes, the *Blue Goose* had one of the first surface radars in the fleet when Pearl was bombed. And from there we went to Alaska. Then convoy duty to Australia and to ports such as Bora Bora and Pago Pago, which were nothing more than fueling stops in those days; now they are resorts. We went back and forth across the equator so that we soon ran out of pollywogs to initiate.

About this time the Japanese began to see the light—Australia and New Zealand were not to be theirs. So they began their stand in the Solomon Islands. Our fleet took a series of losses at Guadalcanal, such that they named the waters off its upper end "Iron Bottom Bay."

We were dispatched with haste to the Solomon Islands. There were light cruisers and destroyers, all that was left at that time (1943) to stop the Tokyo Express. It took a while to stop it, but we did. We lost more ships and men, but our losses were light compared to those of our enemy. In the Battle of Kula Gulf, in July 1943, we took a hit in the bow by a torpedo at the same time the man on the headphones on the fantail called the bridge and reported a torpedo half in and half out of our square stern—unlike the one that hit almost simultaneously in the bow. The stern hit was a dud. The skipper stopped the ship dead in the water for a damage-control check. Nothing serious was reported, whereupon he immediately got underway. When he did, the stern torpedo slipped out in the wake.

In 1942, I transferred to the fire-control gang. In 1945, I went to Fire Control School and was there when the war with Japan ended. On V-E Day, my tin can was returning from the Okinawa campaign.

Cal Fields remained in the navy for his initial six-year cruise and two additional three-year cruises. During his last reenlistment, he discovered that he had tuberculosis. After his treatment and convalescence at the Portsmouth Naval Hospital in Portsmouth, Virginia, and Saint Alban's Hospital in New York City, doctors prepared the necessary paperwork to place Fields on the disability retired list. After twelve years and four months of active duty, including four months in two navy hospitals and one year in a veterans hospital, he received disability retirement pay of 50 percent. His tuberculosis had been arrested rather than cured.

The USS *Tautog*

BILL SEACH

The *Tautog* was one of four submarines docked at the submarine base on the morning of the attack on Pearl Harbor. Tucked away in the eastern corner of the Southeast Loch, the base and the adjacent CinCPac Headquarters were bypassed by Japanese bombers. Ironically, the failure of the Japanese to estimate the power and potential of the American submarine fleet and their inability to employ their own large fleet of submarines effectively led to the downfall of their Pacific empire.

Operation Z, the Japanese plan for the attack on Pearl Harbor, included the use of twenty-seven I-boats and a special attack unit of five additional I-boats, each of which carried a midget submarine. I-boats were the backbone of the Japanese submarine service. Each boat displaced from sixteen-hundred to twenty-two-hundred tons, carried up to twenty torpedoes, had a maximum range of sixteen thousand miles, and had top speeds of more than twenty knots on the surface and from seven to nine knots underwater. Slightly larger, faster, noisier, and more difficult to handle than their American counterparts, they were capable of sinking the US Pacific Fleet as they headed out of Pearl Harbor.

The Japanese knew of the US Pacific Fleet doctrine to get underway in case of attack and to head to open sea through Pearl Harbor's narrow entrance channel, and they positioned their I-boats around Oahu's northern and southern portions, with the hope of engaging the fleeing ships in a major sea battle. The plan called for the midget submarines to enter Pearl Harbor and fire their torpedoes at the larger combat ships of the fleet. Each midget submarine had a crew of two, carried two small torpedoes, and measured about seventy-nine feet in length.

While the Japanese surface fleet was enjoying a major victory at Pearl Harbor, the undersea complement was enduring a total failure. All five midget submarines did not inflict any damage and sunk or ran aground. The I-boats positioned off the coast of Oahu waited for days to attack any ships escaping the harbor. Finally, 10 December, the submarines spotted a quarry. Two cruisers and the aircraft carrier *Enterprise* were their prey. The brief battle was disastrous for the Japanese. Planes from the *Enterprise* bombed the I-170, which sank with all hands. The I-boats remained in the water off the Hawaiian Islands until early January, then headed for the West Coast. The poor showing of the submarine force plagued the Japanese throughout the war. The early failures later affected appropriations and manpower requirements needed to sustain a top-flight submarine force.

In the first days of the war in the Pacific, the US submarine force was essential in fighting the Japanese. The US Pacific Fleet had been weakened from the attack on 7 December, and American submarines were the only offensive weapons available. The aircraft carriers USS *Enterprise*, USS *Lexington*, and USS *Saratoga*, which were the heart of the fleet and last line of defense, were considered too valuable to risk at this early stage of the war.

Six hours after the first Japanese attack planes had struck, naval commanders received orders from the Navy Department in Washington, D.C., to "execute unrestricted submarine warfare against Japan." However, submarine-fleet commanders, clinging to idealistic notions of honorable warfare, ordered that no more than one or two torpedoes be expended upon a merchant ship. Efforts were directed at the larger Japanese warships, such as battleships and carriers, which proved difficult to intercept, much less sink. Submarine commanders foolishly ignored cargo and supply ships in order to chase after the highly coveted combat ships.

The *Tautog* returned from sea duty to Pearl Harbor on 5 December 1941. On 21 October, the *Tautog* and the *Thresher*, under sealed orders, had begun a forty-five-day simulated war patrol in the area of Midway. For thirty-eight consecutive days, the two submarines operated submerged for up to eighteen hours a day. Upon their return, the crews looked forward to some well-earned liberty on Oahu. Bill Seach, chief torpedoman's mate aboard the *Tautog*, expected to spend time with his wife in Waikiki Beach. From the *Tautog*, he witnessed the attack on Pearl Harbor, as well as exploits of the submarine until 1944.

———

As a boy growing up, I used to hear my dad tell about all the different countries that he visited while he was in the navy. Before he retired, his life had been spent at sea—thirty years of which was in the navy and, before that, as a cabin boy aboard old sailing ships. He won the Congressional Medal of Honor in 1901, during the Boxer Rebellion. In 1978, he died at the age of 101. But back to my youth: listening to all these adventures made me very restless. Interest in school studies had no interest for me, and I longed to join the service and go to sea, like my dad before me. After dropping out of the first year of high school, I went to work at a local milk farm. One dollar a day for seven days of hard labor. Four in the morning till after dark at night, all the other farm laborers and I would maintain and care for the cows and do numerous other duties. At about age sixteen, I took a day off and ventured into the big city of Boston and walked down to the recruiting station and tried to enlist. The chief petty officer in charge smiled and told me to come back on my seventeenth birthday, as I was then too young. I went back to the farm and patiently waited for that day to come. When my birthday finally arrived, I hopped on the first train to Boston and headed fast as I could back to that navy recruiter. He gave me papers that needed my parents' signature. Thus I returned home full of excitement for the signing by my parents. My dad and mother were not very happy about me quitting school, but I knew what I wanted to do. They signed the release, and the next day I traveled back to the station to join up with the navy. After a wait of a month or two, I was called in and sent off to Newport, Rhode Island, to the training station. Right away, I began to study and slowly, over years in the service, advanced to the rate of chief torpedoman's mate. I even took and passed the exam for warrant officer. Serveral years of serving aboard a submarine out in the US Asiatic Fleet finally got to me, and, as my time was up, I decided to return to the United States in 1939. They assigned me to the submarine R-2 down in New London, Connecticut, at the submarine base. In 1940, I met my future wife while visiting an old friend in Washington, D.C. He introduced me to his wife's girlfriend, and we married soon after. Both of us moved back to New London, where I was assigned to a new submarine being built at the Groton Shipyard, the USS *Tautog*.

The year was 1941. For a number of years I had been in the Far East, as a crew member aboard the USS *40*. Now at Pearl Harbor I was a torpedoman aboard the sleek new submarine USS *Tautog*. In October we received an order to load our torpedoes with active warheads. Our orders were to patrol off the coast of Midway and its vicinity and to sink any Japanese or German ships that we might chance upon. For almost eighty-nine days and nights, we patrolled. We were submerged from sunup until sundown. At night we surfaced to charge the huge batteries while running our diesel engines. On 5 December, without ever spotting any ships to fire at, we returned to Pearl Harbor a tired and very hungry crew. Mostly we lived on canned Spam and dehydrated spuds. The thoughts of getting back ashore to eat a good steak had all of us excited.

My wife, Ruth, was living in a small cottage near Waikiki Beach, and I couldn't wait to see her and find out if she was okay. As soon as we docked, the liberty began for those of us assigned to the port watch. It was Friday evening now, and I had all of Saturday and Sunday to enjoy at home with her. On Saturday, we went downtown and shopped. Everything was quite normal, and the crowds were busy as we walked in and out of stores. That night we were invited to a civilian friend's house for a party. After midnight, we arrived home very tired.

Early the next morning all hell broke loose. Several concussions from exploding bombs rocked our little house. We both leaped out of bed and ran to the street. Many neighbors were already out there—some in their shorts, and others in housecoats. As we hit the street, a plane roared by at treetop level. It was then that I spotted the huge red ball on its wings and knew from my years in Asia that it was a Japanese plane. Since those who lived on our street were navy people, we ran for our houses and quickly put on our uniforms. Three of us were back on the street in a jiffy and we stopped just long enough to say good-by to our wives.

Running down the main road, we saw a car with a key in it and jumped in and drove back to the base. People on the way were running, and cars were going every which way down the roads. Bedlam had broken loose. As we approached the Navy Yard gate, we saw some Japanese men turn a truck over to block the gate. A couple of marines grabbed them and held them as we raced by. Soon we could go no farther, so we dumped the car and continued on foot.

All this time, of course, the Japanese planes were circling and dropping bombs. Already the *Arizona* was billowing flames and smoke, and the *Oklahoma*, which was nearby, was listing before it went under.

I ran up the gangplank of my submarine, which was tied to the dock. A torpedoman named Pat Mignone, my shipmate, was standing at the rear deck firing a machine gun from his hip. At the time of the attack, so early in the morning, our gunner's mate, who had the keys to the gun magazine, was on shore liberty. The crew lost considerable time getting to its guns. A hole had to be burned through the door with an acetylene torch. Once through the doors, we quickly mounted the guns and we started tossing bullets back to the Japs. As I ran over to Pat to ask where all the guns like his were, a Japanese plane came swooping down at us. It was making a torpedo approach on the battleships across the bay. Pat was blasting away, and, all of a sudden, there was a big explosion and the shock of the noise almost knocked us both over. Pat had hit that plane, and it had blown apart not more than fifty feet from where we were standing.

There was fire from the burning ships, and guns of all sizes were banging away. Bullets and shells from some of our own ships still afloat were falling around us. I ran below and found a gun for myself. Back up the hatch, I went and began running aft for a better spot to fire from. Mine was a thirty-caliber machine gun, and I was so nerved up by this time that it felt like a feather in my hands.

Things remained in a turmoil for many hours after this first attack. Each time a single gun was fired, the whole area came to life and everybody would fire, tracer bullets streamed across the sky after dark that night. None of us ever got to bed, and the next morning, at sunup, we went with a detail of men to help pull dead sailors up from the mass of floating oil.

Bodies were all over the place in that bay. Black gooey oil covered their burned heads. We were churning around in a motor launch and, as we came near the upturned hull of the battleship *Oklahoma*, we could hear the trapped men pounding and trying to alert anyone who could hear them for help. Many of those poor boys never did get out either. For months later dates were found scratched here and there on the bulkheads, telling that they had lived till long after Christmas.

I wasn't allowed to use the telephone to call and see if Ruth was okay. And, of course, she had no way of knowing whether I was still alive, as they wouldn't allow anyone unauthorized near the navy installations. Finally, after a week had gone by and things became more normal, I was given a one-day pass to go and find my wife. She was okay, but had almost been killed when a huge piece of shrapnel came crashing down through the tin roof of our cottage. It landed on the kitchen floor, six feet from where she was standing. The house that was two doors up from ours was blasted away.

We tearfully parted that evening, and I returned to the submarine *Tautog* at the sub base. The following morning our submarine pulled out, and we were off for what was classed as the first big raid of the war of the Pacific—the Marshall Islands.

In 1944, Bill Seach was transferred to the Electric Torpedo group in New London, Connecticut, where he was commended for his work in supervising the output of torpedoes. But the yearning for action soon returned, and he requested and received another overseas assignment in 1945. He was in the Philippines when the war ended. In 1945, after three years of suffering from spinal arthritis, he chose not to reenlist. He was briefly hospitalized at the Chelsea Soldiers Home for treatment and subsequently given disability by the Veterans Administration.

The USS *Pelias*

KENNETH KLEM AND FREDERICK CURNOW

The submarine tender *Pelias* arrived at Pearl Harbor on 9 October 1941 after her shakedown cruise off the New England coast. Six days after her arrival, she began undergoing an overhaul at Pearl Harbor Submarine Base. On the morning of 7 December 1941, she was berthed dockside in the Magazine Loch between the salvage ship *Widgeon* and a group of PT boats. The *Pelias* was credited with splashing one enemy torpedo plane and damaging another during the attack, as they made their runs along the main channel, which was a little more than one hundred yards from her port side.

Kenneth Klem joined the navy in May 1941. He was assigned to the USS *Pelias* directly out of boot camp. His first living quarters after recruit training were aboard the receiving ships USS *Camden* and USS *Seattle*, which were anchored at the Brooklyn Navy Yard. Here they were billeted with crew members from the USS *Panay*, the gunboat that Japanese aircraft had sunk on the Yangtze River, on 12 December 1937. Klem later was transferred to the Brooklyn Naval Reserve Armory while the USS *Pelias* was undergoing conversion from a passenger ship to a submarine tender by the Bethlehem Steel Corporation in Brooklyn. During this four-month period, Klem shared living quarters with the crew of the HMS *Dido*, which was under repair for torpedo damage that a German U-boat in the North Atlantic had inflicted. After the USS *Pelias* was commissioned, Klem was assigned to the quartermaster/signalman gang.

On 7 December, I had just completed the 4:00–8:00 a.m. signal watch on the flying bridge of the submarine tender USS *Pelias*, which was docked at the Pearl Harbor Submarine Base. I was assisting my deck-watch relief with the execution of the colors, which was normal procedure before departure from that watch, when suddenly we were startled at seeing a low-flying group of suspicious-looking aircraft approaching us from a southerly direction. We quickly identified the aircraft as being Japanese, as they were so very low and clearly marked with their red-circle insignia. Almost immediately, they were arriving in waves and began to strafe the entire area. The element of surprise caused pandemonium to set in. At the moment, it was impossible to even think straight, but my first impulse was to notify my superior officer, who was below at the quarterdeck, where he could not see what was happening. I immediately contacted him on the phone and then ran down to our commanding officer's cabin and informed him that we were being attacked. I returned to the bridge as squadrons of planes were still strafing, dropping bombs and torpedoes.

In seconds, it seemed that scores of high-level bombers in formation appeared overhead in a seemingly never-ending stream. At a point, appearing to be directly overhead, the planes commenced releasing bombs, which fell where the warships were moored or in dry dock for repair. The bombs appeared as black specks in the sky and grew larger as they fell gracefully for their intended targets. By this time, there was no doubt about what was happening, and the gun crews had manned their battle stations and were frantically firing at the enemy aircraft. Captain Wakefield, the commanding officer, ran over to the port side of the wheelhouse clearing and started firing his revolver at some of the low-flying planes. At this point, complete chaos set in, everybody was in a state of shock as the enemy seemed to be almost unhampered in its mission to cripple or destroy the US military forces in the area. The force and the intensity with which it was applied was, to say the least, devastating. Instantly, ships were hit time after time, causing explosions and fires. Flak from our own antiaircraft fire was falling all around; ships began to burst at the seams, crack into pieces, and sink. Men were blown overboard into the heavily oil-covered water.

Thank God our ship was spared, and every person not engaged in gunnery or another essential onboard effort was directed to the rescue mission of those injured and/or in the water. Fortunately, we were equipped with large motor launches, which enabled us to search the waters and pick up survivors. Even those who were not seriously injured were covered with the thick fuel oil, and many swallowed large amounts of it, which had floated on the surface. Within minutes of the first launch, the decks were littered with a number of ragged-looking men fished out of the harbor. Many suffered burns and shrapnel wounds. Outfitted with excellent medical facilities, our ship immediately became a base of operations for rescue, treating, and caring for those requiring help. In addition, we shared our quarters and food with those needing shelter until other arrangements could be made. By evening, the injured and wounded had been removed to hospitals and the displaced and rescued returned to their ships.

Without reservation, I can truthfully say that 7 December 1941 was the darkest day of my life, and my prayer is that no other American shall ever have to experience the horror and the feeling of complete inadequacy in accepting the fact that our country had been so completely humiliated.

Kenneth Klem remained aboard the USS Pelias until May 1944, when she underwent overhaul at Mare Island Navy Yard. He was transferred to the submarine USS Tambor, where he remained until the end of the war. He was discharged from the Submarine Service in 1945.

* * *

Frederick Curnow was aboard the Pelias during the attack on Pearl Harbor. Curnow had joined the navy in March 1941, after graduating from high school in Butte, Montana, and working various jobs, including gandy dancing for the Northern Pacific Railroad and copper mining in Butte.

After completion of boot camp and then radio school at San Diego, California, I was given a nine-day leave, which I used to go back to Butte. Before leaving for home, I was given orders to report to Pearl Harbor for further assignment. I arrived in Hawaii on a Sunday in late September 1941, aboard the tanker *Platte*. On that following Monday, I was given orders to report aboard the submarine *Trout* for temporary duty. After six weeks aboard the sub, I was transferred to the Pearl Harbor Submarine Base as part of the Submarine Squadron Six Relief crew. In mid-November, the squadron moved aboard the *Pelias*, which had just arrived from the States. I was one of those who went aboard her.

Like most of the crew aboard the *Pelias*, I was lying on my bunk relaxing when the air-raid alarms went off on that fateful morning of 7 December. I started topside until someone stated that it was an air-raid drill. I then returned to my bunk. When the word came down a few seconds later that this was the "real McCoy," I went topside just as a Japanese plane was passing over the ship. I could plainly see the pilot's face staring at me through his goggles, and the rising-sun insignia on the plane was unmistakable. I was immediately commissioned to carry ammunition to the five-inch gun on the stern of the ship. I made several trips with canisters until those of us carrying ammunition were informed that it was "dummy" ammunition and had to be taken back. This ammunition had unfortunately been piled on top of the real ammunition. After the first ammunition locker was cleaned out, we went to the second one. This one was still locked, as the gunner's mate who had the key was still ashore. Instead of waiting until the situation was settled (the lock was broken off the door), I again went topside, out of curiosity, to see what was happening. As soon as I was on deck, I was handed a line to haul ammunition up to the number-two machine-gun nest. On the gun was a yeoman first class who had just returned from shore liberty. He told me to come up in the nest and help him man the fifty-caliber machine gun. Things did not go smoothly up in the nest. After firing a round and finding that the gun would not eject the spent cartridge, we called for help. A gunner's mate was sent to fix the gun, and, within a minute or two, we were able to start firing again. After another round was fired, the gun again jammed when the spent cartridge would not eject. During the course of the attack, several futile attempts were made to repair this deficiency. We solved the problem by firing a round and prying out the shells by hand. As a result of this time-consuming process, we drastically reduced our rate of fire; we were quite ineffective. Japanese planes came over the *Pelias* several times. One came parallel to our starboard side and was shot down over the stern of the ship. Many crew members said the plane had strafed the side of the ship, but I could find no evidence to confirm this. As for the number-two machine gun, it would have been a minor miracle for us to hit anything in the sky. All we could do was fire one round at a time and watch the planes pass overhead.

The machine-gun nest was high above the *Pelias*'s main deck, and, because it was located at the submarine base, I had an excellent view of Battleship Row and the action taking place. The *Arizona* was engulfed in smoke and fire and already down in the water when I first arrived in the machine-gun nest. I did see the *Oklahoma* slowly turn over bottom-up in the water and later watched the *Nevada* break loose from her mooring and try to navigate the channel before running aground. I watched with inner agony as the battleship sailors fought the fires on their ships, while those who had gone overboard were struggling in the blazing oil, attempting to avoid the strafing planes that periodically flew overhead.

There were so many men moving about the battleships and so much smoke that it was impossible to figure out exactly what had happened aboard each ship. One could not help but notice the men fighting the fires and the men struggling to stay alive in the water.

I have always been keenly aware of my futility as I watched all this with such a helpless feeling. I was so concerned about the men across the harbor that I didn't even take the time to worry about our open position in the machine-gun nest. Even though the Japanese pilots saw us from their planes, they didn't even bother us with a few bursts from their machine guns. I think the situation would have been a little different if we would have been putting out rounds at a rate of fire normal for our gun. The *Pelias* did manage to get boats underway to help fight the fires and to rescue men who were still in the water. About this time, rumors were making their rounds around the ship that the Japanese were landing troops at Merry Point and that the Japanese people in Honolulu were storming the gates of Pearl Harbor, armed with guns and clubs. Fortunately, these rumors proved to be false, but at the time they heightened our apprehension about what was exactly taking place around the island.

At 5:30 p.m., I was relieved of duty in the machine-gun nest and, after a quick bite to eat, took a tour of the ship. There was no damage to the *Pelias*, and I was surprised to find out later that not a single bomb had been dropped on the submarine base. I have always been surprised at this and chalked one up for Lady Luck. Later that night, I was aroused by another alarm, which turned out to be planes from the carrier *Enterprise* coming over the harbor for a landing. This time the guns in the harbor were ready and waiting. Some of our own planes were shot down in the confusion. The next day, while on duty in the radio shack aboard the *Pelias*, we received messages of the presence of a Japanese submarine in the harbor. The following day, its location was pinpointed by sound equipment from the submarine *Tautog* and the *Thresher*. A PT boat was called in to sink the Japanese submarine and it was then raised and taken to Merry Point. We didn't know if the submarine had been sunk before we discovered it or after we dropped a number of depth charges over her position.

—◆—

On 13 December 1941, Frederick Curnow was transferred from the submarine squadron to the USS *Thresher*. He made ten patrol runs on this submarine until March 1944. After one patrol run aboard the USS *Muskellunge*, Curnow was transferred to New London, Connecticut, to work on the construction of new submarines. He ended the war on a submarine school boat and was discharged in March 1947.

Around the Harbor

The USS *Solace*

ED JOHANN

On the morning of 7 December 1941, the *Solace* was moored in the East Loch of Pearl Harbor. Her decks offered a panoramic view of the harbor. The entire US Pacific Fleet seemed within sight. Only the harbor entrance and the south side of Ford Island were hidden from view. The ships appeared to be anchored in such tight groups that one could almost reach out and touch any ship. The USS *Solace* was an excellent spot to see and be seen. She was a hospital ship with large red crosses painted on her sides and smokestack. Against her white hull, the crosses stood out like bull's-eyes on a target. Although the integrity of the Japanese high command in launching a surprise attack could be questioned, the integrity of a number of Japanese pilots who executed it was primarily uncompromised. The *Solace* was untouched by Japanese bombers. There were limited facilities at Pearl Harbor Naval Hospital and other hospitals in Honolulu, and the trained personnel, the medical supplies, and the equipment aboard the *Solace* were critical in aiding the wounded and dying.

Of all the heroic acts during the attack, some of the most coura-geous yet unsung ones were performed by the nonmedical crews of the *Solace*. During the attack, they set out in launches to assist in res-cuing the wounded from the flaming waters and fiery wrecks. They made numerous trips to pick up survivors and entered the inferno of Battleship Row. They were the first to make rescue attempts from a hospital ship during World War II and, perhaps, any war.

To Ed Johann, 7 December was another working day. However, unlike most working days, it offered the chance to relax and watch the fleet enjoy a hard-earned day of rest. For the seventeen-year-old fireman aboard the *Solace*, Sunday duty meant a leisurely day of ferrying sailors to shore for leave and church services. In the early morning hours, the quiet of the tropical harbor conveyed tranquility. While Johann warmed up the motor launch for the 8:00 a.m. run, the sound of propellers over the north horizon shattered this feeling.

"It's some kind of drill or something," I heard someone say. We watched as the airplanes kept coming. They flew low across the water, dropped their lethal parcels with a splash, then flew off unhindered. I was viewing this scene while standing on the deck of the USS *Solace*. With me were three other members of the motor-launch crew to which I was assigned. We had been waiting to take some fellows over to Ford Island for church services. "My God," some yelled, "those are Japanese planes." I hoped that this wasn't true; I had heard about the army's war maneuvers in the States and thought this might be what they were all about.

The planes kept coming out of the sky unmercifully, and smoke was rising from some of the ships that had been hit. The planes flew by so low that we could see the pilots, and we were sure that they could see us. Our ship was painted white with a large red cross marked on her. The planes flew on by us, and I was glad that they at least would honor the hospital ship.

My group jumped into our motor launch and headed towards the disabled ships; we were going to offer any aid available. All around us, other ships in the harbor were taking a horrible beating. As we pulled over to the ships, they would lower their injured to us, then we would take these casualties back to the USS *Solace*. All morning long we made trip after trip, going to each ship for her injured.

During all of this, the battle had become more intense; there seemed to be turmoil and confusion everywhere. It was inhuman and grotesque. The oil that was leaking from the damaged ships was thick on the water, and men everywhere were trying to swim in it or just stay afloat.

Our boat was loaded with wounded men, all pressed together, all in great pain. With a helpless feeling, we tried to maneuver slowly through the swimmers. Some of those in the water were beyond help, and the heavy coating of fuel and oil made swimming almost impossible. I reached over the side to help someone, anyone. Two men grabbed at my arms, but there wasn't enough room in the boat, so our only hope was to hold on to each other until we could reach safety. I found that I couldn't continue to hold on to both men; our grasps were slipping. I had to release one of them, or lose them both. One oil-slicked arm began to slide from my grip, and I could not prevent what was happening. With two hands, I was determined to succeed in holding on to one of them. Slowly, we made it back to the hospital ship with these casualties and returned for more.

The scene was heartbreaking. Once-proud ships were now completely destroyed. The air was black with thick columns of smoke, climbing upward for miles into the sky. The water was now filled with floating debris covered with oil, which hindered the men in the water more.

The planes kept diving down out of the sun, unloading their bombs, and then flying back into the smoke. This made their escape from our gunners easier. The sounds of the screaming engines as the planes dove down on us was terrifying, and the thunder of the explosion as the bombs hit targets filled our ears. Now came the booming noises from the guns trying to drive off these planes and from orders being shouted back and forth. During all of this, one could hear the pained moaning and screaming of the badly wounded men. We could also smell the terrible odor of burnt flesh, gunpowder, and fuel oil.

As we came alongside of the ships, men came hurdling down from the high decks in a desperate effort to save themselves. This was only causing further injury to some of them as they landed on top of one another. I wished that it would all cease and that I would wake up to find that it was all only a nightmare.

The day continued to be hectic even after the planes left; everywhere around us, there were confusion and disorder. Scenes of violence were visible from every direction, and our ship was crowded with casualties who had been collected from many other ships. During the night, we dozed off occasionally, when we were not worrying about another attack from our adversary. Many of our shipmates had not made it through the night because of the seriousness of their wounds. Now we handled them for a second and last time. We loaded them, wrapped in bed sheets, again into our boat. Each man had a name tag tied on his toe, if possible.

During the attack, we had gone to numerous ships in the harbor, and I had seen hundreds of desperate men struggling to survive, but many courageous acts that had been performed that day are unrecorded and are known only to those who were there and were touched by what they had experienced.

After the attack, I wondered how human beings could be so cruel and terrible to each other. I will never forget the devastating scenes that I witnessed.

—◡—

Ed Johann received a commendation for extraordinary courage in pulling alongside the *Arizona* and rescuing sailors from the burning vessel.

The USS *Phoenix*

WILLIAM RUSH

Within minutes of sighting the first wave of attack planes, gun crews aboard the cruiser *Phoenix* were able to open fire on the planes as they made their diving passes over Battleship Row. Despite receiving heavy antiaircraft fire from the *Phoenix*, Japanese bombers paid little attention to it. Of all the ships in the harbor, she appeared to be among the most likely candidates to be successfully attacked. In addition to being anchored in open water between Aiea Point and the northeast tip of Ford Island, the cruiser was behind the hospital ship *Solace* and in alignment with ships along Battleship Row. Unlike the other ships in the harbor, the USS *Phoenix* was not anchored in a group with other vessels. At 10:10 a.m., the cruiser got underway to make a run for the harbor entrance and the open seas. Fearing the cruiser would be sunk in the harbor thus creating another obstacle for the remaining ships, naval command ordered her to return to her moorage in the East Loch. At around 12:00 a.m., she received new orders and made her way to the harbor entrance, passing the burning and sunken wrecks along Battleship Row and the dry-dock area. The *Phoenix* escaped the attack without any major damage or casualties. Most sailors in Pearl Harbor during the attack considered it miraculous that the cruiser was not resting on the bottom of the harbor by the day's end.

At approximately 7:55 a.m. on 7 December, Seaman William Rush, like many sailors and soldiers, had just finished breakfast.

While enjoying the view of the harbor from the USS *Phoenix*'s decks, Rush witnessed the first wave of enemy planes descending over Pearl Harbor.

———

My story begins in 1928, when my parents moved to the heart of the heart of Dixie—Clanton, Alabama. To survive the Depression, I picked cotton for fifty cents per hundred pounds, and strawberries for one-half cent per quart. I could make up to fifty cents a day when I met those requirements. Credit for my enlisting in the navy goes to my mother, who, during those hot August days in the cotton fields, talked about how I should join the navy and see the world, as that was what she would do if she were a young man. The seed was planted, and when the navy recruiting chief came to the high school in 1939 he spoke of careers in the navy and pointed out the invasion of Poland by the Germans. He hinted to all of us that it would be wise to join now in preparation for a better chance of surviving should the United States declare war in the near future. The money I earned picking cotton and strawberries went for clothing, which made it possible for me to continue in school. I graduated from high school on 27 May 1940, after already having enlisted in the navy in February before my eighteenth birthday. The pay was $21 per month, and I enlisted for a six-year tour. My parents signed for me with the understanding that I should not be called for swearing in until after I graduated. I was sworn in with a group of young men on 10 June 1940 at the recruiting station in the post office in Birmingham, Alabama, and was sent to the Naval Training Station in Norfolk, Virginia, for basic training. Upon completion of basic training, I was assigned to the USS *Phoenix*, as were all graduates whose last name began with the letters R and S. In order to get to the *Phoenix*, we had to go to the West Coast on the USS *Helena*, a sister ship, through the Panama Canal, thence to Long Beach, California. There we transferred to the USS *Argonne* for transporting to Vallejo, California, where the *Phoenix* was in dry dock. Going aboard the *Phoenix* in September 1940, we were welcomed by representatives of each division. The radio officer, Lieutenant Mendte, asked of the recruits, "Any of you know how to type?" I was the only one to hold up my hand, as I had taken a typing course in high school, just for the experience. He then said, "Okay, Rush, you are assigned to C Division as a radioman striker." I had never heard anything about the Morse code other than that Samuel Morse was its inventor. I was assigned to one of the crew chief supervisors of a shift that was next in line for duty that day. My first instructor was named Unger, a radioman second class. After I was assigned a locker and bunk in the compartment where all radiomen were billeted, I went to the radio shack with Unger. He started indoctrinating me in the scope of sending and receiving Morse code, which was to be typed as received, and in using the sending key for transmitting signals. I took my task to heart and mastered the required thirty-five words per minute copying and sending Morse code, as well as all practical factors involved, in fifteen months and was promoted to radioman third class in January 1942.

Until the attack, the *Phoenix* was on maneuvers, convoy escort duty operating out of Pearl Harbor. The last convoy trip was to escort a Presidential Liner ship loaded with army soldiers to Manila, Philippines. While in the Pacific on 12 September 1941, we learned of the death of President Roosevelt's mother and also that, should we come in contact with any Japanese warships that were aggressive, we were to fire upon them.

We returned to Pearl Harbor and resumed maneuvers after reporting back to our assigned task force. On Friday, 5 December 1941, the *Phoenix*, along with the USS *Honolulu*, another sister ship, had had installed the new equipment of radar. There were undeciphered objects being projected on the radar screen that were puzzling, so the *Phoenix* was ordered to stay outside of the harbor with the *Honolulu* while further efforts were made to identify the radar ghosts.

The next morning, 6 December, both ships came into the harbor. The *Phoenix* was anchored near Aiea, behind the USS *Solace*, a hospital ship that was anchored behind the USS *Arizona*. There was a nest of destroyers tied to a tender near us to the north, called the East Loch.

It became obvious after the attack that the radar blips that were picked up on the screen must have been the minisubs. A Japanese chart of Pearl Harbor found in a captured Japanese midget sub had pinpointed our position about 5:00 a.m. on 7 December. They entered the harbor at 4:30 and circled Ford Island, returning to their entrance position at 5:30, pinpointing up-periscope positions of ships.

On Sunday morning, 7 December, a shipmate, another radio operator from Louisiana whose name was Gauthier, and I were all dressed in our white short pants, T-shirts, white socks, shiny black shoes, and white sailor hats, in readiness for church services aboard one of the battleships. He was going to Catholic services, and I was going to the Protestant services; they were being held on different battleships.

After breakfast, about 7:45, the two of us went topside to the fantail of the *Phoenix* to finish eating our apples. We were discussing the anticipated motor-launch trip to the church services, noticing how calm the water was when we threw our apple cores into the water. The air was so fresh, and the surroundings were so serene. Suddenly, general quarters sounded. It was very unusual to have general quarters in port, and especially so early Sunday morning. Everyone seemed to take it as an unexpected annoyance, after already having practiced so much while at sea the past two weeks. No one seemed to be in any special hurry to get to their general-quarters stations, even though they were supposed to report to these stations "on the double." Most did not realize that the alarm signaled a devastating Japanese attack upon Pearl Harbor and all the ships. Japanese planes, torpedo bombers, and minisubmarines attacked what was then America's chief naval base in the Pacific.

For the next four hours or so, I was stationed at my preassigned general-quarters station, which was the antenna repair party, laying flat on my stomach, three decks below, near midship. My duty was to man the sound-powered earphones and relay needed messages and instructions between Main Control on the bridge and Executive Control near the engine rooms, decks below, and to receive any instructions given to our party should any radio antennas be destroyed, necessitating that we go repair and restore them as quickly as possible. I also described to the other men in the party what I was hearing concerning the directions of the planes coming toward us. Five-bombers at two o'clock, two at three o'clock, etc., the kind, and what they had hit.

Our ship was stripped for action in record time: main-deck awnings that were in place were cut down and thrown overboard. Even the gangway was cut loose and dropped into the water, as was all unnecessary equipment, such as paint pots, not needed for war. Those officers and sailors caught ashore came back to the ship via launches and had to come aboard by climbing a Jacob's ladder that was lowered over the side. Other officers and sailors from attacked ships that were burning or sinking also came aboard and reported for duty.

We were underway shortly and trying to make it to open sea. On one side of Ford Island there were overturned ships—the battleship USS *Utah* for one—and midget subs. On the other side was burning oil from the battleships along Battleship Row that were bombed or torpedoed and sinking, keeping us from exiting the harbor. "Boom! Boom! Bang! Bang!" in rapid order, all guns blazing aboard the *Phoenix*. Dust haze was all around our area three decks below, shaken loose from the firing topside. Rivets were jarred out of the bulkheads. I remember how amazed I was to see the dust, for each and every nook and cranny aboard the ship was white-glove inspected each and every week.

Around noon, alongside the damaged battleships, we made a run for the mouth of the harbor. At this point when we were passing the *Arizona*, someone from shore made a photograph of the *Phoenix*, and it looked like the mythical *Phoenix* bird, with all the *Arizona*'s burning oil billowing black smoke in the background. As we passed the USS *Nevada*, which had been deliberately beached to keep from blocking the narrow channel and locking in all seaworthy ships attempting to get out to sea, the nets were opened to let us out. I came to the main deck, having been relieved of my general-quarters station by another radio operator so I could go on duty in the radio shack, at one of the positions for sending and receiving coded messages. When I got topside, I looked ahead of us and saw the USS *St. Louis*, another sister ship, headed at full steam to sea, as was the *Phoenix*. Suddenly I heard someone yell, "Torpedo wake to the starboard headed for us." Everybody fell to the deck, awaiting the explosion; it never came, it passed underneath us. Then another one was launched and was coming toward us; it also passed underneath. Having been stripped earlier must have made the ship ride higher in the water and averted torpedoes that were aimed for us. The *St. Louis*, the *Phoenix*, and the USS *Detroit* were the three largest ships to make it safely to sea from inside the harbor. We went looking for whatever was out in the Pacific: Japanese warships, troopships, submarines, whatever. Each ship went in a different direction in order to cover as large an area surrounding Pearl Harbor as possible and to find and destroy the enemy.

Reports, mostly scuttlebutt or misinformation, were making the rounds, such as that a Japanese troopship had landed at Barber's Point. Just before daybreak on 7 December, a small American minesweeper signaled the World War I destroyer the USS *Ward*, a thousand-ton patrol vessel, that it had spotted an unidentified submarine sliding toward Pearl Harbor. Almost four hours later, the *Ward*'s lookouts picked up sight of the conning tower of a green, two-man midget submarine trailing behind an American supply ship. The skipper of the *Ward*, Lieutenant William W. Outerbridge, called his crew to its battle stations. "Commence fire!" he barked. The midget submarine was fifty yards away when a shell from the number-three gun blasted the conning tower. The stricken sub spun crazily, erupted, and sank. The *Ward* dropped four depth charges on it to seal its grave.

As night drew near, rumors became plentiful. I began to get scared. Up until this point, I had not thought of death or dying. The ship was blacked out, and it was an exceptionally dark night. Everyone was hungry, having not eaten since breakfast. We lined up single file, awaiting our turn to enter the mess hall and receive coffee and G.I. Spam and onion sandwiches, which were delicious. We were not permitted to light a cigarette on topside.

No one seemed to get any sleep for the rest of the night. I was either with the radio gang speculating, or was in the radio shack on duty, as additional circuits had to be set up for copying different frequencies for commands: ship-to-ship commands between the different task forces, ship to shore, and an emergency frequency set to be monitored twenty-four hours a day. There was a radio shack that was always manned, where the main transmitters were located, as well as some receivers that were located near the third main turret and below decks.

We started up a third radio shack near the compartment where I was billeted, next to the water-tenders' compartment four decks below. This third radio shack was to be used should any of the other two receive damage or be put out of action. The main radio shack was just below the signalmen's bridge, which was the first deck from the main deck up, leading farther up to the captain's bridge.

On 8 December, while we were at sea, the emergency billeting already considered for war took place. This meant that some or all specialties and ratings—quartermasters, radiomen, signalmen, water tenders, electricians, coxswains, boatswains, yeomen, machinists, storekeepers, etc.—were billeted and quartered in different watertight compartments. This procedure was to safeguard qualified personnel in each specialty. Should the *Phoenix* be hit in any section, the hit would not wipe out the crew of any specialty. I became acquainted with new shipmates from all areas of the States, making many lasting friendships.

The *Phoenix* remained at sea without any contact with the enemy. We were low on provisions and fuel and made Pearl Harbor on 10 December. While the provisions and oil barges came alongside to fuel and provision the ship, I went to the signal bridge and looked through a telescope and saw boxes on top of boxes stacked at Aiea. There were many launches coming and going to the dock at Aiea. While the launches were dragging the harbor, some had lassoed burned material and bodies that had been found, and they floated to the surface. It made me sick and very sad. However, I was able to mail a letter home, and, when my mother received it, most everything had been censored, except the sentences that I was all right, that I still had my appetite, and "With Love, Son." There were three men from Clanton, Alabama, in Pearl Harbor during the attack. Clifford Smith, who had joined the navy with me, was with me aboard the *Phoenix*. Then there was Dr. Samuel Johnson, a commander, who was killed instantly aboard the *Arizona*.

We made sea early on 11 December, full speed (thirty-five knots per hour) on course toward the States. The *Phoenix* docked in San Francisco. We were not permitted to discuss Pearl Harbor with any of the personnel coming aboard to repair one of the gun barrels that had cracked when it cooled after the attack (it had been fired so fast and continuously). This was to keep the full extent of the damage from reaching the Japanese. We refueled, and provisions were brought aboard. Very early the next morning, we were passing under the Golden Gate, headed to sea, escorting a hospital ship with needed medical supplies and personnel back to Pearl Harbor. We made Pearl Harbor in record time without encountering the enemy.

I remember eating Christmas dinner at the YMCA in downtown Honolulu. We again headed for sea the next day, and the course indicated that we were headed for the States. Four days later, we again docked in San Francisco. Again, we were not to tell anyone from shore about Pearl Harbor. We refueled and got fresh provisions (I can still taste the fresh milk). I awoke the next morning bright and early to find that we were again passing beneath the Golden Gate Bridge, escorting the *Queen Mary*, which had been converted to an army troopship and was rumored to have aboard a complete army division. Our destination was known only to those in need of knowing. After several days, it was scuttlebutted that we were on course and headed for the southwest Pacific. Days later, as we approached the destination, it was obvious that we would make port in New Zealand or Australia.

William Rush finished his wartime duty in 1946 aboard the USS *Missouri*. She had recently returned to the States from Japan, where the surrender of the Japanese had occurred on her decks on 2 September 1945. Rush was discharged from the navy on 10 June 1946. Later that year, he enlisted in the army air corps and served in the army until 1947, when the army air corps became the air force. He remained in the air force until 1962, when he retired with the rank of master sergeant.

The USS *Dobbin*

E. J. ABRISCH

The destroyer tender *Dobbin* was moored with five destroyers northeast off Ford Island when the Pearl Harbor attack began. Although dive-bombers singled out this small nest of ships, the damage to them was minimal. Fragments from near misses killed three men and wounded several others aboard the *Dobbin*. Concentrated antiaircraft fire from the *Dobbin* and the destroyers broke up a second attack before any major damage was done. Throughout the attack, small boats from the *Dobbin* plied the harbor's waters, rescuing survivors from burning and sinking ships.

E. J. "Abe" Abrisch was a machinist mate first class in the machine shop of the USS *Dobbin*. After dropping out of the first year of high school in March 1930, he signed up for a minority enlistment at a Baltimore recruiting office. In November 1941, while in Hawaii, he took the bureau examination for chief petty officer. In early December, he anxiously awaited the results of the test.

It was 7:50 a.m. on 7 December 1941. Reveille had been at 6:50, and, as I lay, fully clothed, on my cot, which was spread in the machine shop of the USS *Dobbin*, a repair ship anchored in Pearl Harbor, I half-read the Sunday morning paper and half-wondered why they wouldn't let us sleep in on a Sunday morning. Even though I had duty that weekend, there wasn't one earthly thing for me to do, except to be there in the event of an emergency. Oh well!

At 7:55, the general alarm bell began to sound, and a voice blared over the intercom: "Away fire and rescue party, away fire and rescue party, on the double." Now it was my job to get the keys from the repair office to open the lock on the handybilly pump, which was in its place by the after gangway topside. I jumped from my cot, complaining bitterly about them holding a drill this early, and on a Sunday morning to boot, got the keys, and took off for topside and the after gangway. When I arrived on topside, running aft, I looked out over the side and I could see a large building on Ford Island burning. My God, it was the real thing, not a drill after all. I quickened my pace, and, seconds later, I was unlocking the lock on the handybilly pump when that voice on the intercom reached my ears again: "Belay fire and rescue party. All hands general quarters, all hands general quarters, on the double." Now I was confused; what in the devil was going on? Weren't they going to send us over to Ford Island to help fight that fire? Anyway, obeying orders, I took off for my general-quarters station, which was repair-party one at the forward gangway, top side.

As I ran forward, passing a shipmate running aft, he yelled, "The Japanese are bombing us!" I thought, "Man, are you joking?" But he was gone by then, and so I dismissed it from my mind as being too crazy to even think about. A moment later, I arrived at my station. I looked out over the harbor and became even more confused, not giving a thought to what my shipmate had yelled to me. There, before my eyes, were planes coming in from the north at a low altitude, one right after the other, going right down over Battleship Row, and each had a large red ball painted on its side, the significance of which didn't dawn on me. I could see spurts of water in the harbor shoot into the air like geysers, and the sounds of explosions reached my ears. "My God, this is one realistic drill. They're going to hurt somebody doing that," my thought continued. Then, suddenly, one of the planes disintegrated in a ball of fire with a loud explosion. The oldest destroyer in commission, the USS *Allen*, had scored a direct hit on the plane's bombload as it passed. Flashes of gunfire appeared from the ships in the harbor, and the sounds of explosions were intermingled with the rat-a-tat-tat of machine-gun fire. I was sick.

I looked over the north end of Ford Island and could see the superstructures of all the battle wagons, which were moored at their pylons. As I watched, the superstructure on the north end of Battleship Row began to move; the USS *Nevada* was getting underway. Gunfire and explosions were increasing everywhere. It seemed like the planes coming in over Battleship Row would never stop. Then suddenly, as I looked back to the north end of Ford Island at the superstructure of the USS *Arizona*, a huge ball of fire appeared, enveloping the entire ship, and the sound of a deafening explosion reached my ears. The whole ship had blown up at once. She began to burn, emitting a huge column of black smoke straight up into the windless sky. As I looked up, I could see other planes diving down toward the battlewagons, releasing their bombloads, and zooming up through the column of smoke as if to avoid detection.

At the top of the column of smoke, another plane emerged in a tight left turn and, as it turned, released three bombs, sort of throwing them towards us. I stood frozen on deck, watching those three bombs heading right towards us. All three hit the stern at once, or so it seemed, because the stern felt as if it had been lifted right out of the water, jarring the entire ship with a tremendous jolt. My thoughts were so mixed up that I just couldn't believe everything that was happening; nothing would fit together.

Soon we got the word from repair-party four, which was below deck and aft, in the area of the explosion, that no serious damage had been done to the hull. Then Damage Control called us to send four men to mount machine guns on the bridge. Four of us grabbed our tools and rushed up to the bridge. Another shipmate and I took the port gun tub, and the other two went to the starboard tub. As we were busily engaged in bolting the mounts to the deck, a flight of Japanese planes appeared at about three thousand feet and to the port. On our port side, we had five destroyers that had come alongside for routine overhaul a few days before. All of their five-inch antiaircraft guns pointed their muzzles skyward and commenced firing on that flight of planes as it progressed toward the starboard. Finally, the USS *Phelps*, which was immediately along our port side, was firing her guns. The muzzles not more than twenty feet away were engulfing the gun tube, occupied by myself and a shipmate in flames, heat, and smoke. I were in, engulfing it in flames, heat, and smoke. A little more, and those shells would be hitting the wing tub. We scrambled out of there, but fast.

A few minutes later, when our hearts started beating again, we finished mounting the machine guns, gathered up our tools, and returned to our general-quarters station on the main deck. We hadn't been back five minutes when that voice on the intercom blared forth again: "All men with blood type A-negative report to the sick bay." I was blood type A-negative. I raced aft to the sick bay, and, when I arrived, there with the others; we were told to stand by. It was then we learned that three men, Howard Carter, J. W. Baker, and Roy Gross, had been hit by shrapnel from those three bombs that had straddled the stern. They had been near misses and not direct hits, as I had previously thought. We also learned that Carter and Gross were dead and that Baker was seriously injured and being prepared for a transfusion. The doctor appeared in the hatch of the sick bay a few minutes later and dismissed us. Baker had died on the operating table. I walked back to my station in a fog, my mind racing with thoughts of my three shipmates, and somehow I was not able to accept the fact that they were dead.

Sometime later, after I arrived back on station, the voice on the intercom screamed: "Hit the deck; they're strafing us." I hit the deck right up against the bulkhead and tried to curl up under a small kapok life jacket for protection. It was then that the full magnitude of the situation hit me like a ton of bricks. I was trembling, and fear swept my entire body, giving me a feeling that I shall never be able to describe. As all men do at a time like that, I turned to God and said, "Our Father, who art in Heaven . . ."

It was 7:55 a.m., 7 December 1971. In my full-dress navy chief petty officer's uniform, I stood on the gently rolling deck of a fifty-foot motorboat, which was laying to, over the exact spot where my ship had been thirty years before. They say that you can never recapture the past, but I wonder. As I stood there, vivid memories, much like a kaleidoscope, began flashing through my mind and gradually began to come into focus.

At this point, I felt a light tap on my shoulder, and, as I turned to look through the now-blurred kaleidoscope of my thoughts, I vaguely saw a face and heard a voice say, "Would you like to return to the dock now, Chief?" I remember answering, "No, not yet, just a minute." As I turned the other way; there, coming into clear focus, were two shipmates who had been with me on that day of infamy and who were now again with me on that motorboat. All three of us stiffened to attention and looked up into the clear blue sky over Pearl Harbor.

Once again, I turned to God. As I lowered my eyes, I found that I was looking right over the north end of Ford Island, at the exact spot where that ball of fire had been just a few minutes before, it seemed. Only now, all I could see was the top of a flagpole with a proudly waving American flag. Without a word, the three of us saluted as one. I turned away and looked toward the coxswain and said, "You may return to the dock now, coxswain." The three of us went back to our seats in the stern of the motorboat. We three twenty-year-retired chief petty officers brought out our handkerchiefs and wiped a tear or two from our eyes. The engine in the motorboat roared to life, getting the boat underway and carrying us back into the reality of 7 December 1971.

——•——

E. J. "Abe" Abrisch made chief machinist mate on the first promotion list published after the Pearl Harbor attack. He remained aboard the USS *Dobbin* for the war's duration. In March 1950, he retired from the navy as a machinery repair chief. Pursuing a hobby of woodworking during his retirement, Abrisch has constructed a four-foot-long detailed wooden model of the USS *Dobbin*. He has also built a three-foot-diameter, three-dimensional copy of the logo of the Pearl Harbor Survivors Association, which is on display at Pearl Harbor in the National Park Service's Visitor's Center at the USS *Arizona* Memorial.

The USS *Worden*

JOHN BEASLEY

Contrary to Japanese claims and early American newspaper accounts, the Japanese attack on Oahu did not leave the US Pacific Fleet on the bottom of Pearl Harbor. Estimates show that half the fleet was absent on 7 December. Of the 103 ships in the harbor on that day, only 19 were sunk or damaged. Fortunately for the bulk of the fleet, the attack centered on eight of the nine fleet battleships moored along Battleship Row. Although most ships escaped Japanese bombs, they were not spared from the attack's immediate and far-reaching effects. The destroyer USS *Worden* was one of the fortunate ships. Anchored off the northern tip of Ford Island, among a group of five destroyers, the *Worden* was only one of the many defenseless targets available to bombers, who had missed their primary targets along Oahu's eastern and western sides.

The story of John Beasley is typical of those of sailors who found themselves on ships on the periphery of the attack. For the most part, they were unable to come to the immediate defense of sister ships. But they did fill the sky with a barrage of antiaircraft rounds in a futile effort to thin out and slow down the swarming attack planes.

My story begins in May 1934, when I graduated from Garfield High School in Terre Haute, Indiana. It was very difficult to find work in the 1930s, and I worked wherever I could find a job, including farm, factory, and railroad work. In October 1937, I went to the navy recruiting office to enlist and was put on the waiting list (I only had fifty-nine ahead of me).

Finally, on 22 March 1938, I became number one on the list and was sworn in. After completing sixteen weeks of basic training at the Great Lakes Naval Training Station, I went to Basic Electrical School at the San Diego Naval Training Station for another sixteen weeks. Upon completion of electrical school, I was assigned to the destroyer *Worden*. In September 1939, the *Worden*, along with a large group of our fleet, was sent to Pearl Harbor as the Hawaiian Detachment and was there on 7 December 1941. By that time, I was a second-class electrician's mate and had taken the first-class examination, which I passed. However, my first-class rating was not yet effective. It became so about two or three weeks later.

On 7 December, I had rated liberty and was intending to go over to Honolulu. I had not eaten breakfast, as I planned to eat when I got to town, but was sitting topside reading the Sunday-morning Honolulu newspaper.

For several days, the first division of destroyers, consisting of the *Worden*, *Hull*, *Dewey*, and *McDonough*, along with the squadron leader *Phelps*, was alongside the destroyer tender *Dobbin*, undergoing tender overhaul. On the *Worden*, two of our four boilers, both throttles for our main engines, and our evaporators were torn down. The tender was supplying the *Worden* with steam, electricity, and water.

About the time I had finished reading the comics of the Sunday paper, I heard a series of explosions aft of the ships. There had been work going on at the Ford Island airstrip, and I assumed that the explosions were connected with that work. It was an hour or two before my liberty started, so I decided to walk back to the fantail and watch the work for a while before going ashore. The first things I saw were two or three torpedo planes coming in low over the cane fields and water. I thought to myself, "If they don't fly higher than that, they might hit some ship's mast."

About that time, they dropped their torpedoes, which struck the old *Utah*. The *Utah* began to roll over almost immediately, indicating that none of her watertight doors were closed. As the torpedo planes pulled up and started to climb, I could see big red circles on the underside of the wings. It was like someone had thrown a bucket of ice water on me as I realized what it meant. I took one quick look around and could see numerous columns of smoke and many airplanes, none of which was ours. I knew we had to get going, so I ran to the quarterdeck, where we had a switch to sound the general alarm. I tripped the general-alarm switch without slowing down, and I headed for my battle station in the Internal Communications (I.C.) room. In the I.C. room were the fire-control switchboard, our telephone switchboard, the gyrocompass, emergency generator, etc. The I.C. room was on our third deck, down below the mess hall and directly above the number-two magazine.

It was just five days before my birthday, and I remember thinking that it was too bad I would not live to reach twenty-five. I only had three more months to do on my four-year enlistment, and I was one of the newer men on the ship. Many of the crew had been on the *Worden* since she was commissioned, and they knew every detail of the ship and her machinery. It was nice that we had a well-trained and experienced crew because the *Dobbin* disconnected our steam line, water lines, and electric cables and told us to go to sea. Our crew put the ship back together with only hand lanterns and flashlights, and she ran for eleven months before going to the Navy Yard. In that eleven months, she participated in numerous patrols with the carriers *Lexington*, *Hornet*, and *Saratoga* and took part in the Coral Sea Battle, the Battle of Midway, and in seventy-seven days of fighting around Guadalcanal.

Our captain, most of the senior officers, and several of the chiefs had gone ashore for the weekend and were not back yet. We sent the captain's gig over to the officers' landing to wait for him, and it brought him and several of the other officers and chiefs back. However, we were halfway down the channel, going to sea, before the gig got back, and we picked it up on the run.

We had a first-class electrician's mate on the *Worden* named Charles Ross, from Baltimore. Charley had been aboard the *Worden* for several months and he had been transferred to her from the US Asiatic Fleet. While in East Asia, Charley had been living with a Japanese girl he called "Peachy." "Peachy" had a brother in the Japanese naval air force. During the Pearl attack, whenever a Japanese plane would come very close, Charley would point at it and say, "Don't shoot that one down—he might be my brother-in-law!" Charley always said that he would have married "Peachy," but, before World War II, the navy frowned on it. I always thought that Charley was transferred from the US Asiatic Fleet because he was losing his proper perspective of the American way of life. Nevertheless, Charley was a good electrician and had a very cool head under fire.

We also had a second-class fireman named Kislowski. Kislowski did not smoke. During one of the lulls of the Pearl attack, however, someone offered him a cigarette and he took it. For the next two days, he smoked one cigarette after another, until someone asked him when he had decided to start smoking. He threw away his pack of cigarettes. As far as I know, Kislowski never did smoke again, and we were on the same ship for nearly a year after that.

When I got to the I.C. room, I started the gyrocompass, made the proper setups on the fire-control and telephone switchboards, and put on my telephone headset. I had to listen in on two different circuits in case there were changes to be made in either of the switchboard setups. Although I could not see what was going on after I reached the I.C. room, I could hear everything that was said by telephone on the ship.

Directly below the I.C. room was the number-two magazine, and the exit hatch for the magazine was just outside the I.C. room entrance. Two men in the magazine were sending five-inch shells up on the ammunition hoist. Neither man had more than half the time in the navy than I did, so both looked to me for moral support. A couple of times, one would stick his head up out of the hatch and say, "If this ship sinks, how will we get out of here?" And I told him, "Don't worry about it. If the ship sinks, we're not going to get out." One turned sort of green when I told him that, but he went back to loading ammunition.

Twice over the telephones, I heard claims that the *Worden* had shot down an attacking plane, but I did not see it. So many ships were firing at the planes, I imagine it would be hard to say just who had shot down a plane. I know that several times dive-bombers made runs on us; but because five destroyers were tied up side by side, the antiaircraft fire would be almost impenetrable. Each destroyer of the first division had five five-inch thirty-eight dual-purpose guns, plus four fifty-caliber machine guns. The squadron leader, *Phelps*, had eight five-inch guns and two mounts of four barrel 1.1-inch antiaircraft guns. All this firepower was concentrated in a space of about two hundred by four hundred feet. I could tell that some bombs were coming pretty close by the noise and the feel. When you are below the waterline and a bomb lands close by, it is like being in a fifty-gallon oil drum that someone is hitting with a sledgehammer. Especially on a destroyer, which had side plates that were each three-sixteenths of an inch thick.

Even with all the excitement, our engineers got our boilers, throttles, and evaporators put back together, got up a head of steam, and cleared the channel buoy for the entrance to Pearl Harbor just as the last of the attacking planes were leaving. As we passed the *Arizona*, heading for the channel, I could smell the burning oil and flesh coming out of the I.C. room ventilator.

When the *Worden* got to the open sea, we joined up with a few cruisers and other destroyers and headed northwest at high speed in an effort to contact Japanese ships. We never engaged in combat with them, for which I am very thankful. We gave up trying to locate the Japanese fleet in late afternoon or early evening and returned to Pearl Harbor. It was truly a mess. We got back around 10:00 p.m. and finally got something to eat and drink.

I will always feel that our fleet could have been warned well ahead of time to avoid such a disaster, if President Roosevelt had not wanted to make sure the United States had a good excuse to get into the war in order to help England. The reason I say this is because, in December 1940, we replaced all of our five-inch ammunition with new ammunition. We also took the practice heads off our torpedoes and put on live warheads. And when we had patrol duty around Pearl Harbor and Honolulu, our orders were to sink any ship or submarine outside certain lanes in and out of the area. Not to challenge or chase off, but to sink. If enough was known to put us on that much of an alert, I feel that much more was known.

In November 1942, John Beasley returned to Pearl Harbor to attend Gyrocompass School. Before he could return to the USS *Worden*, she sank off the Aleutian Islands on 12 January 1943. Chief Electrician's Mate Beasley was transferred to the USS *Florikan*. Two years later, he was transferred to the submarine tender USS *Sperry*, where he remained until the end of the war. In October 1945, he returned to the States and was discharged.

The USS *MacDonough*

GEORGE PATTERSON

The USS *MacDonough* was one of five destroyers anchored together in a tight row off the northeast tip of Ford Island. Like her sister ships in the group, the *MacDonough* escaped the attack without any major damage. The destroyer managed to splash one attack plane before heading out to sea to join the other surviving ships of the various task forces in the search for the enemy. For the next three and one-half months, the USS *MacDonough* performed scouting duties in the area southwest of Oahu.

George Patterson was aboard the *MacDonough* on the morning of 7 December 1941. His colorful narrative provides an emotional look at the events before, during, and after the attack.

Times were tough during the 1930s. In 1938, I joined the Civilian Conservation Corps. At the time, I thought I would be stationed in Berryville, Arkansas, my hometown. We were loaded on a bus and sent straight to Little Rock, to what had been old Camp Robinson during World War I. At this time, the Civil Conservation Corps was partly under the supervision of the army, and, after a week's processing and so forth, we were loaded onto a troop train (army) and sent clear up into the panhandle of northern Idaho! They unloaded us right in the middle of the Nez Perce National Forest! Camp O'Hara, Company 5704. The company was composed of Arkansas, Kansas, and Missouri men who were acquainted with delicate instruments such as a double-bit axe and a crosscut saw. The chain saw was unheard of.

This is the most beautiful forest in the United States! It is also full of large game, all sorts. Here we worked with the Forestry Service of Idaho. In winter, rain or shine, we built roads, parks, trails, barns, and the Lowell Ranger Station, on the banks of the Sellway River. When summer arrived, the whole northern panhandle of Idaho caught on fire! We fought forest fires from July until September, and they were finally exhausted by the fall rains.

After one year of this life, I requested a transfer back to Arkansas. This time, I landed thirty miles west of Little Rock in the Ouachita National Forest, located in the Boston Mountains. After another year with the Forestry Service of Arkansas, I was ready to try something besides dust, mud, ditches, and digging stumps!

In October 1940, my friend Frank Stanton of Bentonville, Arkansas, and I requested a discharge from our captain in order to join the navy. However, as he was a captain in the army, and a good one, he attempted in several ways to get us to join the army. When he found us convinced, he gave his consent and provided us with transportation to Little Rock.

I was born with weak muscles in the left eye, at least that's what the navy called them, and this almost prevented me from getting in. An old chief gunner's mate checked my heart and then remarked, "Now we're getting back into battery." I was to learn later that he had used an old gunnery expression, which I'm sad to say one never hears anymore. He simply meant that my heart was good and that he now could continue his examination. I suppose the expression has gone with the sails of the fleet. At any rate, my old Civil Conservation Corps friend and I both made navy and went through boot training together, in the 82nd Company in San Diego.

I completed boot camp, but did not have enough education to be assigned to a school. I can recall one of the questions they threw at me, "Why did you join the navy?" I answered, "To defend my country from its enemies and give my life, if necessary." I have thought back many times at just how close I came to doing that very thing! And at that time, I did not have any insurance with God! I was a sinner.

We had completed boot camp, and Frank Stanton obtained a three-day leave to Los Angeles. Oh, blast his eyes, this is what separated us! While he was on leave, they shipped me out bag and hammock aboard the *Downes*, for further transfer to Pearl Harbor. One week later Frank Stanton shipped out on the *Shaw*.

Oh, how little does the poor sailor know of the uncharted waters that await him. The ill-fated *Downes*, which I first went to sea in, was soon to be pulverized in a Pearl Harbor dry dock. And the *Shaw*, the ship of my old Arkansas forestry friend, was to be directly astern of the *Downes*, and also in dry dock.

I found the crew of the *Downes* to be a swell bunch of fellows. By the time we reached Pearl Harbor, I had become acquainted with most of the first division. The ship's anchor had no more then hit the bottom of Pearl than the word was passed for all recruits to lay over to the port side, bag and hammocks. We were loaded into the port whaleboat to be transferred to another ship. This time for duty, we hoped.

Minutes later, we were climbing over the port guardrail of the only ship in the US Pacific Fleet, my first love and my home. Oh, how proud I was to become a member of that ship's company. The destroyer *MacDonough*, moored fore and aft. Two buoys holding her right in the middle of the Harbor of Pearls! The officer of the deck, Lieutenant Junior Grade Frederick Matthews, was at the guardrail to welcome us aboard. As I came over the life line of this vessel, my first thoughts were that she seemed so clean. I soon found out why; her discipline was very strict. She was an extremely taut ship.

She was commanded by Captain J. M. McIsaac, who must have had thirty years' service at that time. The ship had been shifted to her new home port, Pearl Harbor, as part of Destroyer Division One. Her three sisters were the *Hull*, the *Dewey*, and the *Wardon*, all four had the same class as the *Farragut*. The *MacDonough* was the third ship of this name. Launched at Boston Navy Yard on 22 August

1934, she had been sponsored by Miss Rose Shaler MacDonough, granddaughter of Commander T. MacDonough.

Before the sneak attack of the enemy, I had advanced to the rate of seaman first class (demon seaman) and had learned the basics of seamanship and gunnery. My battle station was number four gun; I was first powder man. This was before the twenty- and forty-millimeter guns; at this time all we had to repel aircraft with was our fifty-caliber machine guns. In fact, the very thought of an aircraft able to destroy a battleship was ridiculous.

My cleaning station was the boat deck, located up between the two stacks. The ship had four whaleboats, two starboard and two port. I had become interested in the boats and had been appointed acting coxswain of the *Captain's Gig*, a whaleboat with a canopy, which took the ship's officer to shore and back. We were told that war was impending, sometime before the sneak attack (we could see it hanging out like a peacoat sleeve), and they compelled us to turn two of our boats in, thus reducing the threat of flying wooden splinters in battle.

Six months or so before the attack, Japanese sampans were off the coast of Hawaii, thicker than hair on a dog's back! We were told that these were Jap fishing boats. We learned later, the hard way, that each and every one of these so-called fishing boats was equipped with the most modern radios and was reporting to Japan every move made by the US Pacific Fleet. As a lookout, I can remember zeroing my field glasses in on them and thinking to myself, "Boy, they must be fishin' up a storm." No doubt, seamen of the *Arizona* thought the same thing.

The Japanese freighters were doing a roaring business with America at this time. We would meet them going in empty and coming out of our western ports loaded down to their Plimsoll marks with good, hard American steel and scrap iron. We would soon learn, but again the hard way, just exactly what they were going to do with their cargo.

The respect shown at sea by the rising sun to the US Pacific Fleet came to a close about a week before the sneak attack. We were at sea, and I had the afterdeck lookout watch, wearing earphones and standing by our streaming colors. My eyes fixed on that fluttering red meat-ball of a rag. I was waiting anxiously for it to dip, with the halyard of Old Glory held tightly in my hand. At last, the order came that I had been listening for, "Stand by the streaming colors." I was at the ready, and the Japanese flag was yet at the peak. Oh, marvel of marvels, as we passed each other, our starboard to their port, my earphones crackled with the order, "Do not dip the streaming colors." In a week's time, we would learn, again the hard way . . . blood. We would view that same red meatball at a different perspective and circumstance.

I was sacked out on Sunday morning, 7 December 1941. Ensign R. W. Clark was the only commissioned officer aboard. He was the commanding officer, as well as officer of the deck. The chief gunner's mate had the gangway watch. Our ship and the *Phelps* were receiving a scheduled overhaul in company of Destroyer Division One. These ships were all alongside the *Dobbin*, berth X-2, Pearl Harbor. As the *MacDonough* was the outboard ship of the nest, her port side was clear. All her power was off, and she was being serviced by the *Dobbin*.

The ship's general alarm was sounded about 8:00 a.m., and, as the word came to "Man your battle stations," I came groping my way out of the hatch on the fantail, blinking like a groundhog in the bright sunlight, and thinking, "We're drilling now on Sundays!" I could hear the distant explosions and was trying to figure out what sort of plane that white one was, with the round red balls on his wing tips. And why was the *Oglala* listing so heavily to port? I could not believe my eyes. As I stood spellbound, her whole topside slid under and she rolled bottom up, and I could see sailors sliding down her wet, glistening bottom, right into the drink.

The next thing I remember was the heavy explosions over toward Battleship Row. All of the battle wagons seemed to be engulfed in a terrible black smoke that raised ever higher and higher. Aboard the *MacDonough*, everyone was running. Automatically, I was headed for the number-four gun on the afterdeck. Our machine gunners were setting up their fifty calibers, breaking out the ammo and belts. Our magazines were all padlocked, and the padlocks were being knocked off with marline spikes, fire axes, or whatever was handiest.

About two more jumps and I could have been at my battle station, when I happened to think of the captain. I had to get to my boat at once and bring the ship's officers back so we could get to the open sea! With these thoughts running through my mind, I had straddled our port-side life line and was catwalking the boat boom in order to get to the rope ladder that dangled down into the captain's gig. I could hear someone shouting at me, and I glanced over my shoulder to see the gangway watch, our chief gunner's mate, with both hands cupped to his mouth. His orders were, "Get to your battle station, Patt; I'll send the quartermaster after the old man!" I can remember, as though it were yesterday, how relieved his orders made me feel, and in three jumps I was on my own, just in time to receive the first case of powder. It was being passed through the hatches by hand.

Below decks, it was black as pitch, and my shipmates had managed to get into those locked magazines and pass the powder and projectiles topside. Without power, all guns had to be trained and elevated by hand. And, above the roar of the main battery, I could hear the constant hammer of our machine gunners.

The heavy smell of powder smoke, the scream of descending bombs, and the roar of our main battery did not seem to faze our gun crew's performance. When I think back now of how determined the crew worked and loaded those old five-inchers, it makes my heart swell with pride. Those grueling, relentless loading drills of the past paid off in times like these. All hands acted automatically.

The dive-bombers came screaming down at us from out of the sun. At the same time, torpedo planes sneaked in low to lay their deadly shimmering eggs. They must have come from every bearing of the compass. All of our guns could bear to port, and we did our best to give them everything we had.

They gave us credit for splashing two Jap planes. Hit by a five-incher, one plane completely disintegrated. Another plane, hit by our fifty-caliber machine gun, disappeared in a trail of smoke and flame and crashed into a cane field. "Pure cane sugar from Hawaii." They flew so close on our port beam that one could reach out with a swab handle and touch them. The Good Lord had to have been with the nest of Destroyer Division One this fatal morning. This is where I first really learned to pray!

Our quartermaster returned to the ship about 9:00. He had picked up the captain and all the ship's officers. The attack was over, and our captain was the first officer to come aboard. The officers boarded by a Jacob's ladder, and, as the skipper's head came even with the life line, he was looking fore and aft. He sang out loud and clear, "Get these lines off. Let's get this vessel underway." This we did, and, if, I remember correctly, some of them were cut with fire axes. We picked up a swimming survivor from the *Arizona* on our way out. The *MacDonough* had expended 172 rounds of five-inch thirty-eight-caliber ammunition.

Frank Stanton, my forestry friend, made it through the war, but I yet don't know how. We shouted at each other from a distance as he was running to catch a plane. Think he said he had married a New York gal. A damn Yankee!

I was discharged from the navy in October 1946. I returned to the knobs of northwest Arkansas, back to my Ozarks, back to the hills that I love so dearly.

—◆—

After his discharge from the navy in 1946, George Patterson enlisted in his hometown National Guard unit. When the Korean War broke out, his field artillery unit was activated, and he was in the middle of another war. After returning home from Korea, he transferred to a navy reserve unit nearby. While in the reserve, he made chief gunner's mate. He served twenty-three years in the military. The postscript to the Pearl Harbor experience of George Patterson serves as the epilogue for many Americans who remember the attack and the years of war that followed: "Every December the 7th, until I draw my last breath of life, I will again and again see that rising sun. May God forgive me, but I shall never have any respect for the Japanese race or their land of cherry trees and flowers."

The USS *Selfridge*

HENRY WRUBEL

In 1940, after two years of operating in the southern California area, the *Selfridge* was reassigned to Pearl Harbor. On the morning of the attack, the destroyer, having just completed an escort run from Palmyra Island, was moored in berth X-9 in the East Loch. Within five minutes of the opening rounds of the battle, the *Selfridge* fired on approaching enemy planes. Because she was on the perimeter of the primary target area, she did not come under direct enemy fire and therefore was undamaged. Throughout both phases of the attack, her crew produced a continuous barrage of antiaircraft fire. By 1:00 p.m., the *Selfridge*, manned by a crew from various ships, was underway to join the makeshift fleet of cruisers and destroyers patrolling off Oahu.

Henry Wrubel had joined the navy in 1936 at a recruiting office in Albany, New York. After boot camp at Newport, Rhode Island, he was assigned to the USS *Selfridge*.

The events leading up to the attack on Pearl Harbor are worth mentioning. I was in the navy, serving aboard the *Selfridge* as acting chief torpedoman, in charge of the torpedo gang.

In late October 1941, we were assigned to escort an inter-island steamer that was taking a group of marines and supplies to Canton Island, in the Gilbert Islands chain, to reinforce the existing garrison. We crossed the equator and I became shellback. While at Canton

Island, the ocean was so deep we were unable to anchor, and it was necessary to cruise back and forth to maintain headway at about three to four knots. The unloading of the steamer had to be done by bringing a barge alongside, as there were no facilities for docking.

This, of course, was time-consuming. After completion of unloading, we proceeded to set course for Christmas Island, where the steamer was to pick up an empty barge and tow it back to Pearl Harbor. The steamer was capable of a top speed of twelve knots and cruised about nine to ten knots. However, after she took the barge in tow, her speed was reduced to four to five knots. All of the slow cruising affected our fuel and food supplies.

About five or six days out of Christmas Island, we received a message from Pearl in which we were advised to "Take all necessary action, as there were hostile submarines in the area." Accordingly, our captain ordered all depth charges to be armed.

The entire trip was about fifty-five days. In the meantime, our food supply was nearly exhausted; we were down to canned Vienna sausages and canned salmon. The cooks did an excellent job of varying different methods in the preparation of the meals.

When we were twenty-four hours of steaming from Pearl, the captain requested that we be released from further escort duty. Permission from the captain of the steamer was given. We then proceeded to Pearl at normal cruising speed. We arrived at Pearl on 6 December, midmorning. Our orders were to proceed to the fuel dock for refueling. On the way to the fuel dock, we received a message canceling refueling until Monday, 8 December 1941. We were assigned to berth X-9, East Loch. The *Whitney* was outboard the *Selfridge*, *Case*, *Tucker*, *Reid*, and *Conyngham*. After the ship was secured, liberty was granted to those off duty.

Sunday morning there was no early reveille, so anyone not on duty could sleep late, which I did and missed breakfast. I woke up shortly after breakfast, and, after cleaning up, we went to the torpedo shack and made a pot of coffee. While waiting for the coffee to brew, I was joined by Joe Witucki, TM first class. Shortly before 8:00 a.m., we got our second cup of coffee and went outside to enjoy the early morning. We were standing by the rail on the port side of the number-two torpedo mount, about midships. From here we could see the east side of Ford Island, where the *Detroit* and the *Raleigh* were tied up, followed by the target ship *Utah*. Joe called to my attention the low-flying planes that were approaching from the east to the west and remarked, "Hey, look, they are making torpedo runs. This is sure a hell of a day to be practicing. Don't they know it's Sunday?" About that time, we saw them launching their torpedoes and heard explosions. Again Joe exclaimed, "They are using live torpedoes!" About the same moment, a plane swooped over our stern, and, when he winged up, we saw the red ball. Joe hollered, "They are Japs," as general quarters was sounding.

My normal battle station was the bridge, manning the torpedo directors. We were in port, tied up, unable to get underway, and I concentrated on making all the preparations we could. I instructed the torpedo crews to top off all the torpedoes with air. I went to the stern depth-charge racks, as they were already armed but set on "safe." We set all charges at six hundred feet. I then instructed one of the torpedo strikers to go to the bridge to operate the remote-control lever, cautioning him to only move the lever aft, which drops a charge into the cradle, at our signal. When he was on the bridge, we signaled by a hand motion to activate the lever. He did this but, in the excitement of battle, forgot his instructions. He activated the lever aft, then forward, and as a result we dropped a depth charge overboard. Luckily, being set at six hundred feet, it did not explode. Needless to say, I went to the bridge to supervise the operation for the port rack.

There was little else the torpedo gang could do from then on. This gave us time to observe some of the action. We could see the dense black clouds over the battleships and hear explosions and antiaircraft fire. Our main battery consisted of four twin-mounted five-inch guns, single-purpose, useless for antiaircraft. We had two mounts of four-barrel 1.1-inch antiaircraft guns each, one forward, one aft. Two fifty-caliber machine guns were mounted amidships on a deck around our number-two stack. Most of the attacking aircraft came in from the starboard side or across the stern. Because our ship was alongside the nest, the fifty-caliber on the starboard side had an arc of about ten degrees to fire. The forward 1.1-inch guns saw little action, but the rear ones had plenty of opportunity. The 1.1-inch guns had a tendency to jam. The gunner's mate in charge did manage to keep the gun firing at all times when a target was available, and even sometimes with only one barrel.

Our captain, Commander Craig, had returned aboard during the attack. Because we were low on fuel and food, he began dispatching work crews to obtain food, supplies, and extra antiaircraft ammo from the tender. Nobody needed any urging. I did notice, from my battle station on the bridge, an officers' mess attendant carrying two boxes of 1.1-inch ammo, one on each shoulder. Normally, two men would carry one box between them. In fact, I could almost swear he was running with them.

Time meant nothing, and it seemed to go on forever. Because we could not get underway without fuel, we were at a standstill. A fuel barge, hell-bent-for-leather, trying to get out of the harbor to a dock, was spotted. Our captain hailed her captain and persuaded him to come alongside and fuel us. After hearing our predicament, he agreed and proceeded to give us our much-needed fuel. The barge didn't fill us completely, but gave us enough to get underway for a few days steaming. At about 1:00 p.m., we pulled out of the nest and headed seaward. On the way out of Pearl, we saw the cruiser *Raleigh*, which had sunk, and her decks just awash. The target ship *Utah* had capsized. The battleship *Nevada* was beached. We made it out to open sea and immediately were ordered to patrol our given sector.

We remained at general quarters all during the day and night. Someone on the beach directed all our movements over the TBS all through the night. All the ships were maneuvering, and whoever was in control did a wonderful job. Running under darkened ships, not knowing who was at sea or what was going on.

I guess it was 10:00 p.m. before I got anything to eat. That ham sandwich and cup of coffee never tasted so good, as I had had nothing to eat all day.

The next day, because of our shortage of fuel and supplies, we were ordered back into Pearl to refuel, take on supplies, and pick up our gig and whaleboat (which we left behind to help as needed) and any stragglers who had not made it back to the ship. The shock and dismay at the devastation are difficult to put into writing. But the anger was there, and the determination to avenge the death of so many.

Henry Wrubel remained aboard the USS *Selfridge* until 1943, when he was promoted and assigned to Australia as the assistant officer in charge of Travelling Circus Number One, a mobile torpedo unit in Townsville, Australia. Later, he was promoted to ensign while aboard the USS *Langley*. After completing Officer Candidate School in Norfolk, Virginia, he was assigned as a torpedo officer aboard the USS *Hugh Purvis*, where he remained until the end of the war. He was discharged from service in San Francisco on 25 January 1946.

The USS *Utah*

MELVIN BACON

The USS *Utah* was moored in berth F-11 on the northwest side of Ford Island, astern of the light cruisers USS *Raleigh* and USS *Detroit* and forward of the seaplane tender USS *Tangier*. Despite having a large number of antiaircraft guns aboard, the USS *Utah* was never able to fire a shot at the attacking planes. Because she was a target ship in current operations, all her antiaircraft guns were covered with steel housing, and her machine guns were dismantled and stowed below deck.

At 8:01 a.m., as the crew began raising the ship's colors on the fantail, the USS *Utah* received the first of two torpedo hits and immediately started to list to port. Within minutes of the first torpedo hit, word was passed to abandon ship. As the ship began to roll, the six-by-twelve timbers used for target practice began to shift, thereby hampering escape efforts. As men scurried topside, Chief Water Tender Peter Tomich remained below to secure the boilers and evacuate the engineering spaces, while Fireman Second Class John B. Vaessen remained in the dynamo room to ensure that the ship had enough power for lights. For his efforts, Tomich received the Medal of Honor posthumously, just as Vaessen received the Navy Cross.

At 8:12 a.m., the mooring lines snapped and the ship rolled over on her beam ends, the keel plainly showing. Sailors still aboard dove into the water and swam to nearby shore, while others sought refuge on the adjacent mooring quays to avoid Japanese strafers still circling Ford Island. Shortly after Lieutenant Commander Solomon Isquith and other crew members reached shore, they heard knocking from within the overturned hull. Ignoring the strafing, Isquith and a handful of volunteers returned to the hull and cut a hole in the plating with a cutting torch from the USS *Raleigh*. Ten men clambered from the hole in the steel tomb. The last man out was Vaessen, who had made his way to the bottom of the capsized ship with only a flashlight and a wrench.

At the time of the attack, Machinist's Mate Second Class Melvin Bacon was working in the ship's water-distilling plant. His account vividly relates the drama that unfolded above and below the decks.

I was on watch in the water-distilling plant, also called evaporators. The distilling plant, which was two decks below the main deck, was used to distill seawater for the boilers, bilges, and the ship's tanks. I had just finished taking the 0800 water meter reading when the first torpedo hit. The whole plant shook violently. Gauges, pumps, and other equipment went haywire. The air-compressor, a reciprocating engine with a large flywheel, started pounding like a dozen war drums. Pump voltages were frantically going up and down. Almost immediately, another torpedo hit and the ship began sharply listing to the port side. The first thing to come to mind was that a Navy PBY plane had struck the ship, since we were right next to Ford Island. I immediately began to secure the plant, which was proper procedure during an emergency. I was closing a six-inch auxiliary steam valve when the power and lights went out. Seconds later, the lights came back on long enough for me to make it topside. I darted through the living compartment to get to the ladder for the next deck. While passing our sleeping quarters, which was to the starboard side and divided by an open hatch, I saw a buddy of mine amazingly still asleep in his bunk and yelled to awaken him. As I pulled myself up the ladder, water was gushing in about twelve feet away. The ship continued to roll as I pulled myself up the last ladder. When I made it topside, the main deck was engulfed in dark, churning water from the capsizing ship. My sense of relief from being trapped below deck was short-lived. Once I got outside, I was afraid of being crushed underneath the weight of the entire ship.

On the main deck, I didn't notice any fire or debris and still had no idea what caused the explosions. I staggered, then crawled to the starboard side of the ship, which was rising higher and higher out of the water. It may have been a few seconds or a few minutes, but I soon found myself crawling underneath the deck rail and scooting and sliding down the side and bottom of the ship. Slipping in to the water, I heard cries for help from other sailors already in the water. I started to swim to shore when I saw a motor launch attempting to rescue five or six men who were grouped near me. The coxswain from the launch asked me if I needed help. I shook my head, hollered, "No," and continued swimming. I made it to a nearby mooring platform and somehow on my first try climbed about eight feet to get to the top. Looking around the harbor, I could see diving planes strafing sailors who were still in the water. I quickly jumped back in and swam to land. I dragged myself from the water and sprinted for a large pipeline ditch only a short distance away. Six of my shipmates were already in the trench. We watched as Jap planes made another run over the harbor. One slowed and dropped a bomb on the ship which was aft of the *Utah*. If I had a rock or a baseball, I believe I could have come near hitting the plane. That's how close it seemed.

When the attack was over, I went with a group of sailors to a nearby building to get a change of clothes. No success in finding any clothes, but I did get covered with Mercurochrome for my scratches. Sometime late in the morning, I caught a motor launch for the mainland. I spent a couple of hours searching for water in nearby military houses, then spent the afternoon riding in a motor launch that was looking for midget subs. At dusk, I was directed to the edge of a field, where I was given an old 30-30 rifle and some ammunition in case of a parachute drop by the Japs. I spent the night in a marine dining hall, which in itself was ironic considering that my two meals for the day consisted of one cracker and applesauce, and later one cracker, one peanut butter sandwich, and a bottle of orange soda. I didn't get a good, hot meal until the next evening when I went aboard the USS *Argonne*, our division flagship, with other *Utah* survivors. There, I was given a toilet pack, underwear, socks, dungaree shirt and pants, and hats. We were then taken to an uncompleted barracks to spend the evening. The morning of 9 December, my group of displaced sailors was placed on various work assignments. Five of us were assigned to the burial detail. Had we known what we were going to do, I'm sure we would have found some way to get reassigned. Our job was to bury the dead in a cemetery outside Honolulu. We were trucked to a sugarcane field and dropped off near a stack of about forty pine boxes. Near the stack were rows of dead sailors and marines, each draped under a heavy canvas cover and tagged with a shipping tag. Our job was to place the bodies in the coffins and stencil each coffin with an identification number. While putting the second body in a box, my partner dropped his end and vomited. He was quickly given the job of stenciling the coffins, but remained pale and sick throughout the whole ordeal. As my new partner and I were placing another body in a box, I discovered there was no head under the cover. Most of the bodies we lifted seemed to be missing some part. Blood and body fluids leaked on our hands. There was a strong smell of fuel oil in the air, which got on your clothes and skin. Some of the bodies seemed to be gasping for air, but this, of course, was only gas. Some of the larger bodies didn't fit the coffins, so the Hawaiians, who were working with us, just stomped them in the box. All of the bodies appeared puffed and swollen, but the ones I lifted didn't require any extra effort to place them in the coffins.

At noon, we were taken to the plantation mess hall for lunch. Although most of us thought we couldn't eat very much, I ate enough for two people. I guess I was really needing food, since I had eaten only a little since Sunday morning. After lunch, we returned to the field, where a bulldozer was digging a large hole. Coffins were then placed in the mass grave in rows of two, side by side. The rest of the afternoon was spent crating bodies. Late in the afternoon, we stopped to rest and estimated that we placed about one-hundred bodies in the pine boxes. While relaxing near the latest stack of coffins, we noticed that the bulldozer had stopped digging. The atmosphere was void of sound when suddenly the eerie calm was shattered by a bugler who began sounding "Taps." I cried for the first and last time. At last, the war finally hit me.

———

For Melvin Bacon, the war ended where it started, in the engine room aboard a ship. As the destroyer USS *Richard P. Leary* was steaming toward Japan, the news of Japan's surrender was piped over the ship's loudspeakers. Bacon, who enlisted in August 1938 and served forty-three months of overseas duty, was discharged under the point system on 1 October 1945.

The attack on the *Utah* resulted in the deaths of six officers and fifty-eight enlisted men. Due to unforeseen salvage costs, efforts to retrieve the ship were abandoned after it had been partially righted, leaving more than sixty men entombed in the hull. Today the *Utah* is part of the Pearl Harbor National Historic Landmark. In 1972, an elevated platform with a small memorial plaque was constructed on Ford Island to commemorate the site.

The USS *Curtiss*

WALLACE BROWN

On the morning of 7 December, the *Curtiss* was moored at the entrance to the Middle Loch. She sounded general quarters at the sight of the first enemy plane and immediately opened fire. At 8:36 a.m., she sighted the periscope of a midget submarine at seven hundred yards south of her position and promptly opened fire. A torpedo from the submarine narrowly missed her and smashed into a dock at Pearl City. At 8:40, when the submarine partially surfaced, the *Curtiss* again opened fire and hit the conning tower with two hits from her five-inch guns. The destroyer *Monaghan*, which had been anchored north of the USS *Curtiss*, was steaming for the harbor entrance when she passed between the *Curtiss* and *Tangier* as both were firing on the submarine. The *Monaghan* put on flank speed, rammed the submarine, and dropped two depth charges. The submarine was later recovered from the bottom of the harbor floor.

At 9:05 a.m., the *Curtiss* was hit by an enemy plane that crashed into her number-one starboard crane and burned on the boat deck below. At 9:08, she splashed a plane. At 9:12, a bomb from another attacking plane crashed in the vicinity of her damaged crane, passed through three decks, and exploded on the main deck, causing extensive damage and fires. The plane was splashed off her port beam. Despite nineteen dead and many wounded, the crew extinguished the fires and began emergency repairs. Fragmentation damage to her piping, wiring, steam lines, and control and engine rooms was extensive. Smoldering cork and poor lighting hampered firefighting efforts.

Wallace Brown provides a colorful account of activity aboard the USS *Curtiss* during the attack. He first joined the military service in September 1935, when he enlisted in the army. At the time, the navy would not accept him because he did not meet minimum height requirement. In 1938, after his discharge from the army, he again attempted to join the navy. This time, due to less rigid standards or because he had grown a few inches while in the army, Brown was accepted. After serving aboard the battleship *Arkansas*, he attended Surface Diesel School in New London, Connecticut. Upon graduation, he was assigned to the *Curtiss*, which was then still under construction at the New York Shipbuilding Company in Camden, New Jersey. He sailed on her from the Caribbean to the Pacific when she was reassigned to the US Pacific Fleet.

———

At the time of Pearl Harbor, 7 December, my rate was machinist mate second class. My station was in the forward engine of the ship. On the afternoon of 6 December, I had gone ashore to visit a shipmate who had his family in Honolulu and to swim a little at Waikiki Beach. Things went so well that I planned to go back on Sunday afternoon for another session of swimming and then dinner with the family.

At around 8:00 a.m. on 7 December, I had just gone through the mess line, sat down at a table, and asked some of the men having breakfast to pass the salt. They were so involved with discussing their liberty the night before that they ignored or didn't hear my request. As I arose to make a few well-chosen remarks in jest about "letting their shipmate starve" while discussing night maneuvers on the beach, the first bomb was heard. The bomb fell on Ford Island, which was to the starboard side of our ship.

When I ran to the cargo hatch on that side of the ship and saw the hangars and planes on fire, with Japanese planes strafing the runways, there was no doubt in my mind that we were under attack, as the Honolulu papers had predicted with huge block letters the day before. As general quarters was sounding, I was already running to my battle station in the number-one engine room. As I made my way below deck, men were scrambling in every direction, bobbing and weaving among bodies without somehow running into one another. When I reached the engine room, I began to start the pumps and make the propulsion plant ready to get underway. Down below, we waited anxiously for the words, "All ahead forward." We heard from topside that a submarine was sighted inside the harbor near our position, and was beginning to attack ships in our sector of the harbor. Everyone in the engine room stared at one another with a look of bewilderment as to why we were not getting the "hell out of the harbor." As the minutes passed, the bulkheads seemed to be closing in on us. We felt like trapped miners or submariners. Our clothes, already wet with hot, sticky sweat from the engine room, were now being drenched with cold perspiration. The longer we waited, the more nervous and fearful we got.

At sometime after 9:00 a.m., an explosion rocked the ship. In the engine room, we thought it was a torpedo from the submarine. Immediately, everyone braced himself for the next hit. The faces now reflected a sense of impending doom. We would either suffer from a direct hit or be trapped when the ship sank or capsized. Many of the men were whispering or silently reciting prayers they hadn't used or remembered in years. Those too nervous to pray simply asked for some kind of forgiveness from their Creator. A few minutes later, when word was telephoned that it was a bomb, there was a little relief. Everybody thought that if we took one hit, we could surely take another, because they had us in their sights. That one bomb was the only one that hit the *Curtiss*. Later, we found out that it was a five-hundred-pound bomb that hit the ship and penetrated the boat deck and radio shack before exploding between the hangar deck and metalsmith shop. Flying shrapnel tore into the after engine room, mess hall, and a section of berthing spaces. This was one of those times when being below ship was more dangerous than being on deck. At least on topside we could hear and see the enemy coming. Those of us in the engine room didn't realize how fortunate we were to escape with our lives. Most of the dead and wounded were from sections of the ship near our engine room. Several of the dead were from different sections of our engine room.

The most memorable thing about the attack on Pearl Harbor was the fact that I never did get breakfast that day. It seems funny that of all of the memorable events of that day there are some rather small ones that somehow stick in my mind and stand out above the others. It's like being at the seventh game of the World Series and remembering only that the guy sitting next to you was eating a hot dog and drinking a beer when the winning run was scored.

One of the engine-room telephone talkers, John Conzone of Oswego, New York, attempted to leave the engineering space after the officer had given word to abandon the engine room. John was in such a hurry to leave that he forgot to remove his headphones, which were still plugged in. For a few feet, he was moving right along, putting as much ground as possible between him and the engine room. When the telephone cord reached its end, he was jerked up short of the hatchway. He was snapped back with such force that he lost his footing and became a doormat for those other men who were escaping the lower compartments of the ship. After the attack was over and some sort of normalcy returned, he said he was sure that most of the men in the engine room and fire room ran over his back twice as they ran back and forth between hatchways, trying to find the safest exit. In all the commotion, no one bothered to bend down and help him to his feet. Most likely, no one even saw him lying on the deck. His problem was compounded by the fact that so many men were hurrying back and forth that he didn't have time to get up on his own.

Pete Glisson of Kansas had a battle station in the starboard shaft alley. When one of the bombs exploded, a large main in the hangar deck broke, and water filled the compartment below and above the scuttle hatch opening to the alley shaft. At the same time, the hangar deck was flooded and the ship took a list to starboard. Pete was trapped in his unflooded compartment by flooded compartments above and below him. When he attempted to open the hatch, not knowing whether the ship was afloat or underwater, he got a shower of salt water. Realizing that he was still breathing air and not water where he was, he stuck to his battle station. When the flooding was controlled and the spaces were pumped out, Pete finally came out of his space. He seemed to be in good shape and rather cool and collected about the ordeal. He was so self-composed that, when he went to light a cigarette, he found himself so nervous that someone had to light it for him.

During the Korean War, I served aboard the destroyer USS *Sproston*. One of my shipmates aboard her had served on the battleship USS *West Virginia* when the Japanese attacked Pearl Harbor. He was coxswain of a liberty boat and was at the fleet landing dock at the time the attack began. All boats at the dock, including his, were commandeered to transport the wounded, ammunition, and supplies to those ships in need. It was almost two days before he was able to get back to his own ship. After the attack, the crew aboard the *West Virginia*, which had been hit and severely damaged, were assembled for roll call. Because the coxswain was not there to answer to his name and nobody could place his whereabouts, he was considered missing in action. The Red Cross or the Navy Department wired his mother that he was missing and presumed to be dead. His mother, who lived in a small rural town in Wisconsin and was a devout Catholic, asked the parish priest to hold a memorial service for her son. When most of the town was turning out for the memorial service, the local Western Union operator received the coxswain's telegram, stating that he was safe and sound. The operator, who knew the family and the circumstances, dashed into the church during the middle of the service with the news that the coxswain was still alive. After the congregation's hugging and tears of joy, the service continued as a thanksgiving to the Almighty for delivering their native son from the rolls of the dead.

Wallace Brown served aboard the USS *Curtiss* until December 1944. The Pearl Harbor attack was the only action that he saw, except for two bombing raids while at anchor at South Pacific islands. In 1955, he retired from the navy, after having served on thirteen ships, the most famous being the USS *Missouri*, which he had been aboard during the Korean War.

8 DECEMBER 1941:
THE DAY AFTER

Waikiki: Securing the First Beachhead

HERMAN J. TRAVERS

For the thousands of soldiers on Oahu, 7 December marked their rite of passage into the art and science of war. In a matter of seconds, they became the army's first combat veterans of World War II. By Sunday afternoon, they had become caught in the emotional drama that was to play for four years. It was the time to contemplate their mortality and to calculate their odds of living or dying. As the sun set slowly in the Pacific, many felt that death would be the only victor. The uneasy calm slowly dissipated as darkness blanketed the island. Fear of the Japanese, the darkness, and death spread like an epidemic. The tension overwhelmed many of the troops dispatched to patrol and defend Oahu. Some tired, hungry, and trigger-happy soldiers opened fire on almost anything that moved or made a sound. Around every corner and behind every tree lurked imaginary Japanese soldiers or, in some instances, civilians and American military personnel. The tension was understandable; America's first military engagement had been in its own backyard, where it had suffered a stinging defeat. To many servicemen, Pearl Harbor was a bad omen.

Private Herman J. Travers was one of the soldiers who participated in the defense of Oahu during and after the attack. After enlisting in the army in September 1940, Travers shipped out from Fort Slocum, New York, to Oahu. In December 1940, he arrived at

Schofield Barracks for basic training. His story provides a view of the hazards of army life on Oahu during and after the attack.

———

For me, at that time a private in A Company, 27th Infantry Regiment (Wolfhounds), I could say my story all began upon my initial arrival to Oahu on 10 December 1940. Little did I realize that just one year and three days hence, I would be involved in a military occurrence that would be looked upon as a "day of infamy" by the president of the United States and its people. Also, those of us who are survivors are inclined to categorize ourselves as an "endangered species."

Immediately after arriving on Oahu, I was transported to my outfit at Schofield Barracks by way of a narrow-gauge railroad train, whose principal purpose was to carry the pineapples and sugarcane from the fields to the factories. Little did I envision that within a year it would be these same fields that would require a search, because it was alleged that an arrow was formed in the cane field pointing in the direction of Pearl Harbor, guiding the Japanese planes to their targets, the fleet anchored in the harbor.

While stationed at Schofield, although the unknown attack was still some time away, you could sense an aura of something developing because near the latter part of the year our training for combat became more intensified, even though some of our equipment was becoming more antiquated every day. For example, the 1903 Springfield rifle was accurate but had no firepower, and the thirty-seven-millimeter antitank gun would be unable to stop even the lightest Japanese tank.

In any event, our training went on, especially the full alerts that were called anytime, day or night. These were becoming too repetitious. In my opinion, these so-called dry runs contributed more than any other factor to the complacency that was to assist the enemy in carrying out its surprise attack with such success. If any one thing is still crystal clear to me after all these years, it is the radio broadcast by the local stations informing the listeners: "This is not an alert, it is the real thing; the Japanese are attacking the island." This announcement seems like it went on for quite some time.

On the morning of the attack, it being Sunday, there was no formal breakfast. You usually went into the kitchen, where the cooks had the goodies on the stove and gave you whatever you desired. Most of the company was off the base anyway. As I recall, it was getting near 8:00 a.m. when I received my breakfast. I sat at a dining table with other members of the company when the bombing sounds reached us, coming from the direction of Wheeler Field, Hickham Field, and the Pearl Harbor basin. For a while we accepted the sounds as being from some of those dry runs, and our forces were practicing target bombing again—another element for complacency. About this time, someone remarked that there were some small holes in the company street, just outside the mess-hall window. On going out, we saw not only what the nicks were but also their cause: the Japanese with their rising-sun emblems as big as life, strafing not only our quadrangle, but anything else that they could take advantage of while making their descent in attacking the fleet at Pearl Harbor, their ultimate objective. At about this same time I saw, for the first and only time in my military service, "The Call to Arms." It was being sounded by the regimental bugler, directed to all corners of the quadrangle. Also, I noticed some of the company men did reach the roof and set up machine-gun positions in the attempt to repel the enemy. Other than the one plane that was shot down in the Schofield area, very little damage was done to the attacking forces in this location. Simultaneously, some noncommissioned officers, prior to the arrival of the company officers, were getting the men to report to their company muster and to standby for further orders that would eventually move the company to its preassigned positions established in defense of Oahu. Before this transfer took place much later in the evening, it was necessary, due to the absence of the supply sergeant, to break open the supply-room doors for the issuing of our combat gear, especially the ammunition that was kept under lock and key.

As we were waiting, confined to the barracks, for the order to move out to our defense positions in the Honolulu area, a once-in-a-lifetime incident, at least for me, took place: the infamous post stockage was said to have opened its gates, releasing the men to return directly to their respective units. To this day, I do not know to what degree the men were released, but I do know the ones that returned to our company were much relieved, even though it may have taken a war to effect their release. Even today, I often wonder how their sentences were finally adjudicated, if at all.

I was quartered in a commandeered Japanese school located in the Kapiolani Park section at the base of Diamond Head. I can recall events and happenings that may be of interest because they show some not-so-glamorous aspects of the initial phases of the war.

When martial law was instantly declared in the islands, it seems the so-called native populace had an immediate change of heart towards the servicemen. Previously, it was only on a rare occasion that the military personnel was looked upon as anything other than a target for exploitation. Now, with martial law in effect, it appears they are now going out of their way to placate the serviceman.

Being in an antitank unit with no enemy tanks to destroy— although the rumor was that the Japanese were on the way and would land on the beaches most anytime—I was assigned to a motorized jeep patrol, with orders to patrol roads, highways, and streets, being on the lookout for martial-law violators and saboteurs. Other times, we had to respond to calls both day and night, especially at night, involving citizens calling for help because Japanese paratroops were thought to have landed in the hills and were presently hiding in the attics. Such troops never landed on Oahu.

I can vividly recall my first encounter on such a call. On reaching the house, it was my duty as the point man to lead the search with a submachine gun cradled in my arms, go up a narrow and dark flight of stairs, open a trap door and search the attic with the aid of a flashlight while acting a big hero, but at the same time hoping to God no one would be there. And, of course, I never found any Japanese hiding in houses.

In the evening, right after the attack, most of our time on patrol was spent enforcing the island blackout orders, which were occasionally violated. And in some instances, after repeated warnings, the exposed lights were shot out, even in some of the homes. This was also true with the vehicle headlights, which were supposed to have a blue blackout coating on them.

I can recall such a car being driven by a civilian going to work at the Pearl Harbor basin, where repair work was going on around the clock. This particular worker passed a checkpoint, where the exposed light was noticed. Only after someone in the car was shot did it come to a stop. The driver left and ran to the side of the road, and then he said that, due to the constant winds that are always prevalent in the area, he did not hear our command to halt and left the car when he became frightened. As was not always the case, little damage was done, and, with our help, he proceeded to the basin.

It is interesting to note that there was a period when the military command threatened to remove our ammunition, as it was being used unnecessarily, against not only civilians but also our own military.

Often things that are sometimes considered mundane also have a way of creating fond memories; such was my assignment as a member of a unit whose duty was to install a line of defense offshore on the edge of a coral reef. This line was to extend from the area of Diamond Head to some distance past Waikiki Beach. This work consisted of placing coiled barbed wire and numerous tetrahedrons in the ocean at a specified height and distance to take into account the high- and low-water marks. This was done in hopes of deterring and possibly preventing the Japanese from successfully making a landing on the island. This landing was a constant threat.

Of course, the landing never did materialize; nevertheless, the job of constructing this barrier was one I can never forget, as it necessitated using infantrymen as engineers. From Diamond Head to Waikiki, for many, many months and ever so slowly, we installed our portion of the barrier. We had to spend all day, seven days a week, in the ocean waters, with a man standing on a floating, bobbing raft and swinging a sixteen-pound maul. He was trying to drive a metal post—held by another man, who was standing chin high in the ocean—into the coral reef and hoping to strike the post between the incoming waves. Sometimes you did and sometimes you didn't. If a miss occurred, you not only went into the ocean with the maul but you could strike or fall on the man holding the post. Fortunately, with progress, injuries were minor.

Often, while standing on the beach, we were informed by the officer in charge that not only was our progress unacceptable but, as punishment, we would not be relieved periodically as scheduled.

All things considered, I feel Oahu could have been Japan's, just for the taking.

In September 1942, after being selected for Officer Candidate School in Fort Benning, Georgia, Herman J. Travers attended Infantry School there, where he received his commission as a second lieutenant. He returned to the Pacific campaign in January 1943. His combat role ended on 30 October 1944, when he was struck by enemy gunfire during combat operations on Pelelieu Island in the central Pacific. On July 1947, after periods of hospitalization in Guadalcanal, San Francisco, and Augusta, Georgia, Travers was finally discharged from Valley Forge Hospital and the army.

Cleaning Up the Navy Yard

MALBURNE PEABODY

The Japanese victory at Pearl Harbor was partially a result of American political and military leaders underestimating the strength and will of a people considered physically and intellectually inferior by many Americans. Japanese leaders, however, did not properly evaluate American's determination to recover from a humiliating and seemingly overwhelming defeat. The ultimate defeat of the Japanese was attributed to their underestimation of the American industrial machine.

After the attack, hundreds of thousands of defense-plant workers in the States worked diligently and became an example of industrial unity and productivity. Working two-week shifts with one day off, they produced the pieces necessary to refit and refloat the crippled ships of the US Pacific Fleet. Their expertise was crucial to the fleet's welfare.

Because the Japanese had not destroyed primary repair facilities and major utilities on Oahu during the attack, or launched a follow-up attack directed at key facilities on land, US military forces were able to regroup and rebuild. After the attack, it was critical that the Navy Yard fulfill its mission. If US military forces were to either mount a counteroffensive or "buy time" in the Pacific, the damage due to the attack had to be minimized. Repairing the damage had to be done as quickly as possible. Both civilians and military personnel ingenuously and determinately restored the fleet. As the last of the Japanese attack planes disappeared over the western horizon, workers poured through the gates of the Navy Yard to begin the enormous task of repairing the damage.

Not all the cleanup and repair activity at the Navy Yard was confined to the areas adjacent to the water. Damage to the base was widespread. Much of the damage on the fringes of the dock area, which included downed lines, ruptured pipes, and cratered roadways, directly affected the ability of the Navy Yard to begin repair and salvage operations. The task of repairing and restoring these vital public utilities belonged to the Navy Civil Engineer Corps. Malburne Peabody arrived at Pearl Harbor on 7 September 1941 aboard the oiler USS *Neosho*. As a young ensign in the corps, he was assigned to the District Public Works Office. On 7 December, three months to the day after his arrival at his first permanent duty station in the navy, he was assigned to stand district security duty.

I lived on Dewey Way, adjacent to old Fort DeRussy by Waikiki, along with several other junior corps officers. On the morning of 7 December, while driving through the far side of Honolulu on my usual route down by the docks, I was intercepted by a fire engine that headed out Kamehameha Highway, with me falling behind in the staff car. Flak was in the air by the time we emerged from the sugarcane fields. The fire engine turned into Hickam Field to the left, leaving me to make my way alone to the Pearl Harbor main gate. The highway seemed deserted; I really felt alone, but not for long. A Jap plane at the bottom of a dive somehow drew a bead on me and got off a couple of bursts. Near miss! Fortuitously, some fast-moving young man had been able to set up a thirty-caliber machine-gun position, protected by a few sandbags, just inside the Hickam fence. He must have drawn a fair bead on the belly of the pilot as he pulled out of his dive. I saw him trying to gain altitude; but, with smoke streaming from his ship, he went out of control and spun in. Later we investigated the wreckage at Hospital Point. The generator we found on the engine, manufactured by the Eclipse Aviation Corporation in New Jersey, became the subject of later correspondence with Senators Henry Cabot Lodge and Lyndon Johnson when we were sending strategic war materials to Communist China. I estimated that I must have been doing from thirty to forty miles per hour when I arrived at the main gate and was waved through without stopping by the marine guard. At about this time the *Arizona* blew up.

I proceeded to the second deck of the Administration Building to relieve Dudley A. Lewis. His words of greeting were, "Isn't this a hell of a mess." Being new at war and not knowing exactly what to do, we decided to put the mattress from the bunk up against the window. I guess neither of us was exactly sure what good it would do, but it seemed proper at the time. It then developed that his extremely provident wife had placed a pint of spirits in his lunch box to carry him through his "arduous" duties. Dudley had not felt the necessity for this source of strength, which remained intact and completely available to ease our uncomfortable state of mind. The devil was the author of confusion that morning. The tidy reins of command had been delegated to uncomprehending junior hands. Word passed that the potable water system was poisoned. I immediately ordered samples taken at strategic points in the system and personally carried them to the laboratory for analysis.

No contamination!

The prospective date with the admiral's daughter for lunch at the officers' club never materialized, and I was left in my Sunday go-to-meeting whites with gold buttons like dangling participles, incongruous and completely out of place.

Sidearms were available at the supply warehouse, so I drew a forty-five pistol. After three days, I was finally able to get the "gunny sarge" at the marine barracks to separate the gun from the Cosmoline, file down the sear pin, and to show me how to work the firearm.

Since the security watch was an adjunct of the captain of the yard, it became my lot to "get the hell down to Dry Dock Number One" when the *Pennsylvania*, *Cassin*, and *Downes* received their visitation from the Samurai. The plethora of documentation of the Dry Dock Number One affair leaves little for me to say on this subject.

Captain Baughman, the captain of the yard, requested my presence in his office. Upon entering, I heard the *Nevada* was desperately requesting permission to sortie. Again and again, *Nevada* requested permission to leave. Captain Baughman replied, "This is a combat force show." Combat force was somewhere ashore. Finally, Captain Baughman (in a World War I helmet) left for the head. Commander Hayes (also in a World War I helmet) took charge when, for the umpteenth time, the *Nevada* asked for permission to leave. Commander Hayes responded, "get the hell out if you can." The *Nevada* got underway for the open sea only to be forced aground at Pearl City after absorbing additional Japanese torpedoes.

About 10:30 a.m., Captain Baughman, having received requests to clean up the harbor, to retrieve the dead, and to repair the damage, asked me if I knew how to get towboat service to Honolulu. Being acquainted with the Young Towboat Company people, as well as the Dillingham organization, I volunteered to go to Honolulu and arrange for towboats and other manpower assistance. Captain Baughman agreed and told me, "Get going."

I drove to the offices of Young Towboat Company, introduced myself, and requested that they send all towboats in operating condition to Pearl Harbor and report to the captain of the yard. Upon receiving assurance that some half-dozen boats would be available forthwith, I proceeded to the office of the chief of police. Upon arriving, I noticed that a solid arsenal of firearms was perfectly laid out on the counter, available for anyone walking in the door. After suggesting that they be more careful with regard to the availability of their firearms, I requested to see the chief of police alone. We retired to his office, where I wrote out a message to be released upon my instructions and delivered later to the radio stations KGU and KGMB.

I then proceeded about a block way to the Navy Shore Patrol Office, where I advised the lieutenant commander in charge of my intention to send workmen to the Navy Yard to repair damage and asked what orders he might have received. He had no instructions and put his forces at my disposal, whereupon I suggested that he await further word, for I was proceeding to the Oahu Railway Station and would phone him from there.

Arriving at the station, I encountered Mr. Walter Dillingham, in his ever-present riding boots, sitting on the desk. In answer to my query as to the availability of his railroad for transporting workers to Pearl Harbor, Mr. Dillingham said, "The track walker will be back soon." At this point, the army had Kamehameha Highway completely blocked, and we reasoned that it would be completely useless to attempt to send workmen over the road to Pearl Harbor. He said, "If the track is in good condition, I can have a train made up and ready to transport five hundred people to Pearl Harbor fifteen minutes after the track walker gets in." Upon receiving this word, I contacted the shore patrol, requesting that they send patrolmen to the Oahu Railway Station immediately, to report to me.

Almost simultaneously thereafter, the track walker returned and reported that the Navy Yard spur was in good condition and that personnel from shore patrol had arrived for instruction. Using Mr. Dillingham's telephone switchboard, which was fully manned, I contacted the chief of police, instructing him to commandeer the services of radio stations KGU and KGMB and to issue the call for assistance that I had earlier prepared. This call was to be repeated at fifteen-minute intervals until they received cancellation of these instructions from me via the chief of police. The shore patrol was directed to commandeer a beautiful park adjacent to the railway station, for use in parking automobiles. The radio message having been released at 11:00, it was noteworthy that the first worker arrived at the railway station at 11:14. From then on it was a madhouse. Workers reported for Kanahoe Bay, Wheeler Field, Fort Shafter, Tripler, Ford Island, Barber's Point, Hickam Field, and various other military installations. It became clear that we were to be a distributing point for worker assistance to all military installations on Oahu. By 11:30 we had loaded five hundred men on the narrow gauge to Pearl Harbor after authorization from Admiral Block's office. We contacted all other military installations on the island, advising that workmen would be available at the Oahu Railway Station, but that they must send transportation. By 1:15 p.m. we had sent some fifteen hundred workers to the various military installations to repair damage inflicted by the Japanese attack.

I stayed in my whites for two days while acting as messenger to the harbor net and boom operation and doing a variety of other odd jobs. My basic job was to handle the dredging at Pearl Harbor and Kanahoe Bay, because I had been in the dredging business before the war. Additional assignments followed in quick succession. I was put in charge of burying the dead after the attack. Real estate was located at Red Hill, where some two thousand bodies were interred. I remember going to my friend Dick Long, who owned a nursery in Moana Valley, and getting him to contribute white and yellow oleanders for landscaping the cemetery. A minor crisis arose when one of the bodies to be buried was that of a Japanese aviator who had been shot down during the battle. I was finally able to make arrangements for his body to be buried in a downtown Honolulu cemetery.

The tank farms, through which passed all fuel for the US Pacific Fleet, were vulnerable from air attack. I was called in to see the Public Works officer and told to do something about it. We changed all pipeline fittings from cast iron to wrought iron, installed portable foam systems, stopped leaks caused by penetration of machine-gun bullets with wooden plugs, and placed a six-inch clay layer throughout the berms in order to prevent oil leakage into the harbor and the resulting fire hazard.

Also at this time, engineering crews were sent around the Navy Yard to inspect aboveground and underground power lines and pipelines. Most of the damage was not extensive, but it was enough to affect certain operating areas of the Navy Yard. Wooden poles were knocked down from the fireworks of the attack. Some were cut in half, cracked and splintered. Some of the aboveground pipeline was gouged with bullet holes. Portions of aboveground and underground pipeline were cracked and ruptured from the concussion effect of the bombing. Since it was imperative that the Navy Yard be fully operational as soon as possible, makeshift repairs were done to restore the needed services. Permanent repairs had to wait until the time and personnel were available. These type of "gum and shoelace" repairs also applied to many of the roads and paved lots. Some of the errant bombs had created very large potholes, which at the time of the attack served as foxholes. Like other workers at the Navy Yard, we worked seven days a week to see that it was fully functional. Although we were overlooked, our job was important to the overall mission of the Navy Yard. In order to get the damaged ships repaired, it was necessary to first get the repair facilities repaired. This was part of our job.

Burying the Dead

MELVIN FAULKNER

In the days following the Pearl Harbor attack, the army prepared for Oahu's defense, the navy furiously worked to repair and refloat the fleet's damaged ships, and members from both branches of service were involved in the important tasks of caring for the injured and burying the dead. Private First Class Melvin Faulkner was one of the men from Schofield Barracks who was assigned to the grim and solemn task of burial detail.

———

I was born on 10 September 1921 at my grandmother's house in the country, near Henderson, Texas. When I was fourteen years old, my father died, leaving my mother with three small children to raise. I felt this was too much of a burden on my mother, so I dropped out of school and traveled around the country, working here and there, and sending home most of the little money that I made. The jobs were mostly laboring in the fields and hills, always involving long hours and little pay. I lived and worked like this until I was eighteen years old. In December 1939, shortly after my eighteenth birthday, I joined the army, agreeing to serve my two years in Hawaii. After traveling around the country during the Depression, I felt that the army—with three meals a day, a place to sleep, and twenty-one dollars a month—was a good deal. At the time, it seemed too good to be true, two years in a tropical paradise in the middle of the Pacific Ocean. And to top off the deal, the army promised to teach me a skill other than manual labor; this part of the deal held true. I learned a useful skill, but, within a year, the tropical paradise became an armed camp.

I arrived in Honolulu on 7 May 1940 and was assigned to D Company, 21st Infantry Regiment. I took my basic training with the regiment. Shortly after basic, I transferred to the H&S Company, Third Engineers, because I felt I might learn something that would help me in making a living in the future. Although I had little experience driving tractors, I was assigned to the heavy-equipment section. I was eager to learn and was given ample opportunity to do so. I worked hard at my job and made private first class in about three months. This was good progress in those days, and the promotion raised my pay to thirty dollars a month. I was proud of myself, to say the least. Before long, I was operating bulldozers, motor graders, draglines, and power shovels quite well. As my abilities increased, so did my pay and promotion chances. I was reasonably happy during this time, but being in the army was quite lonely and boring. There were large numbers of soldiers, sailors, and marines stationed in Hawaii, so social life was out of the question for an enlisted man.

On 7 December 1941, I was quartered in the 24th Infantry Division Headquarters quadrangle, located a few hundred yards north of Wheeler Field. I was still in bed, debating whether or not to get up and eat breakfast, when several airplanes flew very low over the barracks. In a few seconds, there was a big explosion. Thinking that one of the planes had crashed, I ran over to the porch to see the crash. There were no wrecks within sight, only groups of planes diving low over the quadrangles. As the planes made their way over Wheeler Field, you could see bombs falling from them. Big explosions were going off everywhere, one after another. Although it was impossible to make out the debris flying high in the air, I knew it was pieces of men, planes, trucks, and buildings blasted apart and hurtled through the air. People could be seen scrambling from Wheeler Field and leaving the target area as quickly as their feet could carry them. A number of men could be seen falling to the ground, but it was impossible to tell whether they were hit or just diving for cover to avoid a strafing. The whole scene was like a nightmare. I had to reassure myself that this wasn't a dream and that I was not back in my bunk still sleeping. I saw one American fighter plane, a P40, chasing one of the Japanese planes. The gunners on the ground were so excited that they were trying to shoot the American plane as well as the Japanese. Everything was in a state of chaos. No one really knew what was going on, and, by the time the ammunition and weapons were set up, the raid was over.

We expected another attack by the Japanese, so the rest of the day was spent getting better prepared. The night of 7 December was a trying time, because everyone was trigger-happy. To make things worse, all kinds of rumors about saboteurs were being circulated. It was a dangerous time to get out of your area.

The next day, 8 December, I was assigned to work the graveyard detail at the Schofield Cemetery. For the next couple of days, we dug holes in the ground, lowered the dead, and then covered the graves. The dead were all placed in pine caskets and stacked inside the fence at the cemetery until we dug trenches with a large ditchdigger. I estimate that we buried 150 to 200 American soldiers and three Japanese pilots. While we were busy digging holes, other members from the battalion were busy putting together the pine caskets. I'm sure there was a shortage of these items around the island. There was no way Supply could have requisitioned hundreds of government-issue caskets for emergency use. While we waited to cover over the open graves after the bodies had been lowered, people from graves registration checked to make sure names and plot numbers matched up. After we got the go-ahead, I covered the graves with a bulldozer. There was a military funeral with a full ceremonial service for our men, and then later a military funeral service for the Japanese pilots. It was a sad and sobering sight to look on from the edge of the cemetery and watch the ceremonies. These were the first American soldiers lost in this war, and I knew history was being made right in front of my eyes at the Schofield Cemetery. I wondered how many more Americans would lose their lives before the war was over and prayed that I wouldn't be one of those buried so far from home. At this time, I thought Schofield Cemetery was the loneliest place on earth. The smell of the freshly dug earth and the scent of pine in the air from the freshly cut caskets seemed so out of place in the middle of a tropical island. The ugliness of war was leaving the earth scarred, even in paradise. Before I left the cemetery for the last time, I offered a silent prayer for the souls of those men we had just laid to rest.

In May 1943, I was made a training cadre and was sent back to the States. On the same orders, I was also promoted to technical sergeant. I was twenty-one-years old, and this was one of the happiest days of my life.

After assignment at Camp Bowie, Texas, with the 248th Engineer Battalion, Melvin Faulkner was shipped to the European theater. Faulkner not only participated in both major battlefronts but also witnessed two of the most memorable battles of World War II. On 6 June 1944, D-day, Faulkner landed with the 248th Engineer Battalion on Utah Beach at Normandy to establish a beachhead for the Allied invasion. In June 1945, he returned home and was discharged.

A Reunion

LLOYD JOHNSON

a time to be born, and a time to die . . .
a time to kill, and a time to heal;
a time to weep, and a time to laugh . . .
a time to mourn, and a time to dance . . .
a time to keep silence, and a time to speak;
a time to love, and a time to hate;
a time for war, and a time for peace.
—ECCLESIASTES 3

a time to forget, and a time to remember.
—SURVIVOR AT THE FORTIETH ANNIVERSARY
OF THE PEARL HARBOR ATTACK

On the fortieth anniversary of the Pearl Harbor attack, military leaders, politicians, veterans, average citizens, and Pearl Harbor survivors around America gathered to mourn the dead and renew their sense of patriotism. At Pearl Harbor, the ceremonies were a little more elaborate than usual there due to media attention and public awareness.

Admiral James D. Watkins, CinCPac, addressed the USS *Arizona* Memorial gathering, whose honored guests included Bruce Babbitt, the *Arizona* governor; Joseph K. Taussing Jr., deputy assistant secretary of the navy; and Mary Paulsen, the sister of an *Arizona* crew member who had been killed in the attack. Watkins said that "our history lesson is that if we are to survive—if our cherished freedoms are to live—we must pay the bill in full. We must do all we can to avoid the kind of tragedy which unfolded in this harbor. We must never be perceived as other than ready and strong by those tempted to deny us our rights and freedoms."

At 7:55 a.m., the exact time that the attack had begun, a minute of silence was observed at various locations around the island. At the USS *Arizona* Memorial, single flowers from dozens of floral wreaths were dropped in the waters about the sunken battleship. Four Phantom jets flew over in a tight diamond formation, with one soaring up and away from it to symbolize men missing in action. From the concrete quay where the USS *Arizona* was moored, a squad of marines fired a twenty-one-gun salute, while crew members in dress whites aboard the destroyer USS *Rathburne* "manned the rails" as she sailed past the USS *Arizona*.

Not far away from Pearl Harbor, some three thousand members of the Pearl Harbor Survivors Association met at the National Memorial Cemetery of the Pacific for morning ceremonies and services, as well as a sunset observance, which included the playing of "Taps." Six USS *Arizona* crew members joined fourteen sailors who had served aboard her before World War II in a private remembrance at the memorial. At other military installations around Oahu, gun salutes, reenlistment ceremonies, and plaque dedications honored this day.

In Washington, D.C., there was a "Remember Pearl Harbor" ceremony aboard the USS Coast Guard cutter *Taney,* the last active US warship that had been at Oahu on the morning of 7 December 1941. Ironically, Transportation Secretary Drew Lewis could not attend the ceremony aboard her because he was in Tokyo for talks on curbing Japanese auto exports.

For Pearl Harbor survivors, it was a day of remembrance. The memories are bittersweet, a mixture of some of the best and worst times of their lives. Seven December has become the official day when they remember a bygone era, reflect on their youth, and reminisce about friends who were connected with Pearl Harbor. The survivors have become messengers of the past, living links with history, who quietly voice a patriotic refrain about duty and honor to country. The message has remained uncompromised through years of turmoil and change.

Warrant Pay Clerk Lloyd Johnson was one of the survivors who participated in the fortieth anniversary. In December 1981, Johnson and wife, Lee (who, at the time of the attack, was living off base with their young son), returned to Pearl Harbor, where he had received his baptism by fire aboard the destroyer tender USS *Whitney*. His story about a reunion, reflects the thoughts and feelings shared by many of the survivors.

Plans had been made, and at last the day arrived for our flight to Hawaii! There we were to meet and relive our common experiences with other survivors of the bombing of Pearl Harbor on 7 December 1941! During the forty years that have passed since that time, we have all grown a little older, a little grayer, and a little heavier, but time has not dulled our memories of that terrible day!

My wife, Lee, and I flew from Kennedy Airport at 11:00 a.m., 5 December 1981, enroute to Honolulu to attend the Fortieth Anniversary Convention and Reunion of the Survivors Association, arriving there fourteen hours later.

We were both wearing our Survivors Association overseas caps with the name tag "USS *Whitney*" on them. The *Whitney* was a destroyer tender on which I had served as a warrant pay clerk. Lee and our young son, Ronald, were living in Honolulu at that time. During our stopover in Chicago, we met our first shipmate from the *Whitney*. At the time of the attack, he was a chief yeoman who had been the "captain's writer" (i.e., secretary). This was the first of our many contacts.

The convention tour was planned and operated by the Fitzpatrick Travel Agency of Los Angeles. After the long flight, we were all tired when we arrived at the airport, but we all cheered up when we were greeted by Fitzpatrick hostesses, who presented each of us with a lei. We were all assigned to buses, which took us to our respective hotels; ours was the Sheraton Waikiki.

We were pleasantly surprised to find we were assigned a room on the thirtieth floor, with a balcony overlooking the length of beautiful Waikiki, and stretching on to Diamond Head! Gorgeous view, with the world-famous Royal Hawaiian Hotel just below us! Looking to our left, we saw all the high-rise buildings with mountains in the background. We could also see, in the distance, the general area where we had lived, Center Street in Kiamiki, at the foot of Wilhemenia Rise. After a twenty-two-hour day, we finally went to bed at 4:00 a.m. est.—I did not reset my watch to Honolulu time!

At about 8:00 a.m., many of the survivors started gathering and signed their own individual ship's roster, and then they looked for shipmates. Eventually, about twenty survivors from the *Whitney* signed in. Although we had all served aboard the same ship at the same time, none of us knew each other, but we were acquainted by the time the convention was over.

We also talked to survivors from other ships. In 1940, destroyers were assigned to a tender for logistic support and repairs; two of these were the *Case* and the *Tucker*. Both had just returned from Australia and were alongside the *Whitney*. Lee's older brother Bruce was serving aboard the *Case* at that time.

Lee talked to survivors from the *Case* and asked if they knew "Wahoo" (Bruce's well-deserved nickname) and also to a survivor from the *Tucker*. They all remembered "Wahoo," who had been the *Arizona* cowpoke! Lee told them that her brother had died twelve years ago; he had been employed at the King's Ranch in Texas after his retirement as a chief electrician's mate (he had been nicknamed "Sparky").

Talking to many survivors from the *Whitney* and, particularly, from other ships that had been anchored in the same general area, which had not been the main target for the first wave of Japanese attack planes, we were able to compare notes and fit together many pieces of what had taken place. For instance, while talking to a survivor from the *Whitney*, I learned that the three-inch fifty-caliber antiaircraft gun on which he was a crew member had fired about thirty rounds in the general direction of the Navy Yard. Quite possibly, this prevented or turned back the Japanese planes from carrying out their planned attack on the ships in that area.

A survivor who had been a gun-crew member on the five-inch twenty-five-caliber antiaircraft batteries of the *Phoenix* told me that the guns had fired about three hundred rounds before she got underway; this was an unbelievably high number! This information fits into the puzzle, because, when I returned to my ship about 9:00 a.m., the officers' boat went through an area that was littered with countless floating shell cases from the antiaircraft guns of the *Phoenix*. By this time this ship was at sea. How fortunate were the ships in that area that the *Phoenix* had so much firepower! A number of Japanese planes were shot down in this area.

The initial Japanese attack with bombs and torpedoes at 7:55 was aimed at Battleship Row and the berths where the aircraft carriers normally would have been anchored or tied up. The carriers were all at sea, so the ships in their berths all suffered severe damage. Practically every ship targeted in the first Japanese attack was either sunk or badly damaged.

The second attack wave came about a half-hour later. That allowed enough time for the ships in the area off Aiea and Pearl City to get their guns manned and turn back the attacking planes and receive little or no damage. I talked to many survivors from ships that had suffered damage. We all remembered details forty years later as clearly as if it were 7 December 1941! On Sunday at 6:00 p.m., the Sheraton-Waikiki sponsored a courtesy and welcome reception on the lawn of the hotel, for survivors attending the convention.

On Monday, reveille was at 4:00 a.m., breakfast was at 5:00, and then we boarded buses to go to the memorial services at the Punchbowl, site of the National Memorial Cemetery of the Pacific. It was dark when we arrived. While sitting and waiting for the sun to come up, and the services to start at 7:30, we visited with those around us, including four marines, one of whom had escaped from the *Oklahoma* as she capsized. About thirty-five-hundred people attended this service.

At exactly 7:55, the identical time of the Japanese attack, four planes flew over in tight formation. The services were stirring, as we paid tribute to all of our shipmates who had died on that sad day! We will never forget that day. We were glad to have had the opportunity to be a part of the unforgettable ceremony. At 9:00, we boarded buses for return to our hotels. Bad weather started about noon, and the heavy rain prevented many of us from attending the sunset memorial services at the USS *Arizona* Memorial. I had served aboard the *Arizona* from 1932 to 1934.

We took advantage of bus tours around the Oahu on Tuesday and Wednesday. We experienced exceptionally high winds on the Pali around Wind-ward Chau. We saw banana farms, beautiful flowers, Wiamea Falls Park, and high surf on the northern end of the island. We went through sugarcane and pineapple fields on our way back to *Honolulu*.

The finale of the convention was the memorial banquet in the Hawaii Ballroom of the Sheraton-Waikiki with over two thousand in attendance. After an excellent dinner, there was a "roll call" of navy ships and stations, and army and marine units, that had been on Chau on 7 December 1941. This was a fitting tribute to all, both the living and the dead.

We were fortunate in being seated at a table exclusively composed of *Whitney* survivors, thanks to the efforts of Bill Emolovich, who had spent much time and energy in organizing this group. He was the first *Whitney* survivor we had met on Sunday morning, and, by a strange coincidence, we met him practically every place we were. We exchanged many facts about what happened on the *Whitney*; he had been a member of the gun crew that had fired the antiaircraft batteries. He had been a member of the *Whitney* baseball team, which I had watched play a number of times back in 1940–1941 out in Pearl Harbor. We also shared some common acquaintances and had many interesting and informative conversations. As the evening came to an end, a number of pictures were taken of the *Whitney* survivors and their wives. We all agreed that the *Whitney* was a fine ship with an excellent crew. We were all proud to have served aboard her.

It seems most fitting and proper for my wife and me to remember with fond memories, and pay tribute to my "boss" on the *Whitney* at that time, Lieutenant Commander (later Captain) Charles C. Schaaf, our supply officer, now deceased. Without doubt, he was one of the finest officers and gentlemen it was ever our pleasure to meet.

The survivors and their wives who attended this convention were the best-mannered, well-behaved, and orderly group we have ever had the pleasure of being with in our lives. They were well-dressed, and most must have been successful in life. Most of the survivors we met had been young boys on their first enlistment at the time of Pearl Harbor, and most served only during the war and then returned to civilian life. Some had gone to college under the G.I. bill and pursued successful careers. Of course, there were also those like myself who had made the navy a career. I had retired after thirty-three-and-one-half years of service. These were challenging and rewarding years for me!

I discussed this pattern of good behavior with others attending the convention who had noticed it, and we reached the consensus that this behavior was largely the result of having served in the well-disciplined "old" navy. Lee met only three other women at the convention who had been in Honolulu at the time of the attack. This ended the convention for us.

Once home, I had a chance to collect my thoughts and to reflect on the convention. I realized just how close to death most of us had come. Prior to the attack, most of us had paid little attention to the idea of dying. Here we were in a tropical paradise during peacetime, a thousand miles from the coast of Japan. At the convention, we all seemed to make light of our close encounters. Perhaps the closeness of death remained in the back of everyone's mind, but was left unspoken as the common bond among survivors. During the trip, however, I had a number of interesting conversations about the strafing of the road approaching Pearl Harbor and the roads inside the Navy Yard.

I knew that there had been one or more strafing attacks in the general vicinity of the main gate and the enlisted men's landing. For instance, as I entered the Navy Yard, after having driven approximately ten miles from Center Street in Kaimiki in my old 1937 Ford Coupe, I dropped my brother-in-law Bruce "Wahoo" Harrison (of the USS *Case*) off at the enlisted men's landing and proceeded on to the officers' landing.

I learned later that he and others in the vicinity were strafed by Japanese planes. Another friend of mine, Bob Hendon, then a chief gunners' mate, and his wife, Vera, arrived in the Navy Yard and had to hide behind old armor plates stored in the area to avoid the strafing planes!

In my case, planes were dive-bombing as I approached the Navy Yard. One large plane in the area of Aiea was flying low and might have crashed. While I was waiting at the officers' landing for a boat to take me to the USS *Whitney*, I was opposite the sunken and burning battleships and could see the smoke from the Navy Yard and Ford Island. But I never saw any planes while I was waiting. Neither did I see any enroute to my ship. I was unaware of the earlier strafing attack on the enlisted men's landing where my brother-in-law was waiting for a boat.

After I had gotten back to the *Whitney* and gone to my battle station in Ammunition Supply, our AA gun fired a few times at planes flying over us. At the time we thought they might be our own planes; however, from what I have read, they were most likely Japanese reconnaissance planes taking photographs of damage resulting from earlier attacks. By this time, the Japanese attack planes were well on their way back to their carriers. I had heard that a few bombs were dropped on Honolulu and that shells fired from our own ships did some damage with casualties resulting. Possibly this was behind me. I always thought that it was.

A number of inquiries from survivors about strafing attacks on the road to Pearl Harbor brought some other items to light. One survivor asked me if I had seen many abandoned cars and trucks in ditches along the road approaching the Navy Yard. I remembered nothing, and if I saw them, they made no impression on me. I was stopped by a man on a street in Waikiki who saw my survivor's hat, and we engaged in an enlightening exchange. Recently discharged from the army, he had been working in the Navy Yard as a civilian employee when he witnessed the initial attack. He told me that a friend of his was killed on the road during one of these strafing attacks.

At the convention banquet, our waitress told us that her husband, a civilian bus driver, was killed during the attack. Now I knew that all of the attacks took place either ahead of me, behind me, or both. Therefore, I feel it was only by good fortune that I was able to drive ten miles during the attack and get to my ship safely.

Of course, these strafing attacks were of small consequence compared to the terrible damage and havoc wreaked upon the airfields and ships; nevertheless, it is a fortunate thing for those of us who survived. For instance, a gunner's mate first-class from one of the tenders was pressed into service as a gun crew member on a cruiser tied up in the Navy Yard as he was trying to get back to his ship, and he was killed by a bomb! I, however, drove a car perhaps ten miles, waited on the dock in the yard for a while, and road a boat back to my ship, all in lulls between Japanese attacks! How lucky I was!

⚊ ⚊

Since the end of World War II and the development of commercial passenger planes, the Hawaiian Islands have become an affordable and convenient tropical retreat for millions of American and Japanese vacationers. For the majority of tourists, Oahu is an escape to paradise. Despite crowding and commercialization, Honolulu and Waikiki Beach are the pearls that attract the tourist and the tourist dollar. The fact that many tourists exchange one crowded city for another is nonessential. The fact that they can claim to have spent a vacation on a tropical island in the Pacific is all important. Hidden among the clutter and glitter is Pearl Harbor. The harbor today, as it was in 1941, is a strategic waterway that provides a home for the US Pacific Fleet. Pearl Harbor contains the largest naval command in the world, a fact often overlooked by the average vacationer. The command covers an area of almost 102 million square miles, with over two hundred major ships, two thousand aircraft, and more than two hundred thousand navy and Marine Corps personnel.

In addition to being the home port of numerous major warships, mostly destroyers, the six-thousand-acre harbor is also the home of nine separate commands that provide the defensive and offensive arms of the US Pacific Fleet. Among the commands are the Commander Submarine Force Pacific, which controls submarines based at Pearl Harbor; the Naval Surface Group MIDPAC, which oversees a fleet of vessels responsible for refueling, repairing, and supplying fleet ships at sea and in port; and the Commander Third Fleet on Ford Island, which oversees antisubmarine warfare activities and fleet training. With 8.5 square miles of water area and approximately 12 miles of docking facilities, Pearl Harbor is the navy's and Oahu's busiest and most important piece of real estate.

Just offshore of Ford Island, alongside what was once known as Battleship Row, stands one of the most famous landmarks in Oahu, the USS *Arizona* Memorial. The white concrete structure, a lonely sentinel watching over the harbor, straddles the wreck of the sunken battleship. The memorial traces its beginning to the days immediately following the attack, when the navy decided that the USS *Arizona* would continue to remain on the harbor bottom as a monument to the men entombed inside the ship. During World War II, new ships joining the US Pacific Fleet began the unofficial practice of rendering colors to salute the USS *Arizona* as they passed by her berth. In 1950, Admiral A. W. Radford, CinCPac, made the practice of honoring the USS *Arizona* official when he ordered the flag to be flown from atop the sunken ship. The bronze plaque that honors the USS *Arizona*'s role in the Day of Infamy, reads:

DEDICATED
TO THE ETERNAL MEMORY OF OUR GALLANT SHIPMATES
IN THE USS ARIZONA
WHO GAVE THEIR LIVES IN ACTION
7 DECEMBER 1941

"From today on the USS Arizona will
again fly our country's flag just
as proudly as she did on the morning of 7 December 1941.
I am sure the Arizona's crew will know
and appreciate what we are doing."
—Admiral A. W. Radford, USN

MAY GOD MAKE HIS FACE
TO SHINE UPON THEM
AND GRANT THEM PEACE

By 1956, it was no longer safe to conduct the daily ceremony of colors aboard the ship. To insure that the USS *Arizona* would continue to be honored, the commandant of the Fourteenth Naval District invited the Pacific War Memorial Commission to sponsor a public campaign to raise money for a permanent memorial. In 1957, the fund-raising campaign raised $500,000. The following year, John A. Burns, Hawaii's delegate to Congress, introduced legislation calling for a permanent memorial. On 15 March 1958, the Eighty-fifth Congress approved the bill authorizing the construction of a memorial at Pearl Harbor to be designated as a national shrine. Congress appropriated $150,000, and the state of Hawaii contributed $100,000 to the memorial. The remainder of the money was contributed by private citizens, corporations, and a number of nationwide fund raisers. A telecast of the television show *This Is Your Life* and a benefit performance by former GI Elvis Presley helped raise the remaining funds. The AMVETS veterans' association contributed money for the carillon and paid for the Italian marble used in the memorial.

Architect Alfred Preis was chosen to solve the sensitive and controversial problem of designing the memorial. His final design achieved a harmonious composition of space, light, and form. Blueprints and scale models were turned into reality by the Walker-Moody Construction Company, with assistance from the Public Works Center at Pearl Harbor. The total cost for the memorial was $532,000. On 30 May 1962, it was formally dedicated and opened to the public.

The design concept for the memorial was explained in the statement prepared for dedication ceremonies:

> *The form, wherein the structure sags in the center but stands strong and vigorous at the ends, expresses initial defeat and ultimate victory.*
>
> *Wide opening in walls and roof permit a flooding by sunlight and a close view of the sunken battleship eight feet below, both fore and aft. At low tide, as the sun shines upon the hull, the barnacles which encrust it shimmer like gold jewels . . . a beautiful sarcophagus.*
>
> *The overall effect is one of serenity. Overtones of sadness have been omitted to permit the individual to contemplate his own personal responses . . . his innermost feeling.*

The USS *Arizona* Memorial is in the form of an enclosed bridge, measuring 184 feet in length. The center is 36 feet in width, and 14 feet in height. At the ends, the width narrows to 27 feet and the height tapers to 21 feet. The entire structure is supported by two 250-ton concrete girders, which rest on thirty-six prestressed pilings driven into the harbor bottom. No part of the memorial touches the remains of the USS *Arizona*. The inside of the memorial is divided into three sections: a museum room that contains mementos from the ship; an assembly room, which accommodates up to two hundred people; and a shrine room, in which the names of the 1,177 men who died in action while aboard the USS *Arizona* are inscribed on a wall. The oldest memento on display is the bell that had been placed aboard the USS *Arizona* before she was commissioned on 17 October 1916. Contrary to popular belief, the USS *Arizona* is no longer in commission. As a tribute to the ship and her crew, the Department of the Navy permits the United States flag to fly daily from a flagpole now attached to the severed main mast of the sunken ship.

ABOUT THE AUTHOR

For the past twenty-five years, **Paul Joseph Travers** has followed and updated the Pearl Harbor story, most often, in the footsteps of his father and other survivors close to his home in Maryland. He received a BA from the University of Maryland and an MA from Pepperdine University. He served as an amphibious armor officer in the US Marine Corps. A former park ranger and historian with the Maryland Park Service, he is also the author of *The Patapsco: Baltimore's River of History*, *Flight of the Shadow Drummer*, and *The Cowgirl and the Colts*, the story of the first female to take the field in the National Football League with the Baltimore Colts in 1959. In 2009 he thru-hiked the Appalachian Trail (Herm's Hike) as a fundraiser for veterans with Alzheimer's disease. He plans to, hopefully, follow the Pearl Harbor story until the hundredth anniversary. For more information about the author and his books, visit his website at paultravers.com.